Aristocrats Go to War

This book is dedicated to my granddaughter Grace

So that she and her generation will continue to remember

Aristocrats Go to War

Uncovering the Zillebeke Churchyard Cemetery

Jerry Murland

Pen & Sword
MILITARY

First published in Great Britain in 2010 by
Pen & Sword Military
an imprint of
Pen & Sword Books Ltd
47 Church Street
Barnsley
South Yorkshire
S70 2AS

ISBN 978-1-84884-152-9

A CIP catalogue record for this book is available from the British Library.

Typeset in 11pt Ehrhardt by
Mac Style, Beverley, E. Yorkshire

Printed and bound in the UK by the MPG Books Group

Pen & Sword Books Ltd incorporates the imprints of Pen & Sword Aviation, Pen & Sword Maritime, Pen & Sword Military, Wharncliffe Local History, Pen and Sword Select, Pen and Sword Military Classics and Leo Cooper.

For a complete list of Pen & Sword titles please contact
PEN & SWORD BOOKS LIMITED
47 Church Street, Barnsley, South Yorkshire, S70 2AS, England
E-mail: enquiries@pen-and-sword.co.uk
Website: www.pen-and-sword.co.uk

Contents

Foreword

There is still a huge interest in the First World War, some ninety years after its end, as it fades into history with the death of the last British survivor. This book records the tragically short lives of some of those who took part.

No one who has seen the cemeteries in Belgium and northern France can be the same afterwards. It is extraordinary and humbling to see what remains of those four years when so many young men fell while fighting for their countries. The rows of graves and headstones in the beautifully tended enclosures show the extent of the losses.

Among the dead that Jerry Murland writes about is my ancestor William Reginald 'Regy' Wyndham. We know that Regy was a humorous, easy-going man, a good horseman, fond of riotous jokes and adored by his family – someone who loved life. What else can there be to say of such an early death? Who knows what might have happened to him had he lived?

Such is the sadness of war. But this book has revived Regy and its other subjects, bringing them back to life of a kind – a life made by the imaginations of those who read of it. To have achieved this shows how worthwhile a project *Aristocrats Go to War* is.

Max Egremont

Acknowledgements

I am very grateful to Lord Egremont for agreeing to write a foreword and for giving permission to use extracts from Regy Wyndham's letters and diary. I must also register my thanks to my editor, Jon Cooksey, for his encouragement and faith in a book that grew from a discussion we had in his kitchen. Rebecca Jones at Glory Designs in Coventry has produced some excellent maps from my sketches and I must thank her for her patience and understanding in the face of my many revisions.

This book would not have been possible without the enormous number of individuals who have assisted me with the research and preparation. In particular I must thank the Lee Steere family who welcomed me into their home and gave me full access to the papers and effects of John Lee Steere. I am grateful to both His Grace the Duke of Richmond and Gordon, and to Rosemary Baird for assistance from the Goodwood Archive and to Bernard, David, Michael & Andrew Gordon Lennox for permission to print extracts from Lord Bernard Gordon Lennox's diary. I am also indebted to Janine Heaney nee Siewertsen for her assistance with gathering information on her great uncle, Walter Siewertsen.

In the course of my research I have visited numerous archive collections and the help and assistance I have received on every occasion has been outstanding. I must thank the staff at: the National Archives at Kew, Alison McCann at the West Sussex Records Office, Elaine Mundill at Glenalmond College, Jennifer Thorp at New College, Oxford, Penny Hatfield at Eton College, Dr Anthony Morton at Sandhurst, Rita Boswell at Harrow School, Eleanor Whitney at the Westminster Archive, Carole Standeven at Minstead, Colonel Seymour at the Grenadier Archive, Guardsman Gareth Goodwin at the Coldstream Archive, Mrs Sue Cole at Charterhouse School, Clem Webb at the London Scottish Archive, Adam Green at Trinity College, Cambridge and John Lloyd at the Household Cavalry Archive.

I must also record my thanks to Tom Waterer and Paul Webster who spent three days with me walking the ground at Ypres in March 2009 and to Pastor

Odile Denorme at Zillebeke for allowing me access to the church tower to photograph the bells.

The author and publishers wish to thank the History Press for their kind permission to quote from The Crofton Diaries. We are also grateful to the following for permission to reproduce photographs: the Lee Steere family, Janine Heaney, Goodwood Collection, New College Archive, Petworth House Archive, The Household Cavalry Archive, The Queen's Royal Lancer's Regimental Museum, Grenadier Guards' Archive, Coldstream Guards' Archive, Soldiers of Gloucestershire Museum, London Scottish Archive, Glenalmond College, Charterhouse School and Harrow School. In all instances every effort has been made to trace the copyright holders where any substantial extract is quoted. The author craves the indulgence of literary executors or copyright holders where these efforts have so far failed.

Finally a big thank you to my wife Joan for putting up with the disruption to family life that writing a book of this nature often creates.

Vitai Lampada

There's a breathless hush in the Close to-night
Ten to make and the match to win
A bumping pitch and a blinding light,
An hour to play and the last man in.
And it's not for the sake of a ribboned coat,
Or the selfish hope of a season's fame,
But his Captain's hand on his shoulder smote
'Play up! play up! and play the game!'
The sand of the desert is sodden red,
Red with the wreck of a square that broke;
The Gatling's jammed and the Colonel dead,
And the regiment blind with dust and smoke.
The river of death has brimmed his banks,
And England's far, and Honour a name,
But the voice of a schoolboy rallies the ranks:
'Play up! play up! and play the game!'
This is the word that year by year,
While in her place the School is set,
Every one of her sons must hear,
And none that hears it dare forget.
This they all with a joyful mind
Bear through life like a torch in flame,
And falling fling to the host behind
'Play up! play up! and play the game!'

Sir Henry Newbolt (1862–1938)

Introduction

The last great battle of 1914 took place in Flanders and much of it was within sight of the spires of the ancient walled city of Ypres. By its conclusion many of the British Regular Army battalions that had taken part in the retreat from Mons and fought on the Marne and the Aisne had been reduced to little more than cadres. More significantly, the experienced core of officers and NCOs that fell in those grim days of October and November were an enormous and irreplaceable loss to the raising and training of the New Armies already answering Kitchener's call to arms back in Britain. By December 1914 the British Expeditionary Force (BEF) was all but gone; their epitaph encompassed in the words of Brigadier General James Edmonds in the Official History of 1914:

> *'The old British Army was gone past recall, leaving but a remnant to carry on the training of the New Armies; but the framework that remained had gained an experience and confidence which was to make those armies invincible … If they had done naught else, the men of the Expeditionary Force would have done far more than could have been expected of their numbers.'*[1]

The focus of this book is on the lives of eighteen men who are commemorated in the small churchyard cemetery of Sint-Catharinakerk at Zillebeke and who fought in the first battle of Ypres as part of the BEF in 1914. The cemetery, often referred to by battlefield guides as the 'Aristocrats' Cemetery', is noted for the proportionally high number of individuals from the families of the aristocracy and landed gentry who are buried and commemorated therein. I have always been drawn towards the social history of the Great War and the lives and circumstances of those who took part in it and while this book is not intended as another history of the First Battle of Ypres, in order to fully appreciate the impact of the business of war on the individual it is necessary for the reader to have a broad understanding of the chronology of the battle itself. To this end the circumstances that brought each of the eighteen officers and men to Ypres in October 1914 have been placed in the context of the fighting that was taking place at the time.

Needless to say, there is often a direct correlation between social status and the amount of research material available. Thus those who were born into aristocratic or well-known families tend to have a wealth of family history already in existence, albeit sometimes difficult to track down. The same is true of military records; researching an officer is generally a more straightforward task than that of trying to piece together the movements of a soldier in the ranks. The death of an officer is usually recorded in the regimental war diary and in the case of the early Great War deaths they may also have an entry in databases such as the *Bond of Sacrifice*. But for many soldiers serving in the ranks it is only possible to build up a picture if their actions have been recorded. This may be as a result of wounds received or gallantry in the field but even then an element of luck is required. Additional family information can be obtained from census returns or where a surviving family member still exists, but for the purposes of telling their battlefield story a certain amount of conjecture is impossible to avoid. Such is the case with Private Walter Siewertsen, Lance Corporal James Whitfield and Private William Gibson. The exact circumstances of their deaths were not recorded in the respective war diaries or in any of the regimental histories; thus we can only speculate how they died in the light of what was happening around them at the time.

The great majority of the men who appear in the following pages were regular soldiers who were already serving when war was declared in August 1914, the remainder, with the exception of Second Lieutenant Baron Alexis de Gunzburg, were either reservists or former soldiers with a military pedigree. All did their duty as soldiers to king, country and regiment and in doing so occasionally demonstrated courage and gallantry that was above and beyond the call of duty. As a former soldier I have always marvelled at the manner in which the BEF stood their ground before Ypres in the last months of 1914. The horrors of sustained shell fire and its impact on the men occupying the trench lines, many of which provided very little protection, must have been the stuff of nightmares. So too must have been the relentless onslaught of the German infantry that outnumbered them and reduced some of the finest battalions of the British Army to a mere handful of men. The very fact that they remained in their positions day after day, often in the most appalling weather conditions, says a great deal about the quality of the men who fought in France and Flanders in 1914.

Typical of the resolute tenacity to be found along the thin line of defence that stretched from north of Ypres to La Bassée in the south was the mindset of Second Lieutenant John Lee Steere who was fighting with the 2nd Battalion Grenadier Guards (2/Grenadier Guards).[2] After being on the receiving end of a heavy artillery bombardment at Klein Zillebeke that lasted most of the day,

Lee Steere apologizes in one of his letters to his mother for the 'rather disjointed' nature of his writing, 'I must confess to being rather jumpy at the moment' he wrote, 'I hope it will pass off.' When I first read John Lee Steere's letters I had to remind myself I was reading the words of a teenage subaltern who had been at the front for less than a week and not those of a seasoned regimental officer.

The personal letters of John Lee Steere, Lieutenant Colonel Gordon Wilson and Lieutenant the Hon William Reginald Wyndham have without doubt enriched the text and provided an insight into the character of the men who wrote them. The Lee Steere letters present us with a personal glimpse into the trenches of 2/Grenadier Guards from the perspective of a novice platoon commander while the letters of Gentleman Cadet Wyndham, writing home from Sandhurst in 1894, rarely mention anything of a military nature and reflect very much the gentlemanly disdain for any form of professionalism that was prevalent at the time. On the other hand Gordon Wilson's letters to his wife recount his regiment's actions and reveal his growing concern at the number of casualties and his pride in their achievements. If he had any fears for his own future he kept them very much to himself. 'I keep well,' he wrote on 30 October, 'and am standing the life very well. I think of you always.'

A prolific letter writer, Regy Wyndham also kept a private diary that fortunately survived his death and was eventually returned to his mother at Petworth House.[3] His first entry was on 5 October on the SS *Indore* as he steamed towards Zeebrugge with the 3rd Cavalry Division, his last entry being two days before his death a little over a month later. The Wyndham diary in particular contains one of the very few personal accounts of 7 Cavalry Brigade's fight at Zandvoorde on 30 October 1914, an action that is to some extent still cloaked by obscurity to this day. Similarly, Major Lord Bernard Gordon Lennox's diary began on the sea crossing from Southampton on 12 August and concluded a few days before his death in November 1914. His diary covers the retreat from Mons, the struggle on the Aisne and the fighting around Ypres and is a classic account of a battalion of the Grenadier Guards at war. The extracts from both diaries appear as they were written except for the addition of the occasional word to aid clarity or the identification of an individual referred to in the text.

These men were part of a regular army that had evolved from nearly a century of reform and reorganization. Many had fought in South Africa in the second Boer War and most were typical of the Edwardian officer corps in their social origins and outlook. The book traces the historical and political processes that saw the British Army emerge from being the plaything of the aristocracy to the professional organization it became in the early twentieth century. By 1914 the regimental system that fostered regimental pride and spirit was at the very heart of British military tradition. A good proportion of officers were bound to their regiments by strong family ties and were part of a close knit community that knew each other well; many like Lord Bernard Gordon Lennox had married the sister of another officer in the regiment and followed his father and grandfather into the regimental fold.[4] His brother, Charles Gordon Lennox, married a daughter of Thomas Brassey the railway pioneer and the eldest of the Brassey brothers, Henry Brassey, was his brother-in-law. All the Brassey's served either in the Household Brigade or, in the case of Henry, in the Northamptonshire Yeomanry. These military dynasties were commonplace as family names became linked to regiments with the result that, even in 1914, connections rather than ability still continued to cloud judgement to some extent when it came to promotion.

Despite the reforms, the officer corps that went to war in 1914 was still very much educationally and socially exclusive. The previous dominance by the aristocracy and landed gentry was, however, in decline. In fact by 1912, apart from the Household Division and the Foot Guards regiments, the aristocracy and landed gentry comprised only forty-one percent of the entire officer corps and some sixty-four percent of the officers holding the rank of major general and above. There is no doubt the officer corps was still influenced very much by the values of the gentry and officers were expected to behave within the largely unwritten code of gentlemanly behaviour. When on active service it went without saying that regimental officers were expected to display leadership and gallantry and, if they could do so, retain as much gentlemanly demeanour as possible. Historian Gary Sheffield has made the point that 'officer man relations were characterized by the deferential conduct of other ranks in exchange for the paternalism of their officers.' This paternalistic behaviour would have included an expectation from the rank and file of appropriate behaviour from their officers both on and off the battlefield. The Canadian military historian, Desmond Morton, suggests appropriate behaviour on the battlefield for regimental officers was quite straightforward:

> '*They gave leadership, took responsibility, and set an example, if necessary, by dying ... Implicit was the assumption that the officer would be the first to die in battle. Officers were the first out of the trench in an assault ... and the last out in a retreat.*'

The close knit exclusivity of the army of 1914 meant that few officers were unaffected by the casualty lists that took up so many column inches of the daily press. I will always remember first reading my grandfather's diary of 1914 where he listed the names of his friends who were appearing in the casualty lists. The lists stopped rather abruptly in early October when he wrote, 'I have stopped recording now; the list is becoming too long.' Apart from losing personal friends, of which there were many, both Bernard Gordon Lennox and

Regy Wyndham received news of brothers who had been badly injured in the fighting around Ypres during October 1914. As you might expect, the deaths of friends and family members filtered through via the casualty lists, letters from home or by word of mouth. Lieutenant Michael Stocks, fighting with the Grenadiers on the Aisne in September, had news from home that his cousin Lieutenant Francis Levita had been killed with the 4th Hussars (4/Hussars) whilst on a cavalry reconnaissance, and before his death on 17 November 1914, John Lee Steere read in the press of the death in action of two of his cousins.

The gallant Brigadier General Charles FitzClarence VC, who was killed leading his men in December 1914, was not only related through marriage but was also a personal friend of Gordon Wilson. The distressing news of Wilson's death at Zwarteleen would have reached FitzClarence's headquarters at FitzClarence Farm via brigade staff by late evening or early the next day. Lieutenant Colonel Lord Henry Crichton, who was killed commanding the Composite Household Cavalry Regiment on 31 October at Messines, was related to Captain Richard Dawson serving with the Coldstream Guards. The sad account of Crichton's death quickly travelled through the units of the Guards Brigade and was passed on to Dawson in the trenches at Polygon Wood. The casualty lists of 1914 were the death knell of the Regular Army and I can understand my grandfather's grief when he wrote in January 1915, 'all the old families are disappearing, so many of my friends are gone and we have only just begun this dreadful war.'

Over the past two years I have come to know the Zillebeke men and their circumstances well. My research has led me to make numerous visits to the churchyard at Zillebeke and the surrounding area. I have walked the front line they so resolutely defended and stood on the ground where they fought and died. I have been privileged to read the letters they wrote and the diaries they kept; I have made visits to the schools and universities they attended and the places at which they lived and worked. They died in a war that was fought in our name over ninety years ago, a sacrifice we, and future generations, should never forget. This is their story.

Jerry Murland
Coventry
August 2009

Chapter 1

Zillebeke Churchyard

I first came across the Zillebeke churchyard cemetery almost by accident. I was driving through the village in February 2006 looking for the larger Maple Copse cemetery when my attention was drawn to a small cluster of Commonwealth War Graves Commission (CWGC) headstones in the churchyard. After a closer inspection of the dates on the headstones it was apparent that this was the final resting place of a number of officers and men who had been part of the original BEF of 1914 and who had fought in the First Battle of Ypres.

As with all such cemeteries the location and the manner in which they are laid out can often provide the historian with clues offering some insight into the circumstances that led to a particular locality being used. The rather random layout of headstones at Zillebeke, a known hot-spot in the Ypres Salient, suggested that the cemetery had suffered badly from the effects of enemy shell fire and the apparent empty spaces were possibly the unmarked graves of men whose names have been lost. I was instantly captivated by the poignancy of the place and resolved to find out more about the small number of men who lay in this peaceful spot at the centre of the village.

These were the men who had sailed for France in the early months of the war and who had 'played the game' to the last just as they had been taught throughout their boyhood years at school. They were men of a different character and disposition than those who followed; they were part of the last legions of Edwardian gentlemen: chivalrous, privileged, stubbornly proud of their traditions and patriots to the core. Above all, they epitomized the professional British soldier of 1914, earning the devotion of their men and the respect of their opponents. As an officer class we shall never see their like again.

Apart from the seventeen 1914 burials at Zillebeke, there is one other British officer whose death in November 1914 is commemorated inside the church itself. Although his name appears on the Menin Gate at Ypres, his family paid for a memorial plaque to be laid after the church was reconstructed. Lieutenant Alfred Felix Schuster was killed at Hooge serving with 4/Hussars and even

Table 1: The register of 1914 burials at Zillebeke churchyard cemetery.

Grave	Rank	Name		Regiment
A.1.	L/Corporal	**Whitfield**	James William	2nd Coldstream Guards
A.2.	2nd/Lieutenant	**St George**	Howard Avenel Bligh	1st Life Guards
A.3.	Private	**Gibson**	William	1/14 London Scottish
A.4.	Captain	**Neill**	Norman	13th Hussars
B.2.	Lt/Colonel	**Wilson**	Gordon Chesney	Royal Horse Guards
C.3.	2nd/Lieutenant	**Petersen**	William Sinclair	2nd Life Guards
D.1.	Lieutenant	**Tufnell**	Carleton Wyndham	2nd Grenadier Guards
E.1.	Lieutenant	**Stocks**	Michael George	2nd Grenadier Guards
E.2	Lieutenant	**Parnell (Congleton)**	Henry Bligh Fortescue	2nd Grenadier Guards
E.3.	Major	**Gordon Lennox**	Bernard Charles	2nd Grenadier Guards
E.4.	Private	**Siewertsen**	Walter Frederick	2nd Grenadier Guards
E.5.	Major	**Rising**	Robert Edward	1st Gloucesters
E.6.	Captain	**Dawson**	Richard Long	3rd Coldstream Guards
F.1.	Lieutenant	**Lee Steere**	John Henry Gordon	2nd Grenadier Guards
F.2.	Captain	**Symes-Thompson**	Cholmeley	2nd Grenadier Guards
SM1	Lieutenant	**Wyndham**	William Reginald	1st Life Guards
B.1.	2nd/Lieutenant	**De Gunzburg**	Alexis George	11th Hussars

though his body was recovered by the regiment after his death, there is no record of where he was eventually buried. Surviving members of the family are unable to shed any light as to why the plaque was placed at Zillebeke but the fact that his memorial is in the church suggests he might have been buried after his death on 20 November by his regiment in the churchyard. The churchyard is a little over a mile away from the chateâu on the Menin Road where he was killed.

The men recorded in the Zillebeke cemetery register, and in the church, took part in all the decisive engagements of October and November 1914: Langemarck, Gheluvelt, Hollebeke, Zandvoorde, Messines and the battle for the woods around Zillebeke. They served principally with Sir Douglas Haig's I Corps and Sir Edmund Allenby's Cavalry Corps and of the British burials that took place in 1914, fourteen are either from, or attached to The Foot Guards and Household Cavalry regiments, one is a 13th Hussar and one is a senior officer from an established county infantry regiment. Two private soldiers and an NCO from 1914 rest with their more distinguished counterparts, serving as a sharp reminder that death in battle does not discriminate.

Without exception all of the British officers commemorated at Zillebeke attended public schools before being commissioned and of these, eight passed through Sandhurst. Thus, as a group, they are very much representative of the Edwardian officer class that went to war in 1914. Zillebeke is also more of an aristocrats' cemetery than appears at first glance, eight officers and their families are listed in *Burke's Peerage,* one is a Russian aristocratic and three have entries in *Burke's Landed Gentry.* The remainder either have links to the aristocracy or are sons of wealthy professional families. Of the three rank and file soldiers, two are regular soldiers each with at least eighteen months service and one is a territorial volunteer.

Zillebeke and most of the commune were in British hands for the greater part of the war but even by November 1914 Zillebeke village, although behind the British front line, had suffered severely from German shell fire. One of the 2nd Life Guards (2/Life Guards) officers, Captain Sir Morgan Crofton, who served with 7 Cavalry Brigade, recorded his first impressions on 20 November:

'*We decided to walk back to Zillebeke which was about a mile off to see what the damage there was like in the daylight. We got there about 10, and found a fearful state of wreckage. Every house had been hit, whole fronts were torn away. The steeple had been knocked off the church which was filled with bricks and rubbish. The Altar had been hit and was covered with rubble under which the Altar cloth could be seen torn and stained. All the Candelabra, Pictures, Statues, etc were lying on the floor, broken and torn off the walls. In one corner a cupboard had been broken open, and the gold embroidered vestments were lying about on the floor covered with bricks and mortar. All the windows were broken but the organ was untouched. Outside in the churchyard, marked by rough wooden crosses were the newly made graves of Lord Bernard Gordon Lennox, Lord Congleton and Symes-Thompson, all of the Grenadier Guards, also Lt Peterson [sic] of my regiment, and about 20 others, all of whom had been killed in the attack of Nov 6th when Dawnay and O'Neill were also killed. Every house had its windows broken and in some cases the whole façade had fallen down and lay in a heap below, making the house look rather like a Childs Doll's House with all its floors showing ... I counted 15 shell holes in the street each large enough to buy a good sized cart. I felt so glad that it wasn't an English village.*'

Crofton's reference to twenty other burials is an interesting one. The continual shelling of the village and the church destroyed a number of graves over the course of time, many of the grave markers becoming lost or damaged. More significantly, the names of several of the dead became indecipherable, particularly if they were written in pencil as some were. Of the thirty-two headstones in the churchyard that we see today, six mark the unidentified remains of men whose names are engraved on the Menin Gate. It is a great tragedy that, for thousands of soldiers who fought in and around the Ypres Salient over the course of the war, their names will never stand over them in permanent memorial.

Of the unidentified soldiers at Zillebeke churchyard, all the indications point to one of them possibly being Alfred Schuster and another, the Mid-Antrim Member of Parliament, Captain the Hon Arthur Edward O'Neill of 2/Life Guards. Although there is no official record held by the CWGC of O'Neill's burial, contemporary 1914 accounts describe him being buried alongside Gordon Wilson and Second Lieutenant William Sinclair Petersen in the churchyard. William Petersen and Gordon Wilson were killed on 6 November 1914 along with Alexis de Gunzburg, Norman Neill and Regy Wyndham. In the same action on 6 November Arthur O'Neill and another Life Guards officer, Major the Hon Hugh Dawnay, who was commanding 2/Life Guards, was also killed and at one time both were thought to have been buried at Zillebeke. Hugh Dawnay's remains were later identified in 1924 as the unidentified Life Guards officer exhumed in Harlebeke New British Cemetery. Despite the high probability that Arthur O'Neill is buried next to William Petersen in an unmarked grave, the final word from the CWGC remains non-committal:

'It is possible that Captain the Hon O'Neill was buried in Zillebeke Churchyard and that his grave was lost, destroyed or became unmarked during subsequent fighting but we have no way of knowing this for certain.'[1]

There is a good case for the CWGC to re-examine the evidence and at least give Arthur O'Neill the chance of having his remains officially recognised with his name on a headstone. Until such time as that happens, his name continues to rest on the Menin Gate.

The destruction of Zillebeke and the churchyard from shell fire continued through November into 1915 destroying, amongst others, the grave markers of Private William Stewart and Regy Wyndham. Today the exact location of their remains is not known, hence the two special memorials on the west wall that have the rather unsettling epitaph, 'known to be buried in this cemetery.' In February 1915 Sir Morgan Crofton had another opportunity to go back to Zillebeke and he again noted the names of four officers whose grave markers were still intact:

'The body of Zillebeke church had almost disappeared, and so had the steeple, the ruined tower alone remained ... In the porch of the church, the only habitable place, lived a French guard of a corporal and four men, though for what reason they were there nobody knew. Inside the church lay the remnants of a 10th century font, and several broken plaster saints. The Church yard had several enormous shell holes in it, which had uprooted the monuments, smashed open the vaults and laid bare the coffins and the dead. These vaults were half full of rainwater, and in many cases the zinc or tin coffins were floating about, with their occupants exposed or bobbing over the sides ... I was very glad to see that the graves of Bernard Gordon Lennox, Congleton and Stocks of the Grenadiers, and Peterson [sic] of my regiment were untouched, though their names, which had been written in pencil on wooden crosses were in danger of being washed out by the rain and bad weather.'

By 1917 a network of front line fortifications with connecting communication trenches had been created in the Zillebeke sector. Communication trenches theoretically allowed movement to and from the firing-line to be conducted in comparative safety; one of these trenches ran right through the churchyard itself and was regularly used by the poet and writer Edmund Blunden during his service at Zillebeke as an officer with the Royal Sussex Regiment. He recalled:

'The [Zillebeke] Church tower was not yet altogether down, but had lost its architectural distinctions in one's quick movement over the road under German observation; one's eyes managed to register nevertheless a number of wooden crosses.'

Two of these wooden crosses would probably have marked the graves of John Lee Steere and Alexis de Gunzburg. At the end of hostilities they were replaced by the only two private memorials in the churchyard, erected and paid for by the respective families. They are unusual in that they break the CWGC's 'equality in death' principle that the Commission was founded on, to 'avoid class distinctions that would conflict with the feeling of brotherhood that had developed between all ranks serving at the front.' However, once the CWGC began its work, graves were marked in the uniform manner which is commonplace today in the silent cities of white headstones that populate the battlefields of the Great War.

Inside the church are two more permanent memorials to British officers, the more obvious is an elaborate stained glass window commissioned by Mrs Evelyn St George in memory of her son Second Lieutenant Howard Avenel Bligh St George who was killed on 15 November 1914. The window, designed and created by Reginald Bell, is one of a number of memorials commissioned by Evelyn St George in memory of her son. The Zillebeke window depicts the warrior knight St George killing the dragon and framed by the coats of arms of the nobility related to the St George family. The second memorial is less obvious but serves as a daily reminder every time the church bells ring out. After the war, when the reconstruction of the church and village began, the de Gunzburg family paid for the manufacture and installation of two bells that first rang out on the eve of the village fair in August 1924. Made by Slegers-Canard Tellin of Luxembourg, the larger of the two bells is called 'Catharina' and weighs 744kg, while the second bell, weighing 397kg, and appropriately named 'Alexis', carries the inscription 'Given by Baroness Henriette de Gunzburg to remember her son, the soldier Baron Alexis George de Gunzburg who fell in Zillebeke in the year 1914.'

Three French soldiers have their names commemorated inside the church and interestingly one of them, Petrus Joseph Chambourd, was also killed at Hooge. Was he brought to the churchyard by his regiment and buried with his two comrades-in-arms as I suspect Alfred Schuster was? Initially, there were a number of French graves in the churchyard which were later removed to the nearby main French National Cemetery at St Charles-de-Potyze. Their removal accounts for the open space in the eastern corner of the cemetery.

*   *   *

There are of course nine other identified burials in the churchyard that took place after November 1914 and it is not my intention to relegate their sacrifice in any way. However, as they did not take part in the First Battle of Ypres and, apart from Arthur de Courcy Scott, were not regular soldiers, they fall outside the scope of this book. Nevertheless, they did give their lives and for that alone they should not be forgotten. A brief biography of each of them can be found in Appendix 1.

With the exception of Arthur de Courcy Scott, Neill Thompson and William Stewart, the remaining six were all soldiers who fought with the Canadian Expeditionary Force (CEF). Three of them emigrated to Canada from various parts of Great Britain, two were Canadian nationals and one was an American by birth. Thousands of young men in Canada rushed to join up in 1914, many of whom had only recently arrived as immigrants to begin new lives and make their fortunes in what was seen as a country of new opportunity. The enormous exodus of young men from Great Britain in the second half of the nineteenth century continued into the first decade of the twentieth century with many of them returning post-1914 as part of Commonwealth expeditionary forces. Some though, like my great uncle Archibald Goode, decided to return home and join local regiments, others cut all emotional ties with the motherland and were happy to fight as Canadians.

Table 2: The register of 1915 and 1916 burials at Zillebeke Churchyard.

Grave	Rank	Name		Regiment
B.3.	Private	**Croft**	William John	24th Battalion CEF
B.5.	Sergeant	**Davison**	Walter William	52nd Battalion CEF
C.4.	Corporal	**Coyde**	Charles	15th Battalion CEF
D.4.	Private	**Sime**	John Carron	24th Battalion CEF
F.3.	Lieutenant	**Watson**	Frederick Johnston	43rd Battalion CEF
H.2.	Sapper	**Ilsley**	Charles Preston	6th Field Company CEF
H.3.	Lt/Colonel	**Scott**	Arthur de Courcy	1st Cheshire
J.1.	L/Corporal	**Thompson**	Neill	11th Royal Scots
SP2	Private	**Stewart**	William John	11th Royal Scots

Whereas the Australian Imperial Force was not slow in ensuring its part in the Great War was commemorated on every battlefield on which it fought, Canada's considerable contribution to the war effort was characterized more by the modesty and selflessness that mark the Canadian character. Canada supplied more than 600,000 soldiers to the war effort, while industrial and agricultural production, for war purposes, was also considerably increased. The first seventeen battalions of the CEF had sailed for England by 3 October 1914 and by the end of the war there were 260 Canadian battalions in existence. In the end, more than 60,000 Canadians lost their lives in the Great War.

The war of mobility that characterized much of 1914 had come to an end by Christmas of that year. The two sides entrenched themselves as they had done on the Aisne in September and shell fire became a feature of the daily routine of death. Artillery from both sides regularly targeted crossroads, assembly points, working parties and other strategic areas to harass opposing forces and disrupt movement. It was this random lottery of death that claimed the lives of Neill Thompson and William Stewart in December 1915 when their respective working parties were shelled. A shell also killed John Sime and William Croft while they were walking through Zillebeke with their platoon early on 7 June 1916. An hour and a half later a shell, possibly from the same German battery, killed Walter Davison at the ration dump behind the Maple Copse trenches.

*   *   *

The reconstruction of the new church in Zillebeke began in 1923, and apart from one or two improvements suggested by the Ypres architect, Georges Lernould, it is an exact replica of the old building. Prior to 1923 the church shared a temporary wooden building with the village school on Stationsstraat. Almost exactly a year after the first stone was laid the new church was ready to receive its congregation, which since 1919 had gradually returned to begin the task of reconstruction. This was not without its hazards. The deadly legacy of the war years was responsible for killing four Belgian workmen and seriously injuring four others at Zillebeke in September 1921 when workmen levelling the ground detonated an unexploded shell. The iron harvest of unexploded shells is still a feature of the Ypres battlefields today. Shells in various stages of decay are recovered annually from the fields in Flanders and they are just as dangerous today as they were after the war when there were far more of them.

Just as the war-ravaged landscapes were being reconstructed and revitalized, so were the myriad battlefield cemeteries that bore testament to the titanic struggle that had reduced a once peaceful countryside of farms, villages and fields to a muddy and desolate wilderness. In 1919 the Ypres area contained hundreds of small soldiers' cemeteries that were found in clusters where men had fallen in battle. Others were on the sites of casualty clearing and advanced dressing stations and there were, inevitably, the remains of many of the dead still lying unburied on the old battlefields.

As the task of reconstruction gathered pace so did the more gruesome undertaking of taking care of the dead. Most of the larger cemeteries such as Zandvoorde British Cemetery were left in place but many of the dead from smaller burial grounds were exhumed and gathered into larger cemeteries nearby. Of course, in 1914 there were no established war cemeteries in the Ypres area and quite naturally many of those who fell in battle were buried by their comrades in local churchyards. Zillebeke churchyard is one of those sites that became the collecting ground for those killed in the fighting around Klein Zillebeke and Zwarteleen. It is a sad fact, however, that less than twenty per cent of the 10,500 who were killed in the First Battle of Ypres have known graves; the remainder were either never recovered from the battlefield or were unidentified when they were found. These are the men who have their names commemorated on permanent memorials to the missing such as the Menin Gate.

The Imperial War Graves Commission (IWGC) was established by Royal Charter in May 1917. Its founder was Major General Sir Fabian Arthur Goulstone Ware. During the Great War he commanded a Red Cross ambulance unit and as the war continued he became more and more concerned about the fate of the graves after the war. With the help of Edward Prince of Wales, in 1917 he submitted a memorandum on the subject to the Imperial War Conference. The Prince of Wales became the Commission's first president and Ware its Vice-Chairman, a role that he held until his retirement in 1948.

From the beginning the IWGC – which later became the CWGC – set out to create memorials and cemeteries that would stand the test of time and, through their design, become a fitting memorial to the dead and missing. By employing the most eminent architects of the day, Sir Edwin Lutyens, Sir Frederick

Kenyon, Sir Herbert Baker and Sir Reginald Blomfield, to oversee the architecture and layout of the cemeteries and memorials, the Commission ensured future generations would be able to 'gaze in wonder at them and remember.' However, progress was not without its difficulties and the decision not to repatriate remains and to veto private memorials produced a storm of opposition. The debate continued into 1920 with the IWGC finally winning the argument that fellowship in death crossed 'all boundaries of race, creed or wealth'. By this time though the two private memorials to John Lee Steere and Alexis de Gunzburg at Zillebeke had already been put in place and it was sensibly decided not to replace them when the cemetery was designed in 1920.

The War Graves Commission section of Zillebeke churchyard was designed by William Harrison Cowlishaw under the direction of Frederick Kenyon. Cowlishaw also designed the Prowse Point, Rifle House and Devonshire Cemeteries in the Ypres area. CWGC cemeteries generally adhere to a standard design that takes the form of a walled cemetery in a garden setting with the precisely positioned Cross of Sacrifice as the focal point. A Cross of Sacrifice is usually only found in cemeteries with more than fifty burials and thus is absent from Zillebeke churchyard.[2]

So what of the other unidentified graves in the churchyard? Sir Morgan Crofton's diary suggests that they could be the men of 7 Cavalry Brigade who were killed on 6 November. In addition to Dawnay, O'Neill and Petersen, 2/Life Guards' war diary for 6 November 1914 records thirty-eight rank and file killed, wounded and missing, while the 1st Life Guards (1/Life Guards) recorded one officer, Regy Wyndham, and four men killed. In the same action the Royal Horse Guards lost their commanding officer, Gordon Wilson, and Alexis de Gunzburg, together with three other ranks killed. It is highly likely that a number of these men were buried in the churchyard alongside their officers.

In June 1915 twelve men of the Canadian 24th Infantry Battalion were killed by a single shell while walking past the church on their way to the front line trenches. The official history of the battalion tells us the dead were buried in the churchyard but today only two of them have marked graves, the remainder were either so badly injured that they were not able to be identified with any degree of certainty or had their graves later destroyed beyond recognition by shell fire. While the churchyard itself was never a battleground, it must have been a dangerous place to loiter in, particularly when it was under direct German observation.

A striking reminder of this was brought to my notice while I was at the Coldstream Guards regimental archives at Wellington Barracks. Having located the personal file of Captain Richard Long Dawson I was intrigued by the contents of a bulky package that had been sent to the regiment in 1991 by Colonel Richard Crichton, himself a decorated former officer of the regiment.

Richard Crichton was a cousin of Richard Dawson and had presented the regiment with the original metal nameplate that had been fixed to Dawson's cross after his burial in the churchyard. Although accompanying paperwork from the regiment indicated that the nameplate was intended as an exhibit in the Guards Museum along with a photograph of Dawson's temporary grave at Zillebeke, it has remained buried in the archives ever since. The nameplate has a rather eye-catching feature in the form of a jagged bullet hole, which is evidence enough to account for the apprehension Edmund Blunden felt when crossing the road by the church in 1917.

Chapter 2

Reform and Reorganization

Hanging in the aisle next to the St Edmund's Chapel in the Cathedral at Gloucester are the regimental colours of the 28th and 61st Regiments of Foot who fought for sovereign and country from 1694 through to Waterloo and the Crimea. Later, when they were reorganized as the 1st and 2nd Battalions of the Gloucestershire Regiment, they fought in India during the Mutiny and in South Africa at the turn of the twentieth century. The regiment has more battle honours on its colours than any other in the British Army, battle honours that recall the regiment's long and proud service from the time they were first raised as Gibson's Regiment of Foot to the famous last stand on the Imjin River during the Korean War of 1950. But perhaps more interestingly, for the military historian, those same battle honours highlight the significant watersheds in the development and restructuring of the British Army from the relative amateurism of the late eighteenth century to the professionalism of the 1914 Regular Army represented by the officers and men recorded in the cemetery register at the Zillebeke churchyard.

As the end of the eighteenth century drew to a close the British Army was in a poor state. It was by and large, albeit with some exceptions, incompetently led by the aristocracy with the rank and file said to be drawn from the worst of society; a body of men who would later be described by Wellington as the 'scum of the earth'. However, it must be said that this so-called rabble that Wellington led to a final victory on the field of Waterloo, fought its way up and down the Spanish peninsular for six long years and proved to be a highly effective fighting force in both victory and retreat.

In Wellington's army entry to the commissioned ranks of the Guards, cavalry and line infantry regiments had little to do with the ability to lead and command men. In almost every case a commission was bought and thereafter promotion carried a price tag which in most cases, providing one had enough cash and influence, enabled command to be bought without any previous experience of the battlefield. King George I had established a tariff of prices for commissions in 1721 and while these varied from regiment to regiment, in practice they were usually exceeded by as much as twice the regulation price. A lieutenant in the Grenadier Guards could expect to pay anything from £1,700 for his commission in 1798 while a lieutenant colonel could be looking at a starting figure of £5,400. Even then there could be a further delay before a vacancy in the regiment of choice became available.

This of course contrasted hugely with promotion through ability that was commonplace in the Royal Navy. Fortunately for all concerned Britain's navy did not achieve its formidable reputation through incompetence. On His Majesty's ships of war midshipmen had to pass stringent examinations and demonstrate practical skills before promotion to lieutenant could be secured. Senior naval officers were generally highly skilled sailors who had learnt their trade the hard way serving on the decks of the fleet. However, the winds of change were beginning to blow in the army and the first tentative steps in moving away from an assortment of amateurs towards a more professional officer corps were taken in 1849 when it became compulsory for all candidates for a commission, regardless of whether they bought them or not, to pass an examination. Although a small step, it heralded sixty years of reform that saw the army transformed from its status as a gentleman's club to a twentieth century professional fighting force.

In 1854 the Crimean War broke out and over the next few years the scandal of official ineptitude and consequent hardship and suffering caused nationwide concern at the state of the army and its leadership. Britain's soldiers have frequently suffered from the ineptitude of their commanders, however, on this occasion the military leadership excelled itself in setting new standards of incompetence. Unfortunately any immediate post-war reform beyond the formation of the Medical Staff Corps was short-circuited by the Indian Mutiny of 1857 which set army reform back by years. In the fifteen or so months it took to restore order after a widespread and bloody uprising, the army redeemed itself in the eyes of the general public and to an extent had its reputation restored.

While 1857 did see a Select Committee established to report on the purchase of commissions, incredibly it wasn't until fourteen years later that Edward Cardwell, the Secretary of State for War, finally addressed the issue with his Army Regulation Bill which he introduced to a sceptical Parliament in February 1871. The Bill was quite simple in its direction: it abolished purchase and ensured all potential officers for the army would now have to pass an examination overseen by the civil service commissioners. Promotion, albeit now inexorably slower, would depend on seniority and ability. Much to the chagrin of the Conservative peers and a vocal opposition group led by no less than the Duke of Cambridge, the Commander-in-Chief of the Army himself, the Bill was skilfully manoeuvred into legislation by Gladstone and Cardwell, who by-passed the Upper House by invoking the powers of Royal Warrant and in so doing guaranteed Cardwell a permanent place in British legislative history. Unfortunately the Commander-in-Chief would continue to be resistant to any change until he was sidelined and forced to resign in 1895.

The abolition of commission by purchase did not, however, effect a change in the social blend of the officer corps that had perhaps been hoped for. Cardwell did not take this opportunity to review officers' pay and conditions which left the door of recruitment open to the upper classes and wealthy landed classes and firmly shut to those without private means. Regrettably the continuing necessity of a private income was arguably in itself a purchase system that maintained the restrictive practices of officer recruitment.

However, having removed purchase, Cardwell continued to fly in the face of tradition and next turned his attention to the basic structure of Britain's Army. Under his localization scheme the country was divided into sixty-six brigade districts each based on county boundaries and population density. All line infantry regiments would now consist of two battalions, sharing a regimental depot and an associated area from which it could recruit. One battalion would serve overseas, while the other would be stationed at home for training and home defence. Included in his reorganization were the part-time militia units that were now to be brought under the administrative umbrella of the regimental depot and re-numbered. Thus the 28th and 61st of Foot became the 1st and 2nd Battalions of the Gloucestershire Regiment and the two Gloucestershire Militias became the 3rd and 4th Battalions. Many regiments, including those in Gloucestershire, were required to amalgamate to form the new two battalion structure. This inevitably resulted in a complicated internal wrangle involving much debate over regimental traditions and seniority, an aspect of military restructuring that continues even today when long established regiments and traditions fall victim to so-called modernization.

It took another war and a further series of military humiliations to bring about the next raft of change. The backlash from the reverses suffered in the South African War of 1899 to 1902 served two functions; it highlighted the army's shortcomings in the field but more importantly it served as a national wake-up call. The Royal Commission, chaired by Lord Elgin, that reported on the conduct of the war, was scathingly critical of the army's performance and in particular its inability to respond quickly to national emergency abroad and have sufficient reserves to draw upon. The South African War was a timely rehearsal for the future that provided the catalyst for further reform. However disastrous the South African War was to Britain's international prestige, without it and the subsequent changes it brought about, Britain would have been unable to mobilize as quickly and as efficiently as it did in August 1914.

Richard Burton Haldane's far reaching reforms that he introduced to Parliament on 25 February 1907, brought into being the Territorial Force and disbanded the Militia replacing it with the Special Reserve. Up until 1908 the

Militia was an accepted route by which a permanent commission in the Regular Army could be obtained. Rather than pass through Sandhurst, many potential officers, after passing the necessary examination, went straight from the Militia into their regiment, often as a second lieutenant. In 1890, when the young Winston Churchill was considering his future, he expressed his desire to enter the army through the Militia in a letter to his father,[1] 'It is a well known thing that a fellow who goes through the Militia is always much more use than a Sandhurst Cadet.' In the event Churchill did enter Sandhurst, albeit by the skin of his teeth, and ultimately was appointed to 4/Hussars as a second lieutenant.

Historians will argue that the Cardwell reforms fell short in two respects, firstly by not removing the Duke of Cambridge and more crucially, by failing to create a General Staff. With the Duke of Cambridge now gone Haldane moved to complete Cardwell's work and created the Imperial General Staff with Sir Neville Lyttelton as Chief of the Imperial General Staff. He also placed the final piece of the jigsaw into place by laying the foundations of an Expeditionary Force that would respond quickly to situations in Europe and the Empire. In doing so, Haldane was not only responding to the recommendations of the Elgin Enquiry of 1902 but was demonstrating a consciousness of Britain's future role in Europe.

Sadly the Territorial Force, one of Haldane's most innovative reforms, was never thoroughly tested in 1914 and was largely distrusted by Lord Kitchener who failed to appreciate the potential of these units as a reserve. In the event several territorial units did fight in Flanders during 1914 when the need for reinforcements became acute and one of these, the 1/14th London Scottish, a territorial infantry battalion, was brought into action at Messines on 31 October. Typical of the part-time soldiers that had signed up with the battalion was William Gibson, a 29-year-old Commercial Clerk from Ilford. William was mobilized early in August when the London Scottish were placed on a war footing and landed in France on 16 September 1914.

*   *   *

Just as the arrival of the twentieth century began a new era of military efficiency and professionalism for Britain's army, so it also began to sweep aside the old Victorian order that had underwritten the training of gentlemen cadets at Sandhurst but this did not happen overnight. By the time my grandfather, Lieutenant Colonel Howard Murland, entered Sandhurst in 1901, Regy Wyndham, the third son of Henry Wyndham, the 2nd Lord Leconfield, had already graduated and joined the 17th Lancers. However, in the seven years which separated the two cadets, military instruction at Sandhurst had hardly changed. In 1901 my grandfather was being instructed from the same military manual and drill book that the young Wyndham would have been familiar with in 1894. Astonishingly, cadets in 1901 were still being taught how to form a hollow infantry square to receive cavalry, with the front rank kneeling and the rear rank standing behind. Almost certainly the last time such a square had been used on the battlefield was at Ulundi on 4 July 1879 during the Anglo–Zulu War, although there were some later defensive formations based on the square used in the Sudan in 1896 and at Omdurman in 1898.

Training was also deficient in one other important skill that is fundamental to infantry soldiering, that of musketry. Even in 1902 cadets were not taught to shoot either with a rifle or a revolver despite the fact there was a range nearby. The shooting skills of British soldiers in the South African War, which had concluded twelve months previously, had been ridiculed by the Boers and generally shown to be below standard. Yet Sandhurst cadets who wanted to shoot had to pay an additional £1 per term to join a shooting club in order to become at least familiar with the mechanism of the rifle and revolver. In fact, more importance was placed on pipe clay than on the teaching of tactics.

However, it was the 1902 intake of cadets who were the first to benefit from the new order. The old blue serge uniform with the blue and red forage cap which Regy Wyndham and my grandfather wore was replaced by khaki for everyday wear. This coincided with khaki being adopted by the whole of the army and the introduction of the Sam Browne belt, so called after an Indian Army officer who was responsible for its design. Later, in 1902, a long overdue revised drill book was issued which probably caused more problems for the drill sergeants than it did for the cadets and the infantry square was at long last consigned to history where it belonged. Moreover, instruction in military strategy was brought up to date. Also abolished along with the blue serge was the post of Governor which was replaced with a new post of Commandant and the first to hold this post was Lieutenant Colonel Gerald Kitson, who had recently served as commandant at the Canadian Royal Military College at Kingston.[2]

Gerald Kitson took a keen interest in the education of officers and had given evidence to the 1902 Parliamentary Commission on Military Education that examined whether the instruction at Sandhurst and the sister establishment at Woolwich should be purely military and technical, or whether it should embrace general scholarly education as well. In the event a more rounded curriculum was introduced and Kitson's appointment was the beginning of a new period of development for Sandhurst which was begun just in time for the next generation of cadets. While the majority of cadets of my grandfather's era were senior captains in 1914, many of those cadets who entered Sandhurst during Kitson's tenure as commandant found themselves on the front line in 1914 as platoon commanders and suffered the most appalling losses.

The Royal Military College, Sandhurst was now the principle conduit for entry to the officer corps for both the British and Indian Armies and for many, the preferred method of obtaining a commission. Cadets who intended to make a career in the artillery and engineers attended the Royal Military Academy at Woolwich which had opened twenty years before Sandhurst in 1781. The two institutions would remain apart until 1947 when they were amalgamated into the Royal Military Academy.

From the tone of his many letters to his mother while he was at Sandhurst, it would appear that the 18-year-old Regy Wyndham found his military education rather hum-drum. Writing to Lady Constance in September 1894 he gives his first impressions of his new surroundings:

> '*This is a rather fearful place. I am in F Company which I am told is about the best for getting leave which is a good thing. I sleep with 2 others as present but shall probably get a room alone next term It is rather difficult to get fed which is a bore. One is only allowed to wear either uniform or regulation flannels with leave. It is a very pretty place with a huge lake in front of it. At present I am dressed like an ordinary private soldier which does not mean comfort. One feels rather like a convict without the broad arrows on. We do no riding school until our second term, tomorrow we work all day without a minute to ourselves.*'

Apart from his obvious enthusiasm for horses and riding to hounds, none of his letters contain very much about the military training he was receiving although he does mention firing a 'cannon' which he considered to be 'rather fun', which for a potential cavalry officer I suppose must have been a bit of a novelty. There is very much of the gentlemanly disdain for professionalism in his letters, an attitude that was very much prevalent amongst officers in the cavalry and the foot guards at the time. In December 1894 a letter home reported a typhoid outbreak that would have caused Lady Constance some considerable anxiety:

> '*I have nothing to record about this place but a chapter of accidents, one man in the company is very ill with Typhoid and it is very doubtful if he will get round. It appears that they have lately been picking several dead rats out of the hot water system and I suppose he must have drunk some of this water, probably out of a kettle for tea. One of the instructors here has broken his leg, he was a great football player and had played for England once or twice.*
>
> *PS please ask papa to send me some money some time this week.*'

It is refreshing to know that teenage students in 1894 differed little from their modern counterparts in their requests for money from home and their apparent relish in reporting incidents of doom and gloom. His father responded with a five-pound note sent from the Sussex family seat at Petworth with a reminder to 'be thrifty'. A month later Regy added to his poor mother's stress with an account of a fire:

'The whole place had a near escape of being burned down the other day while I was in the Gymnasium. One of the large cupboards in our mess was apparently fastened to the wall with wooden pegs and one had been burned through into the kitchen flue.'

In another letter, smarting from being admonished by his father for spending too much money on 'unjustifiable fripperies', he attempts to give reasons for his spending:

'I hope you don't think I have been spending money as I still have some left out of the former £5 and have spent absolutely nothing except on travelling expenses and what I have to give to my servant.'

Nevertheless, despite all the disasters and his apparent apathy towards all matters military, Gentleman Cadet Wyndham did pass out of Sandhurst unscathed and presumably with some military knowledge and understanding as his overall report described his three terms at Sandhurst as, 'very good', 'good' and 'very good'. At his passing out parade in January 1896 he marched in review order past the Duke of Cambridge, who in one of his last appearances as Commander-in-Chief took the salute. Two months later, on 24 March, the newly appointed Second Lieutenant Wyndham joined the 17th (Duke of Cambridge's Own) Lancers at Fulford Barracks, York.

*   *   *

Before 1914 an army career had been a popular vocation for the sons of the aristocracy and landed classes. Plenty of sport, particularly hunting and riding, provided these gentlemen officers with an occupation and a hobby. Undoubtedly being able to be a gentleman was probably why most men joined the army in the first place. It enabled them to perpetuate their lifestyle and social status at a time when other occupations connected with trade were not considered suitable employment for a gentleman. Other career choices such as the clergy and the law were unpopular; entry into the clergy required at least a measure of faith and decorum to be present and practising law demanded not only hard work and application but a university degree to boot!

Consequently the distribution of aristocrats and the landed gentry in the officer corps at the beginning of the twentieth century was fairly evenly spread across most regiments in the army, although this tended to fluctuate. Between 1875 and 1912, for example, there was a sharp decrease in the number of titled officers in the Guards and a noticeable increase in the Life Guards. Moreover, War Office figures show that by 1912 1/Life Guards had become the most exclusive regiment of all, seventy per cent of its officers had titles, eighteen per cent were from the landed gentry and only twelve per cent were from the middle classes. Interestingly, this degree of exclusiveness was only found in English regiments and amongst those, it was the preserve of only a small number, particularly in the Household Division and the cavalry. Few, if any, officers in the Indian Army for example, were titled or came from the affluent landed classes. Generally speaking, after 1870, regular officers were products of the public school system. Understandably so as the great majority of officers were recruited through open competitive examination at age eighteen, an examination that required passes in eight papers. These requirements practically guaranteed the public schools had control of admission to the officer corps through their special classes that specifically prepared students for the exam.

While a large number of army officers came from the upper and landed classes, as the nineteenth century drew to its close, the professional classes were beginning to make inroads into the ranks of the officer corps. Irrespective of class, however, by 1914 nearly half of all army officers were either the sons of serving or former officers or had a military tradition in the family. This was certainly the case with the Wyndham family. Regy's father, Henry, served in the Life Guards and his uncle, Percy Scawen Wyndham, fought with the Coldstream Guards in the Crimea. Percy Wyndham's son, Guy, followed his father into the army and joined the 19th Queen's Lancers, eventually retiring as a lieutenant colonel. Further back, Regy's great uncle, General Sir Henry Wyndham, fought at the Battle of Waterloo with the Guards in 1815 where he was severely injured. He took part in the famous closing of the gates at Hougoumont where his life was saved by Corporal James Graham, the soldier said to be responsible for slotting the bar home after the North Gate was shut.

Another cadet who entered Sandhurst in August 1896 was 20-year-old Bernard Gordon Lennox who had a long and illustrious military tradition behind him. The family's Sussex seat at Goodwood House was established at the end of the seventeenth century and has housed more than ten generations of the Lennox family. His great-great grandfather, Charles, the 4th Duke of Richmond, is probably best known for his unfortunate duel with the Duke of York in May 1789 while serving as commanding officer of the Coldstream Guards. Meeting with their seconds on Wimbledon Common,

'both parties were agreed to fire at a given signal The signal being given, Lennox fired, and the ball grazed His Royal Highness's side curl: the Duke of York did not fire.'[3]

Despite shooting at the second son of King George III, the incident did not prevent him from later becoming ADC to the King and, in 1814, a full general. Lennox was also appointed Lord Lieutenant of Ireland in 1807 where the young

Arthur Wellesley, who would later become Duke of Wellington, became his secretary. Their paths crossed again in 1815 when Charles' wife, Lady Charlotte, hosted the renowned Duchess of Richmond's Ball on the eve of the Battle of Waterloo.

Also at Waterloo, serving as ADC to the Prince of Orange, was Bernard Gordon Lennox's great grandfather, the 5th Duke of Richmond. He fought in the Peninsular War as ADC to the Duke of Wellington and was wounded at Orthez in 1814. He was later ADC to Queen Victoria. Not to be outdone, Bernard Gordon Lennox's grandfather also became ADC to the Duke of Wellington during his service with the Royal Horse Guards. Charles, the 7th Duke and Lord Bernard's father, was the first of the family to be educated at Eton and purchased a commission in the Grenadier Guards in 1865. Described as 'a stern military figure,' he not only lost Bernard in the Great War but also a cherished grandson, Lieutenant Charles Henry Gordon Lennox, in the North Russian Expeditionary Force in 1919.

No young man joining the army was under any illusion that it would make them rich. On the contrary the costs of serving could be quite high. Parents had to pay fees to enable their sons to go to one or other of the military colleges at Sandhurst or Woolwich. Even after being commissioned, officers needed a private income to sustain the lifestyle which regimental tradition demanded as a gentleman. The exception to this was to be found in the Indian Army where officers were generally able to live on their pay. Officers did not actually begin to earn a living wage until they were promoted to captain, which usually occurred after nine years of service. It was generally considered that a newly commissioned officer in a line infantry regiment in 1900 would require at least £200 to purchase his uniform, furniture, civilian clothes, servant's wear and an incoming mess payment. Another £100 to £200 per annum drawn from a personal income would be needed be cover his essential expenses of socialising and sport. Officers in the Guards and other exclusive regiments would need considerably more and for those in a cavalry regiment additional personal expenses could run to as much as £600 per annum.

In 1900 a second lieutenant in a line infantry regiment earned about £95 per annum and an officer of similar rank in a cavalry regiment about £120 per annum, a figure that had not changed substantially since 1800 and was quite inadequate given the demands made on a subaltern's pay. If we also consider that in 1903 Charles Booth published the results of his survey of London's poor and estimated that a family income of between £46.80 to £54.60 per annum was the baseline below which a family should be considered to be living in poverty, we get some idea of how badly young officers were paid. It was a similar story in the ranks. In 1914 an infantry private was receiving less pay than all other trades in civilian life, the poorest agricultural worker was paid two shillings more than a soldier with two or more years service.

No surprise then that army pay and conditions was the subject of a parliamentary question raised in the House of Commons in November 1902. The Secretary of State for War, William Broderick, was asked whether he would consider the advisability of appointing a committee to inquire into the position, pay, and allowances of the combatant officers of the army. Broderick's reply underlined the expectation that officers in the home army would have access to a private income, reinforcing the grip the wealthy landed classes had on the officer corps:

> *'No change has taken place in the position of officers in the Army of recent years, and the demand for commissions shows that it is impossible to satisfy the large number of candidates available. Efforts are being made, especially in the cavalry, to reduce officers' expenses, but I fear I cannot hold out any hope of a general reconsideration of the pay and pensions of officers.'*

Nevertheless, the enquiry into officers' pay did take place in the form of a select committee chaired by Lord Stanley in 1903, which unsurprisingly found that officers were grossly underpaid. Again rather predictably, the committee, bowing to political pressure, failed to make the recommendation that an officer should be able to live on his pay. This simply confirmed, as Broderick had the previous year, that a private income would remain a requirement for a commission in the army. However, it did agree that some items of an officer's expenditure could be reduced.

When he joined the 17th Lancers, Second Lieutenant Wyndham arrived complete with two horses and equipment supplied at personal expense which, when added to the cost of uniforms and other equipment, including furniture for his accommodation, produced a startling figure of around £1000! For the Wyndham family perhaps this sum would hardly be noticed – although his father did think it excessive at the time – but for others it represented a considerable outlay. In recognition of this disproportionate financial demand the Stanley Committee, rather reluctantly it seems, proposed that the state could provide mounts for the cavalry and even some items of essential kit. It would take another eleven years before officers' pay was finally increased in January 1914.

* * *

Once an officer had joined his regiment he was expected to adhere to the regimental code of ethics and behaviour and that included all the customs and standards imposed by his brother officers. Failure to keep within the acceptable social code and 'fit in' could, and did, result in social ostracism and ragging. There are numerous documented cases of excessive ragging which, by their very nature, could be quite brutal and degrading, being conducted by other officers in the regiment designed to force an individual to resign their commission. Some of these inevitably became public and were widely reported in the pages of *The Times*.

The infamous Guards Ragging Case of March 1906 involved a Second Lieutenant Arthur Clark-Kennedy who was an officer in the 1st Battalion Scots Guards. Clarke-Kennedy was subjected to a mock court-martial by the other subalterns in his battalion for allegedly being in a 'dirty state'. It appears from the reports in *The Times* that he had been infected by scabies, possibly from his reported contact with London prostitutes and had just returned from an extended sick leave. 'On changing into mess dress he went down to the ante-room where he noticed his brother officers received him very coldly and would not speak to him'. Later that evening after a court-martial in the billiard room he was found guilty of 'being dirty' with 'the itch' and subjected to an oil bath during which he had jam poured over his head and was then feathered. Later in the evening his room was broken into and he had to resort to jumping out of the window to avoid further punishment.

The official public enquiry was chaired by Lieutenant General Sir Gerald Morton and 'attended by a small army of reporters who filled the body of the hall.' The findings of the enquiry led to the removal of the commanding officer of the battalion and stringent reductions in leave and seniority for the subalterns who had been involved. The unfortunate Clarke-Kennedy resigned from the regiment.

A year later in 1907 there was a five day public hearing at Chelsea Barracks involving Lieutenant H Woods of 2/Grenadier Guards and his brother officers, who were alleged to have been involved in a conspiracy to have him removed from the regiment. Woods maintained he was picked on because he was studious and did not gamble and go to the Guards Club. Woods, who had six years service and until shortly before the inquiry was considered to be a good regimental officer, was ostracised by the other officers in the battalion who considered him to be 'unpopular'. The case drew in Lord Bernard Gordon Lennox, then a captain in the battalion, who was called as a witness for the defence. His evidence and that of other officers contributed to the case being dismissed. The army closed ranks and found no evidence of a conspiracy. Woods was found unfit to be a regimental officer and it was made it clear by the regiment that resignation was his only option.

It could be argued that the culture within the officer corps developed from the public school ethos of team spirit, loyalty and gentlemanly honour. The army's values still championed the leisurely lifestyle of the gentry and an officer was expected to be a gentleman and a gentleman was by definition educated at a public school. At school important links were made that could be used later on in the army to provide a common point of contact between junior officers and their more senior colleagues. With typical disregard for surroundings and circumstances the old Etonian tradition of celebrating Founder's Day with a dinner was continued during the Great War. Old Etonians of all ranks gathered together on 4 June in every theatre of war, an occasion which frequently saw the most senior Old Etonian officer in the brigade invited as the guest of honour.

One of the characteristics of the major public schools at the time was the degree to which they were essential to the recruitment of candidates for the officer corps. There is no doubt that between 1890 and 1910 the public school hold on the military academies tightened. In 1910 for instance, eighty-five per cent of entrants to Sandhurst were drawn from the major public schools while at Woolwich the figure was slightly higher at eighty-eight per cent. Is it any wonder then, that for many, the officers' mess was merely a grown-up extension of public school where those who did not 'fit in' were ostracised?

The public school emphasis on team games and sport taught those cherished virtues of self-reliance, loyalty, courage and selflessness which were replicated on the battlefields of the Empire and later, in 1914, on the 'playing fields' of France and Flanders. By the 1860s boys at Eton and Harrow were spending up to twenty hours each week playing cricket and other team games, the whole emphasis it seems being on character building and a determination not to let your team down. There is no better illustration of this than the occasion in the late 1860s when Clifton College were playing Marlborough at rugby football. Clifton played the (soon to be outlawed) hacking rule and Marlborough did not. Appealing to the Marlborough referee for the carnage to end, the Marlborough side were told to win the game first and adjust the rule book afterwards. They did exactly that. For the Marlborough players the game represented a basic fundamental of the battlefield: despite injury, suffering and being at a disadvantage, you fight on unselfishly, thinking only of your team and victory. Whether it be on the playing fields of Marlborough or holding the line in the trenches at Zandvoorde, surrender was unthinkable.

Bernard Gordon Lennox's school career at Eton was marked largely by his sporting achievements. As keeper, or captain, of the school Fives team in 1896 he won the school Fives championships that year with JC Tabor as his partner. He was also a member of the Oppidan Wall and Mixed Wall Game and the Field XIs. Eton has two games of football peculiar to the school, the Field Game played by the whole school and the more famous Wall Game which is played between a team of Collegers (scholarship holders) and a team of 'Oppidans' (the remainder of the student body). However, it was cricket that was probably the game he enjoyed playing most and although he did not represent Eton at the sport he was a regular member of the Household Brigade XI. In 1903 he made an appearance for Middlesex in the County Championship and in August 1912 he captained the public schools side against the MCC at

Lord's. His last major appearance was as a member of the I Zingari Cricket Club when he toured in Egypt with the side during March 1914 scoring twenty-four runs against the Egyptian national XI.

* * *

Some form of military training had been provided in public schools since 1860 but it was not until the Haldane reforms of 1908 that this was placed on a more formal basis. In 1908 the new Officer Training Corps (OTC) organised the existing school units into a Junior Division and a Senior Division which prepared university undergraduates for direct entry commissions. OTCs were directed to provide a standardized military training and Certificate A was introduced to test and certify proficiency. Certificate A was still in use when my father gained his in 1941 at Wellington College prior to joining the RAF. Holders of Certificate A were looked upon favourably when applying to Sandhurst and Woolwich and could alternatively obtain a direct commission into the Special Reserve or the Territorial Force. In 1914 nearly eighty per cent of public schools had OTC units and once the war began, membership became almost 100 per cent in all schools.

Overall Sandhurst probably supplied the most suitable education for potential cavalry and infantry officers but Haldane, in creating the opportunity for university students to become members of the University Officer Training Corps (UOTC), was obviously looking to attract the sons of the professional upper middle classes to train for regular and reserve commissions. The university route into the army was not a new one; all Haldane did was place it on a more formal footing by facilitating military training through the UOTC. Previously, up to 1894, university students were admitted on special terms to Sandhurst and Woolwich, a process that was streamlined a year later when they were able to be commissioned directly into the army providing they had successfully passed their degree.

The university route into the army was one that Robert Edward Rising took advantage of. After leaving Charterhouse in 1890, he began life as an undergraduate at Trinity College Cambridge in October of that year. Whether he intended to complete his degree or not, his period as a student was a short one, as he was admitted to Sandhurst after his first year at Trinity in September 1891. William Petersen was also a Trinity College student who graduated with a degree in History in 1913. Petersen had also been in the UOTC before being commissioned in May 1914 into the Essex Royal Horse Artillery, a territorial unit based at Colchester. William had clearly not considered the army as a career, preferring to serve initially as a part-time soldier but the events of 1914 short-circuited his plans to become involved in the Petersen family shipping empire.

Another university entrant into the army was Henry Bligh Fortescue Parnell who was a 16-year-old schoolboy at Eton when he succeeded his father, Major General Henry Parnell, as the 5th Baron Congleton in 1906. 'Harry' Parnell was a New College Oxford graduate and having spent three years in the UOTC was commissioned straight into the Grenadier Guards.[4] Like Regy Wyndham and Bernard Gordon Lennox, he was also born into a family with a strong military tradition. His father had spent nearly half a century in the army and fought in the Crimean War and at the Battle of Inyezane in 1879 during the Zulu Wars. In 1895 he commanded the Malta Infantry Brigade for seven years until his retirement in 1902.

* * *

So was the Edwardian Army that went to war in August 1914 a more professional body after nearly a century of reforms? The answer has to be yes. The officer corps was still a very select, elitist body and regardless of a growing influx of officers from the well-heeled professional classes such as Robert Rising, the wealthy upper and landed classes retained its overall monopoly, a state of affairs that continued well into the late 1960s.

The South African War taught the British Army a number of much needed lessons. The last of the so-called 'gentleman's wars', it provided a necessary transition from the old style colonial battlefield tactics to the more advanced use of aircraft, high explosive and poison gas that was to come after August 1914. Needless to say, military training had improved considerably since 1902 and was now embodied in the first of the four editions of *Field Service Regulations* which opened the way to imposing, what David French describes as, 'order on chaos'.[5] The infantry of 1914 were able to maintain a rapid rifle fire of fifteen aimed rounds per minute which was much superior to any of the major European conscript armies and they were well versed in the principles of fire and movement. Because of reluctance from government and to an extent the military leadership, to provide the army with enough machine guns, more attention had been placed on the British soldier becoming proficient in the use of the rifle. British musketry in South Africa had been largely ineffective against the sharp shooting Boers who delivered a harsh lesson to British infantry tacticians.

The other important lesson from the South African War, the ability to mobilize quickly and effectively, had also been absorbed and by 1914 national mobilization was taken very seriously and practised regularly with annual field exercises for all arms becoming the norm. Fortunately the cavalry had also been issued with the Short Magazine Lee Enfield rifle and cavalry troopers had become as proficient as their infantry counterparts in its use. It is almost providential that the far sighted Sir Horace Smith-Dorrien had insisted on this in 1909 when he succeeded Sir John French in the Aldershot Command. Smith-Dorrien was an infantryman and expected the cavalry to shoot and fight as infantry if called upon to do so. That time would soon arrive and the cavalry's dismounted actions in the battle for Ypres would become crucial in maintaining the integrity of the front line.

The British Regular Army that mobilized in August 1914 had an establishment of 260,000 men made up from thirty-two cavalry regiments and 154 infantry battalions supported by artillery, signals, medical services and supply companies of the Army Service Corps. Of this establishment only 150,000 men were able to be formed into a BEF of six infantry and one cavalry division, although this was increased to seven divisions by October 1914. Each infantry division of 18,000 men, usually commanded by a major general, comprised three infantry brigades, each commanded by a brigadier general. Brigade commanders in 1914 had four battalions at their disposal, a body of men and equipment that would take up to two and-a-quarter miles of road and up to two hours to pass a given point. Cavalry divisions were formed from a number of cavalry brigades, each of which contained three or four cavalry regiments with their supporting horse artillery units. Cavalry tactics were now standardized in a new edition of the *Cavalry Drill Book and Cavalry Training*, both of which had contributions from Sir Douglas Haig.

The quality of the very best British infantry battalions and cavalry regiments that fought with the BEF in 1914 was very much to do with a regimental system that fostered morale and a loyalty to the ethos of the regiment. Many of these fighting units were also characterized by exceptional commanding officers, typical of whom were Noel Corry, who commanded 2/Grenadier Guards until early September 1914 and his successor, Wilfred Smith.[6] Both these men were considered to be outstanding commanders and held the respect of every officer and man in the battalion. Cavalry commanders such as Gordon Wilson of the Royal Horse Guards and Algernon Ferguson of 2/Life Guards were of the same ilk; strategically able, good cavalry commanders and first-class managers of men and resources.

The battlefield self-sufficiency of infantry battalions and cavalry regiments fighting with the BEF, demonstrated so well during the retreat from Mons, was largely brought about by the battalion organisation of four fighting companies, or squadrons in the cavalry, that could, and often did, operate independently. In the First Battle of Ypres this professional ability and leadership of individual commanders from the most junior officer upwards would make a significant contribution to the outcome of many engagements. Robert Rising's Distinguished Service Order (DSO) was awarded in these very circumstances, while commanding his company in the face of overwhelming odds at Langemarck. Bernard Gordon Lennox directed operations and held the guardsmen of his Number 2 Company together during the engagements at

Landrecies and Villers-Cotterets and again in the Zillebeke front line. Commanding a troop of Life Guards, Regy Wyndham looked upon the welfare of every man in the troop as his prime responsibility both in and out of the firing line and earned their undying respect. Harry Parnell led his platoon of Grenadier Guardsmen with a bravery and battlefield aptitude that inspired his men to stand firm on 6 November in the face of considerable odds. In doing what they saw as their duty, all of these men demonstrated a personal bravery and leadership that bolstered the courage and confidence of the men under their command.

Leadership that encompassed personal gallantry on the battlefield was expected of all officers and very few were found wanting in this respect; those that failed to rise to expectation were quickly returned to the reserve battalions at home. But gallantry in the field is a costly business and the attrition rate of officers in the First Battle of Ypres was extraordinarily high, some battalions losing most, if not all, of their officers in a single engagement. Interestingly the rank and file soldier's point of view sometimes differed. John Lucy, who was serving in the ranks in 1914 with the 2nd Royal Irish Rifles (2/Royal Irish Rifles) at Neuve Chapelle felt that:

> '*The acme of officer leadership seemed to be to expose oneself in the most dangerous positions as an example to the men. All very gallant, but not very practical, and useless to us. We did not require any good example to fight in those days. Some of us resented the implication in such an attitude, and soon, in the still more difficult and more disastrous days to come, we heartily wished that our lost officers had taken more care of themselves. Their presence certainly always did inspire us, but a little more directing, and less example of studied bravery, would have suited us better.*'

Although the strength of the regular army was its regimental structure, the two battalion system brought about by the Cardwell reforms did have some disadvantages. Whereas in theory, both battalions would take turn about, one battalion serving overseas while the other remained on home service providing drafts for overseas, an equal balance was never quite achieved. The historian, Ian Beckett, draws attention to the home battalions of the regular army often being under-strength with 'young recruits or servicemen reaching the end of their term of service.'[7] Certainly the 1st Battalion Gloucestershire Regiment (1/Gloucesters) was very much under strength in August 1914 and only achieved war strength after the reservists were called up. Beckett also points out that in 1914 British regulars 'were not that experienced. Only 4,192 men having over fifteen years service, with 46,291 men registering under two years service with the colours.' However, this was compensated for to a degree by the overseas units which had a higher peacetime establishment of men and consequently required few reservists to make them up to war strength.

By comparison the German Army was a conscript army with a field strength estimated at five million men at arms in 1914. National service was established in Germany after 1893, each man served an initial two years followed by a five year term as a first line reservist or *Landwehr* followed by seven years as an *Ersatz Reservist*. Had the Siewertsen and Schuster families remained in Germany they would have been in uniform long before 1914. There was a further period of service up to the age of 45 in the *Landsturm*. German infantry were generally trained in the use of close order tactics with troops advancing shoulder to shoulder in broad waves some 500 yards apart. German commanders believed that this was preferable to troops advancing in open order on the battlefield which would be more difficult to control despite the heavier casualties.

The British Regular Army had practically re-invented itself since the Gloucestershire men of the 28th of Foot last took their regimental colours into battle at Alma in 1854. The companies of officers and men that stormed the heights of Alma suffered severely from a lack of effective command at brigade and divisional level and co-operation between artillery and infantry was non-existent. Furthermore, the rank and file were generally not well looked after by their officers and as a consequence, suffered badly. In direct contrast, the first seven divisions of the 'Old Contemptibles' of the British Army that landed in France in 1914, although not entirely free of their own difficulties at staff level, set the highest possible standards for the people's army that followed them. That standard was set at Mons, Le Cateau and finally at Ypres, where they held a wide frontage for weeks against an enemy which vastly outnumbered them in both men and artillery, but not in spirit.

Chapter 3

Officers, Gentlemen and Public Schools

On 2 March 1882 Queen Victoria was travelling from Windsor railway station to the castle when Roderick Maclean, a 32-year-old former grocer's assistant, stepped out of the crowd and fired a pistol at her carriage. Victoria was no stranger to violent assaults on her person, Maclean's attempt on her life was the seventh occasion on which a member of the public had attempted to harm her. The first and most serious was in 1840 when Edward Oxford tried to assassinate her and the following year there were two further attacks including one from a former officer of the 10th Hussars who struck her with his cane! On this occasion, however, many Eton College schoolboys were in the crowd hoping to catch a glimpse of the Queen, amongst which were Gordon Wilson and Murray Robertson. As Maclean raised his revolver and fired the two Eton boys rushed forward and helped to overpower and disarm him. Later that day the boys of the school marched up to Windsor Castle and the two young heroes were presented to the Queen. For Gordon Wilson this was the beginning of thirty-two years of service to his monarch.

Gordon Wilson was born in August 1865 in Melbourne, Australia and was the eldest son of Sir Samuel Wilson, the Irish born multi-millionaire who, after emigrating to Australia with his brothers in 1852, made a fortune from mining and sheep farming before returning to England. Sir Samuel was reported to be one of the richest men in England and apart from leasing Hughenden Manor, the former country house of Benjamin Disraeli, he owned property in Grosvenor Square in London where he lived until his death in 1895. In December 1861 he married Jean Campbell, and together they produced four sons and three daughters.

The fighting in South Africa during the second Boer War and later in France and Flanders took a terrible toll on the Wilson Family. Gordon was the eldest of the four Wilson brothers, three of whom, including himself, would not survive beyond 1917. All four brothers fought in the South African War, the youngest, Wilfred, was a lieutenant with the Northumberland Imperial Yeomanry and died of wounds received in February 1901 at Hartebeestfontein. Herbert Hayden

'Bertie' Wilson was a well known international polo player and a member of the successful English Olympic Polo team that won the Gold Medal in 1908 at the London Games. He won a DSO in South Africa serving with the Nottinghamshire Yeomanry and was later killed in action with the Household Cavalry in April 1917. The only male survivor of the Wilson family was Lieutenant Clarence Chesney Wilson and he was so badly wounded in the action near Geluk in May 1900 while serving with the 8th (King's Royal Irish) Hussars that he was invalided home. His wounds were such that he was unable to serve in the Great War, something perhaps his family was thankful for in retrospect.

Eton was the choice Sir Samuel made when it came to the education of his four boys. Gordon arrived in 1879 and soon established himself as an all-round performer in the classroom and a star on the playing field. Apart from the 1882 episode with Maclean which elevated him to almost legendary status amongst his peers, he was an outstanding sportsman whose talents ranged from membership of the school rowing eight to winning the one-hundred yards sprint, the half-mile and the hurdles in 1883. In February 1884, during his last year, he came second to Lord Newtown-Butler in the school mile and from all accounts would have won the race if he had not been hampered by spectators. *The Eton College Chronicle* clearly felt Gordon was robbed of his victory:

> *'Wilson was most unfortunately prevented from achieving a brilliant performance ... It is not for us of course to say that he would have won, but it is true to say his chance was entirely marred by the enthusiasm of the onlookers.'*

However in March, during their second encounter in the steeplechase, one of the major athletic events of the school year, he famously beat his rival into fourth place. *The Eton Chronicle* again:

> *'Once more Wilson was to the fore and proved still more conclusively that, as an all round runner, he forms a class by himself amongst Etonians and is possibly one of the best runners we have ever seen here.'*

From Eton Gordon Wilson went up to Christ Church College, Oxford, in 1885 but he did not complete his degree course. Student life obviously came a poor second to the more exciting lifestyle offered by the army. He had joined the Militia in 1885 while still a student, being commissioned into the 3rd Battalion, the Duke of Wellington's Regiment, with the rank of second lieutenant. However the glamour of the cavalry soon took precedence and after leaving Oxford in December 1888 he was commissioned into the very select and expensive Royal Horse Guards as a lieutenant.

Four years later in November 1891 he married Lady Sarah Spencer-Churchill, the sister of Lord Randolph Churchill. The wedding was a society event and one of the smartest of the year. The couple were married by the Archbishop of Canterbury at St Georges Church in Hanover Square. The Prince of Wales, who was a personal friend of Sarah's, headed a guest list that included nearly everyone that mattered on the London society circuit. Moving to one of the large mansion houses in Great Cumberland Place the couple lived a very privileged lifestyle attended by nine household servants.

During the South African War Gordon was seconded from the regiment as ADC to Major General Robert Baden-Powell during the siege of Mafeking. Captain Gordon Wilson, as he was then, was twice mentioned in despatches for his service in South Africa and was made a member of the Royal Victorian Order (MVO) in May of that year. Yet it was his more famous wife and her part in the Mafeking siege that grabbed the headlines in 1900. Having shut down the house in Cumberland Place, leaving two of the household staff as caretakers, she travelled in 1889 from England to Mafeking to be near her husband. While at Mafeking she was recruited as a reporter for the *Daily Mail* newspaper and from her vantage point in the besieged town soon gained a following amongst *Mail* readers in England. One of the many individuals she featured in her reports was a young Royal Fusiliers Captain, Charles FitzClarence, who had led a bayonet charge to retake some captured trenches at Mafeking. Charles FitzClarence and Sarah were related through marriage; Charles having married one of Sarah's cousins, Violet Spencer-Churchill, in 1898 whilst in Cairo. On returning to England he and Violet lived at Lowndes Street in the fashionable Belgravia district of London. FitzClarence's bravery on a number of occasions was rewarded with the Victoria Cross in 1900 and later, in 1914 as a Brigadier General, he commanded the troops of 1 Infantry Brigade on the Menin Road at Ypres.

Baden-Powell was altogether unhappy with Lady Sarah's presence at Mafeking and eventually succeeded in persuading her to leave in November 1889 for her own safety, a journey that ended in her capture by the Boers. From her captivity she wrote to her husband explaining her circumstances and passing on the Boer commander's terms for her release:

'*My dear Gordon*
I am at the laager. General Snyman will not give me a pass unless Colonel Baden-Powell will exchange me for a Mr Petrus Viljoen. I am sure this is impossible, so I do not ask him formally. I am in a great fix, as they have very little meal left at Setlagoli or the surrounding places. I am very kindly looked after here.'

Gordon Wilson replied from Mafeking on 3 December with the characteristic reserve that so typified the Victorian upper classes:

'*My dear Sarah*
I am delighted to hear you are being well treated, but very sorry to have to tell
you that Colonel Baden-Powell finds it impossible to hand over Petrus Viljoen in
exchange for you, as he was convicted of horse-stealing before the war. I fail to see
in what way it can benefit your captors to keep you a prisoner. Luckily for them,
it is not the custom of the English to make prisoners of war of women.'

Despite their obvious regard for each other, not a hint of his concern for her safety was betrayed in his letter and even in the later deal that was struck with the Boers for Lady Sarah's release, their letters to each other remained polite and concise. Eventually she was released and returned to Mafeking to work in the hospital and presumably to continue her work as a correspondent.

In January 1903, after his return to England, Gordon Wilson was promoted to major and four years later, in 1907, to brevet lieutenant colonel. In 1911 he achieved his ambition of commanding his regiment when he was promoted to the substantive rank of lieutenant colonel, taking over command from Lieutenant Colonel Arthur Vaughn Lee.

* * *

In April 1885 Robert Rising made the journey from Norfolk to Godalming to begin his first term at Charterhouse School. At 14-years-old Robert was already a natural athlete and the public school emphasis on games allowed his sporting talents to flourish. He soon became a regular batsman for the 'Weekites' cricket side and in 1889 he reached the pinnacle of sporting prowess by being picked for the School Football XI.[1] Charterhouse has an historic joint claim to having founded Association Football, a game which remains a major sport at the school to this day. Selection to play in the Football XI was a position many aspired to. The team of 1889–90 was certainly a distinguished one; the Captain was Gilbert Oswald Smith, who after graduating from Oxford University captained the England team on at least thirteen occasions and during the period 1894 to 1900 scored eleven international goals. Also in the side were Edward Buzzard and Edward Bliss, both of whom went on to have successful amateur football careers. As for Robert, he was described in *The Carthusian* in 1890 as, 'a good back who kicks well and stops cleverly, he makes good use of his weight and pace.'

In his last year at Charterhouse he won the senior long jump event and was second in the quarter mile and, as one of the school's leading athletes, was a member of the School Fire Brigade. Charterhouse had its own fire brigade in the late nineteenth century which was a very small and select body into which only the foremost athletes were admitted after election by their peers. Although the chief function was that of filling the water-jump for the steeplechase, occasionally the brigade did assist in putting out local fires. On one occasion the brigade turned out to a fire in Godalming without leave from the headmaster. The result was the appearance of two notices on the school board; one from the owner of the burnt property, thanking the 'young heroes' for their gallantry, the other from the headmaster, sending the 'young heroes' to detention for going out of bounds without leave.

Another Charterhouse student and a recipient of a junior scholarship was Alfred Schuster who arrived in the autumn of 1896 from Stoke House Preparatory School. He was following in the footsteps of his two older brothers, Edgar and George, who had already established themselves amongst the school's intellectual elite in Gownboys and it was not long before Alfred added to the academic reputation of the family by joining his brothers as a senior scholar.[2] But academic reputations were not held in the same regard as those achieved through sport. George Schuster later wrote of his time at Charterhouse:

> 'My five years there were a colourless period of my story. Social status in the school depended entirely on skill at football or cricket in which I ranked very low ... my general impression is that in my five years at Charterhouse I got practically no true education.'[3]

However, amongst their more academic contemporaries they were held in some considerable esteem. All three brothers went on to New College Oxford as 'exhibitioners', Edgar graduating with first class honours in Zoology in 1901 and George with a first in Classics two years later. Alfred left Charterhouse in 1901 and graduated with a second in Classics in 1905. What is clear is that all three of the Schuster boys left a lasting impression on their contemporaries at Charterhouse and just as Robert Rising achieved his standing amongst his peers through sporting ability, Alfred achieved his through his considerable intellect and ability to endear himself to practically everyone he came into contact with.

Whilst at Oxford Alfred was a prominent member of the Shakespeare Club, which had been in existence since at least 1867 and was formed for the simple purpose of reading Shakespeare's plays. There is no record of whether any performances were staged and like many of the college clubs and societies it did not restart after the Great War. There is, however, a photographic record of the membership which features Alfred during his association with the club and in one photograph he is pictured seated on the ground in front of his great friend Frederick Murray Hicks. Hicks was another gifted individual who graduated in 1906 with a first class honours degree in Classics and in 1914, as with many of that generation, was caught in the web of the Great War. In September 1914 he was commissioned into the Hampshire Regiment and went on to become Flight Commander in the RAF. He saw active service in Gallipoli where he was mentioned in despatches and was awarded the Croix de Guerre. Unlike Alfred he survived the war.

Despite his German name Alfred Schuster was a second generation British national. His father, Dr Ernest Joseph Schuster, had been granted British naturalisation in June 1875 after emigrating with his father and two brothers from Frankfurt in 1866. The moves towards German unification and the increasingly militaristic climate that accompanied it had prompted many to leave the country to avoid conscription and when Prussia annexed the free city of Frankfurt in 1866 it was the last straw for the Schuster family. Little did Ernest Schuster realize when he left Frankfurt for London in 1869 that forty-five years later the military aspirations of his old country would enmesh all three of his sons.

Once in London Ernest entered the family firm of Schuster and Sons, the bankers and merchants of Cannon Street, and by 1890 he had been called to the Bar, soon establishing himself as the leading expert on German and international law in England. Of his two brothers, Sir Felix Schuster was governor of the National Provincial Bank and Smith's Bank and Sir Arthur Schuster was professor of Physics at Manchester University and an eminent scientist. Little wonder then that Ernest Schuster's three boys were so gifted.

The outbreak of war in August 1914 placed anyone with a Germanic name under suspicion, regardless of their occupation or how long they had lived in England. The Schuster family were targeted by the press along with numerous others including Lord Haldane who had been educated in Germany and Prince Louis of Battenburg who had been a British national since 1868.[4] The Schusters were no exception and apart from calls for Alfred and his father and brothers to be interned, there was a more public case involving the family which resulted in court action in early 1915. Alfred's uncle, Sir Arthur Schuster, was accused in *Pearson's Weekly* of communicating with the enemy with a radio transmitter. Sir Arthur's chief protagonist was Lady Glanusk, the self-appointed spy catcher and chairman of the Women's Home Protection League. The Schusters were wealthy enough to take action over this completely unfounded allegation and sued for libel. Arthur Schuster won his case and was awarded costs and damages by Mr Justice Sargant who delivered a scathing address to the penitent owners of *Pearson's Weekly* who had published the story.

A less public incident was the demise of George Schuster's political career in the Liberal Party. Having been called to the Bar at the end of 1903 he first stood as Liberal candidate for Chelsea and then in 1911 for North Cumberland. He must have been regarded as a promising prospect as several members of the cabinet travelled north to support him at local meetings. On the very day that John Simon, the Attorney-General, was intending to speak at a political meeting in Carlisle in support of George, war was declared. As a candidate with a German name George Schuster had no recourse but to resign.

But for others such as the working class Siewertsen family who lived the East End of London, anti-German feeling often manifested itself in a more violent form. Hans Christian Siewertsen was German born, and like the Schusters, had been resident in England for a considerable period of time. Hans had married in 1890 and in 1914 he and Mary Anne were living at Rosher Road in Stratford East with their six children. Hans was a fur skin dresser with a local firm and his eldest son, Walter Frederick, began his adult working life in the same trade after leaving school. But like many young men of the period he wanted more out of life and a release from the overcrowded conditions in the family home. His father was very proud when, soon after his nineteenth birthday, Walter enlisted in the Grenadier Guards. In 1914, after war was declared and Walter had left for France with his battalion, the family was subjected to constant verbal abuse and had their property vandalised by neighbours who had previously been counted as friends. A heartbroken Hans could not equate this with having a son serving with the regular army at the front with 4 (Guards) Brigade. He was never to see Walter again.

* * *

In May 1897 Second Lieutenant Regy Wyndham received notice that 17/Lancers were to move from York to Ireland and to be stationed at Ballincollig and Cork. To Regy's delight the regiment took over the Muskerry Hounds from 12 /Lancers on arrival at Ballincollig and he was chosen to be Whip. Regimental duties aside, he and his brother officers spent a large proportion of their time riding to hounds and enjoying the country sports that the area around Ballincollig offered. Consequently it was with some personal regret that his squadron moved in 1898 to the Cork barracks. At Cork, disaster struck; Regy contracted typhoid in January 1898 and became so seriously ill that his mother was sent for. In February his condition was described as 'critical' and his father was preparing to go to Cork to see his son possibly for the last time, but the crisis passed and by early March he was on the road to recovery. The recovery process was slow and Lady Constance brought her son home to Petworth to convalesce until he returned to the regiment in 1899.

His return to Ireland was overshadowed by the clouds of war that were gathering in South Africa. These soon became reality when embarkation orders arrived for the regiment to report to Tilbury Docks on Valentine's Day 1900. Regy was one of the three officers who remained behind at Ballincollig with the reserve squadron and did not arrive in South Africa until nearly a year later in March 1901. He arrived in time to see some of the major actions in which his regiment fought and to be under the command of his cousin Lieutenant Colonel Guy Wyndham who temporarily commanded 17/Lancers for two months in May 1901.

Back from South Africa in 1902 the regiment moved to Piershill barracks at Edinburgh where they settled back into peacetime duties. Here Regy's military career with 17/Lancers was again disrupted by a serious riding accident in 1903. Hunting was his great passion and after spending time in Ireland with the regiment he was a frequent visitor thereafter. On this occasion he remembered very little of the actual accident. Writing after the event it is clear he had already contemplated the future of his army career:

> *'I have at last got leave to write my first letter, late enough. I think I remember the day of the mash up to about ten minutes before it occurred. Everyone has been very kind to me. Mother has faithfully sat by me in the best of ways and seen nothing of the spring enjoyments that take place here … It is no use in my keeping my horses as I shall probably be away from my regiment a good time.'*

He was right about that. The accident brought about the end of his army service; he had been badly concussed in the accident and had broken several bones. Recovery was again a lengthy business and by the time he was considering his return to duty, the regiment was under orders to move to India. This may have been the deciding factor that persuaded him to resign his commission, the prospect of being buried away on service in India away from his beloved horses and hunting was probably too much to bear. Although his accident gave him the prefect pretext for leaving the army it does not seem to have prevented him from leading a thoroughly active life in Africa and later in the Rocky Mountains in America. In 1912 he was elected a member of the Jockey Club and settled down to pursue his great passion in life, horses and hunting.

* * *

The young Harry Parnell was an all-round sportsman. He was an excellent shot, a good athlete and regularly ran with the beagles both at Eton and later at university. In his last two years at Eton he represented the school in the Rugby XV; a game he continued to play at Oxford. In 1908, during his last year at the school, he was joined by his younger brother William Alastair Damer Parnell who would follow him into the Grenadier Guards in 1915. When Harry left Eton College in 1909 for New College, Oxford, to study for a degree in Modern History, he initially thought the place to be 'dull.' In a letter to his mother, Elizabeth the Dowager Lady Congleton, on 8 October 1909, he gave her his first impressions of his new surroundings:

> *'I saw my tutor this morning – Mr Fisher – he seems rather nice … I have got quite nice rooms on the second floor … my packing cases arrived from Eton all right. It seems pretty dull here but I expect it will be more exciting next week when the term really commences.'*

His tutor was in fact Herbert Albert Laurens Fisher who became Minister of Education in 1916 during the Government of David Lloyd George and was instrumental in much of the content of the 1918 Education Act. Fisher later returned as Warden of New College in 1926. There is no record of Fisher's thoughts on his young charge but he must have despaired at his lack of academic commitment. Harry Parnell's first year at Oxford was not an altogether successful one. He clearly saw student life as an opportunity for a very wealthy young man to behave badly and enjoy himself in the company of like-minded individuals; an attitude that was in direct contrast to that of Alfred Shuster and one that gave Lady Congleton much cause for concern over her son's conduct. In January 1910 he wrote to his mother about his plans for the summer and added a hint of what might be the result of his lack of application:

'My examinations start on 10 March so they will not interfere with going abroad unless I have to come back in the middle of the time for a viva voce exam which I believe is quite possible.'

In the event it wasn't, as he seems to have managed to pass his first year examinations but he was involved in a serious episode two months later which resulted in him being 'gated':

'I am gated for the present, which means I have to be in college by 9pm. This is owing to a bonfire we had on Wednesday past I and some other fellows built it in the middle of the quad and after dousing it with spirit set fire to it. Unfortunately it occurred to 2 fellows to break into the Don's dining room and place all the furniture on the bonfire.
  NB I have not been here a year yet!'

The bonfire was the work of the New College Twenty Club, a shooting club for wealthy students that Harry belonged to. While some of the group were sent down for their part in this incident, it appears Harry was not. Even so the bill for the destroyed furniture was £60 and placed firmly in the hands of the perpetrators. Harry's second year at New College was marked with another incident that resulted in him being sent down for two weeks in April 1911 and later for the remainder of the term. He was only readmitted for the start of the autumn term in 1912. The Warden of New College was William Spooner and although he was instrumental in Harry's exclusion, as well as having fined him on several occasions for riotous behaviour, he does seem to have had a liking for his wayward student. Spooner himself was well respected by the students and it was largely his influence, supported by Herbert Fisher and Lady Congleton, which achieved a remarkable turnaround in Harry Parnell's attitude to his

studies. When he finally graduated in 1912 with a second class degree, Spooner
wrote to Lady Congleton:

> *'I feel very much indebted to you for your tolerance and courtesy in circumstances,*
> *as you say, have been trying for us both. I feel he [Harry] has made full use of*
> *his time here to gain so distinguished a class in addition to getting through his army*
> *examinations. I hope this will be the beginning of a prosperous and successful*
> *career.'*

After Harry joined the Grenadier Guards in 1912 he continued his wealthy,
privileged lifestyle that included extensive foreign travel and shooting
expeditions to the Rocky Mountains in America. He clearly had an adventurous
spirit and after meeting J Forster Stackhouse in 1913 he was determined to
accompany him on his proposed Antarctic expedition to King Edward VII Land
in 1914. In November 1913 he wrote to his younger brother William, who was
still at Eton, outlining his intentions:

> *'I have been interviewing a J F Stackhouse who is head of the Antarctic*
> *Expedition that is leaving England this time next year and I think of*
> *accompanying him as he is thinking of making a sort of round trip by the Cape*
> *and back by New Zealand and the Panama Canal and will take about 18 to 24*
> *months. I think I could probably get seconded for it and would go as a surveyor.'*

Harry was a qualified surveyor and his interest was just what Stackhouse
needed to publicise his expedition, particularly as he had no previous Antarctic
experience apart from assisting Scott in arranging his expedition in 1910.
Stackhouse desperately needed the patronage of establishment figures such as
Harry Parnell if he was to raise the substantial funding necessary for the
expedition to go ahead. Apparently before Scott left on his ill-fated 1910
expedition, he had urged Stackhouse to lead a scientific expedition to King
Edward VII Land and Stackhouse was intending to use Scott's old ship,
Discovery. The project was doomed from the start, the funds failed to
materialize, the public preferring to support the better known explorer Ernest
Shackleton, who was also intending to leave from England for the Antarctic in
1914. Despite the outbreak of war Shackleton left for the Southern Ocean on 8
August by which time Harry had been mobilized. Stackhouse was tragically
drowned on 7 May 1915 when the RMS *Lusitania* was torpedoed and sank off
Ireland. Even if the Stackhouse expedition had gone ahead it is doubtful that
Harry would have gone with them, the great adventure waiting across the
Channel would have been far too tempting to miss out on.

* * *

John Lee Steere was born on Friday 14 June 1895 and was the only child of Henry and Anna Lee Steere. Descendants of the family first settled in Ockley during the sixteenth century and today the Lee Steere family estate at Jayes Park still sits above the Surrey village of Ockley nestling in the shadows of Leith Hill, the highest point in south-east England. John's family was well connected, his grandfather, Lieutenant Colonel Lord Charles Fitzroy fought in the Peninsular Wars with the Foot Guards and later at Waterloo where he was military secretary to the Duke of Wellington. In October 1825 Charles Fitzroy married Lady Anne Cavendish, a daughter of George Cavendish, the Earl of Burlington, whose brother, Lieutenant General Henry Cavendish, was Colonel of the Queen's Bays from 1852 until 1873.[5]

The family also has an extensive Australian connection, principally through Sir James George Lee Steere who as a midshipman entered the East India Company's mercantile marine in 1845 eventually rising to command the *Devonshire* in 1854. In 1855 his younger brother, Augustus, emigrated to Western Australia and James decided to follow. James and his wife built a house, naming it Jayes after the ancestral estate, and there they raised their family of eleven children. In this colonial environment Lee Steere quickly prospered and in 1868 was elected to represent the south district which was to be the beginning of a career in business and politics that culminated in 1898 when he was appointed KCMG and made his final visit to England.

In 1908, aged 13, John Lee Steere arrived at Eton College from Wixenford Preparatory School where he quickly settled in under the watchful eye of his tutor Ernest Churchill. His first impressions were the subject of one of his first letters to his mother:

'*I am now beginning to get accustomed to life here, I am sure I shall love it. It is such a lovely place, I am quite happy here. I begin fagging on the 5th, I am going to fag for Dawkes the head of house, he has two others, Taylor and Glasbrooke.*'

His Eton school report for 1908 described him as a capable boy who asked 'rather tiresome' questions in his mathematics lessons. His tutor concluded with:

'*Altogether I am quite content with him and his progress. I am quite clear he is not at all stupid. He is a good little chap and you need have no anxiety on his behalf, he is doing all right and is sound in both head and heart.*'

While such a report would be unacceptable today, it did at least indicate that John had settled into school life and by 1909 he had become a regular member of the school beagling fraternity, reporting his many hunting adventures in his letters home. Beagling is still a popular activity amongst the boys at Eton and its origins go back as far as 1858 when there were two beagling packs at the college. Many boys brought their own dogs for the season and one hound called 'Bellman' was owned by a young Bernard Gordon Lennox while he was at the school in 1896.

Apart from running with the beagles John Lee Steere was also focused on his future career. Described as 'always good-tempered and cheery with an undercurrent of seriousness in his character' he had clearly decided on joining the army from an early age; a choice which was probably influenced by his grandfather and demanded some academic application in order to enter the Army Class which prepared boys for the army examinations. In December 1909 he assured his mother that he was working 'as hard as I can in trials (school examinations) to get into the Army Class.' This he managed to do and three years later he entered Sandhurst as a prize cadet in February 1913.

Another keen beagler was Howard St George who began life at Eton in the same term as John Lee Steere. Howard's elder brother, George Baker St George was already a senior boy at the school and no doubt this eased Howard's transition from his preparatory school at Hazelwood to the harsher rough and tumble of life at Eton. Described in the *Eton Chronicle* as one 'who had no taste for book learning' Howard was a keen follower of the beagles at Eton and in 1912 was elected one of the Whips. He was also an accomplished distance runner and came third in the steeplechase in his final year. John Lee Steere and Howard St George would without doubt have known each other at school, coming into frequent contact through their common interest in beagling.

The St George boys were related to the County Galway Irish aristocratic family through their father Howard Bligh St George who is described in Irish census records as a 'gentleman of means'. In 1891, much to her father's surprise, he married Florence Evelyn Baker, the daughter of George Fisher Baker, the American financier and philanthropist who was chairman and co-founder of the First National Bank of New York. George Baker was spectacularly wealthy. In 1909 his shares in the First National were said to be worth twenty million dollars. Initially the St George family lived in the small town of Screebe in the west of Ireland, where George, Howard and their sister Gardinia were born, but in 1905 relocated to Clonsilla Lodge near Blanchardstown, just outside Dublin.

It was at Dublin that Evelyn St George was introduced to the painter William Orpen by her husband's cousin Annie.[6] Orpen was commissioned by the family to paint two full length portraits of Howard and Evelyn, an enterprise that began as a formal business arrangement but blossomed into a love affair with the latter that was to last for fifteen years and resulted in the birth of a daughter, Vivian, in 1912. Their deepening relationship is apparent in the series of portraits Orpen painted of Evelyn concluding with his monumental portrait of her which was completed in 1914.

Initially their affair was conducted in secret but became public after 1912 when Evelyn moved to Berkeley Square in London where she had a flat. At Berkeley Square the lovers continued their liaison and began appearing together with increasing frequency in London society. This did not go unnoticed by the press and was often commented upon in the popular press society pages, particularly as Evelyn St George was over six feet tall and her lover was only just over five feet tall. Inevitably they became known as 'Jack and the Beanstalk'.

In 1912 the St Georges were also renting an estate at Ashorne Hill near Leamington Spa in Warwickshire but by this time the relationship between Evelyn and her husband Howard was beyond repair and although they ostensibly led separate lives they still maintained a public façade. Despite this, Evelyn was from all accounts a loving and devoted mother to the children and William Orpen was instrumental in helping her overcome her grief when Howard was killed in 1914.

*   *   *

The Stocks family fortune was made in the north of England and dates back to 1603 when a John Stokes began mining coal in the Shibden Valley near Halifax. Later members of the family ran and developed the Stocks brewing empire along with the mining interests and by 1850, when the family were living at Upper Shibden Hall, their property consisted of 'extensive quarries and coal mines and one of the largest breweries in the country.' As prominent businessmen the family also became involved in local politics having a great influence in the incorporation of Halifax as a Borough in 1848.

Michael George Stocks was born in November 1892 and was not the first of his family to attend Eton, his cousin Francis Ellison Levita had been an Eton scholar since 1903 and Michael followed three years later in 1906. The family wealth and prosperity were at their height when their paternal grandfather, Michael Stocks, returned from the battlefields of the Crimea and retired from the army. He married Jane Maceckran in 1863 and inherited Upper Shibden Hall and the family businesses on the death of his father in 1872. Major Michael Stocks, served as a captain in the 1st Royal Dragoon Guards and took part in the disastrous charge of British cavalry led by Lord Cardigan during the Battle of Balaclava on 25 October 1854. He also fought in the attack on the Redan and at Sebastopol where he received the Turkish Order of Mejide. He returned home a local hero after lengthy reports of his personal bravery in the battle were published in the *Halifax Courier*.

Not content to remain in the north he purchased the Norfolk estate and manor house at Woodhall, near Downham Market. Becoming lord of the ancient manor at Woodhall gave Stocks the pedigree he felt was missing from his life and an entry in *Burke's Landed Gentry*. Major Stocks died five years after his first grandson was born and although his own son did not choose the army as a career, by insisting on his two grandsons being educated at Eton he left them a legacy that set both boys on their inexorable march to the Great War battlefields of 1914.

* * *

In the south aisle of All Saints Church at Kenley there is a memorial tablet to Laura Gertrude Tufnell who died aged 52 at Watendone Manor in 1911. The 1901 census describes her husband, Carleton Fowell Tufnell, as an insurance broker and underwriter. The Tufnell family lineage in *Burke's Landed Gentry* begins with Richard Tufnell of Surrey who was MP for Southwark in 1640. Thereafter, through marriage and public appointment, the family wealth was accrued. Carleton Fowell was also a very capable county cricketer and after leaving Eton College in 1872 made several appearances for Kent County Cricket Club in 1879, taking fifteen wickets and scoring a total of 108 runs. It was at Watendone Manor that Carleton Wyndham Tufnell was brought up with his sister and three brothers and, as one might expect, followed his father and elder brother to Eton in 1905. The young Carleton Tufnell inherited his father's sporting talent and soon established himself amongst Eton's sporting elite, quickly surpassing the achievements of his elder brother, Neville Charsley Tufnell, who had made a name for himself as a sportsman before going up to Trinity College, Cambridge in 1906.

At Eton if a boy excelled at games the world was his oyster. While the school was happy to reward mediocrity in the classroom the academic rewards were nothing compared to the prizes to be won by the sporting hero. Carleton Tufnell was certainly a sporting hero in the eyes of his peers; between 1908 and 1910 he played in the Field XI, Eton's version of football, in 1911 he captained the Eton Cricket XI and was keeper of the Oppidan and Mixed Wall games from 1909 to 1910. Carleton Tufnell was also President of the Eton Society in his final year at the school. The Eton Society, or Pop as it became known, was founded in 1811 as a social and debating club. Membership of Pop is held in high regard by the student body particularly as election is by a ballot and carries a number of privileges which include a more ostentatious style of everyday dress. Pop is also the school's prefectorial body responsible for internal school discipline and before corporal punishment was outlawed members of Pop administered such punishment on their peers.

By the early twentieth century the intellectual element of Pop with its debates and discussions had been largely replaced by the sporting elite of the school. Not so when the young Regy Wyndham was at the school; his only sporting accomplishments were riding to hounds and beagling, but he was a member of Pop in 1893. In one of his letters to his mother he wrote, with his characteristic indifference, of a forthcoming debate:

> *'We have a debate tonight on a subject proposed by Donaldson: Whether the casino at Monte Carlo should be allowed or not. These may not be the exact words but its something like that.'*

But by 1913, when Howard St George was elected to the Eton Society, the debating element had all but gone.

Tufnell's final honour was the award of the Victor Ludoram Cup in 1911 which is presented to the boy who wins the most points in school sporting events. Carleton Tufnell was the epitome of the public school sporting culture and rather appropriately his headstone in the Zillebeke Churchyard carries the epitaph *Floreat Etona*, an expression that not only describes the sporting ethos of Eton, but is also identified with courage and gallantry. When Lieutenant Robert Elwes rode to his certain death at Laing's Nek in 1881 during the first Boer War his last words were reported to have been *Floreat Etona*. H Rider Haggard in his autobiography *The Days of my Life* remembers meeting Elwes at dinner the night before the British forces left Maritzburg:

> *'The only name that I can remember is that of young Elwes, who within a week or two was to die charging the Boer schanzes and shouting "Floreat Etona!" I sat next to him at table.'*

It leaves one to wonder if those same words were the last gasp of Carleton Tufnell when he fell in action on 6 November 1914.

*   *   *

The Perthshire public school, Glenalmond College, formerly Trinity College, lies on the River Almond near Methven and was the school chosen for William Sinclair Petersen. It was one of a number of minor public schools that were founded in the mid-nineteenth century and modelled largely on the successful system that had been in use at schools such as Eton, Harrow and Charterhouse. The culture of duty and service was embodied in the school motto, *Floreat Glenalmond*, an ethos that 157 former students took with them to their deaths during the four years of the Great War. The first of these was Lieutenant Colonel Alfred McNair Dykes who was killed commanding the 1st Battalion King's Own on 26 August 1914.[7] His obituary in the *Glenalmond School Chronicle* described his 'sacrifice' and thrilled the Glenalmond schoolboy readers with the account of Dykes falling in battle after shouting encouragement to his men. By the end of 1914 there were 113 old boys serving as officers in the army but by then the casualty figures included several more of the school's former students.

William Petersen was born at Newcastle in July 1892 and was the only son of Sir William Petersen, the Danish born shipping magnate who was chairman of Petersen and Co Ltd, ship owners. Petersen was also founder and a director of the London-American Maritime Trading Company and a director of the Thompson Steam Shipping Company. He had also founded the Royal and Uraneum Passenger Line which ran between London, Canada and the United States. He married Flora McKay in 1889 and from 1917 until his death in 1925 he owned the Scottish island of Eigg where he kept a house and estate.

As the only son, William was brought up as heir to the Petersen shipping empire and from an early age travelled extensively worldwide on his father's ships. After leaving Cargilfield Preparatory School he entered Glenalmond in September 1906; it was to be a relatively short stay as he was only on roll for two years before he left in 1908 to work with a private tutor in Dieppe. There, this charming and personable young man also became fluent in French before going up to Cambridge as an undergraduate in October 1910. Trinity College records indicate he gained his degree in History and Political Economy. In 1913 he continued his studies in Germany, adding the German language to those he spoke fluently.

The notions of duty and service, which were very much embodied within the core of the public-school ethos, were at their height at the turn of the twentieth century. Duty to one's house, to the school and to country demanded fortitude, endurance and physical courage. Schools recorded and applauded the military achievements and sacrifices of former pupils and it went without saying that anyone making the ultimate sacrifice would be held in high esteem. 1914, and in particular the First Battle of Ypres, would provide the arena in which the sacrifice would begin.

Chapter 4

From Mons to Ypres

T he lengthy *Times* leader of 5 August 1914 referred to the declaration of war on Germany as 'momentous in the history of all time.' Since 29 July, when all regular officers and men were recalled from leave and officers of the Indian Army on leave at home were retained by the War Office and attached to other units, there had been a general expectation that war was imminent. This was further fuelled by army units on annual training being ordered to strike camp and return to their home stations and by the naval reserve being called out on 2 August. The rumblings of war continued to reverberate for another twenty-four hours until Asquith's statement to the Commons on 4 August which was greeted with cheers from both sides of the House.

Despite the debate aired in the pages of the *Times* as to whether Great Britain should honour Belgian neutrality, the declaration of war was greeted in London with widespread public excitement and people took to the streets in an enthusiastic demonstration of public approval. There was a more subdued reaction at the Knightsbridge cavalry barracks where the Life Guards were quietly beginning to mobilize for war, those that remembered the South African War knew there was little to be jubilant about. R A Lloyd witnessed the public's reaction in London with some bemusement:

> '*it was difficult to recognise the reserved, highly respectable, live and let live Londoner of the 3rd of August in the wildly excited, cheering, bloodthirsty patriot of the 4th of August The ranting roaring mob that cheered and sang Rule Britannia in the streets little realised the extent to which the conflagration would spread.*'[1]

To be fair very few had any perception of the extent to which the war would envelop people's lives. Many of those who cheered the outbreak of war on 4 August would, before long, be in uniform themselves after answering the call to join Kitchener's New Armies and those that didn't would find themselves conscripted as the struggle moved into 1916. But in the heady days of August there was a general public assumption that Britain's Regular Army would be dispatched across the Channel quickly, send the Hun packing and be home by Christmas.

Fortunately mobilization had been the subject of detailed military planning and practice and once the order to mobilize had been given, the process went remarkably smoothly. Most regimental depots had already anticipated the declaration of war and the pre-written telegrams recalling their reservists were stacked in boxes in battalion orderly rooms waiting to be dispatched. In at least one instance anticipation ran away with itself. At Portland, where the 2nd Battalion Royal Welch Fusiliers were based, an orderly room blunder actually sent out telegrams in advance of the official order to mobilize which resulted in the switchboard jamming with the number of calls that came in from puzzled reservists and irate staff officers.

At Aldershot, the headquarters of the 1st Division received the order to mobilize at around 4.30pm on 4 August, the order being passed down to the four infantry battalions of 3 Brigade within the next half hour. As with the majority of the regular army battalions, 1/Gloucesters was very much under its war strength. Having returned prematurely from their annual training camp at Rushmore Bottom, the battalion began the business of exchanging peace-time equipment for war kit and preparing for the influx of reservists.

During the practice mobilization some six weeks earlier, the commanding officer, Lieutenant Colonel Arthur Lovett, had established that at least nine officers and 600 reservists were required to bring the battalion up to a war-time establishment and there had been some discussion as to the quality and number of reservists that the battalion could immediately absorb into its ranks. The most useful would be those whose regular service had recently terminated and those who may have had experience in the more recent South African War, others who had been away from military service for longer would require a greater induction, while some would inevitably be unfit for front line duties. Almost as soon as the telegrams had been dispatched the Gloucesters reservists began to turn up, the first being 28-year-old Corporal Reginald James Minahan – who managed to make the journey from London to arrive that evening.[2] Over the next three days reservists poured in and by midnight on the 7 August, 1/Gloucesters was fully mobilized and awaiting brigade orders to move. Many of the reservists were rejoining the same companies in which they had served as regulars and were able to quickly renew the bond of command with officers and NCOs.

The actual number of reservists that were required by the Gloucesters to bring them up to war strength in August 1914, raises the question of how 'regular' the regular army of 1914 really was. Clearly it was the reservists who made up the greater part of the fighting strength of the 1st Battalion, a factor that was in evidence across all of the regular battalions of the BEF, which was of course exactly why Haldane had created the reserve in the first place. The late John Terraine estimated that in most of the British battalions that left with the original BEF in August 1914, reservists amounted to fifty per cent of the total strength, while overall, the proportion for the whole BEF was sixty per cent.[3] However, despite their hasty return to the colours and the inevitable protests from sore feet, the reservists were soon to demonstrate their mettle in the most trying of circumstances.

As one of the four company commanders of 1/Gloucesters, Captain Robert Rising would be relying on the mettle of these men in the coming weeks and months and took full advantage of the time left before departure to hone the men's shooting skills. Movement orders arrived all too quickly and in the early hours of Wednesday, 12 August 1914 the battalion joined 3 Brigade and left Bordon for Southampton to embark on the SS *Gloucester Castle* for Le Havre. Arriving on French soil just after midnight the next day, they were some of the first British troops to set foot in France on a war footing since Waterloo.

*   *   *

At Knightsbridge barracks former officers and men of the Life Guards were not slow to respond to the order to mobilize. Arriving with the main body of reservists were several retired officers who, regardless of their age and lengthy absence from military service, wanted to get back into uniform and fight. One of these was Regy Wyndham, now aged 38, who had managed to secure a commission in the Lincolnshire Yeomanry and, with some considerable string pulling, was now attached to 1/Life Guards with the rank of lieutenant. His commission had been considerably eased by the family connection; two of his younger brothers were currently serving officers with the regiment and his father, Lord Leconfield was a former officer of the same. Regy Wyndham's first appearance at Knightsbridge caused a few eyebrows to be raised, Lloyd remembered the occasion well:

'*In the very first days of mobilization we were startled by the appearance of an officer who had come back from retirement dressed in a rig-out which was a sight for the gods. His khaki jacket fitted him where it touched him; his riding pants were of coarse material, baggy, and reminiscent of knickerbockers at the knees. He wore in addition a pair of thick greased hob-nailed ankle boots, rough puttees, and a cap from which the wire had been removed and which looked as if it had been slept on. On his Sam Browne belt was a stout iron hook from which dangled a pair of hedging-and-ditching gloves. Before he had advanced ten paces inside the barrack gate he was unanimously christened "Sinbad the Sailor". The nickname seemed to jump to the minds of all those who saw him, and Sinbad he remained. In spite of his weird uniform, Sinbad was a fine soldier and a fine gentleman.*

When somebody chipped him about his turnout, I heard him reply in the deep deliberate voice with which we were soon to be familiar: "My dear sir, you'll all be dressed like this, or worse, before Christmas." He was right.[4]

Another officer who was returning from the reserve list was the grandson of the Earl of Dartrey, Captain Richard Long Dawson, who, after leaving Sandhurst, was Gazetted second lieutenant in the 3rd Battalion Coldstream Guards (3/Coldstream Guards) in 1898. The family had a long connection with the Guards, Thomas Vesey Dawson was killed at the Battle of Inkerman while serving with the Coldstream Guards as a lieutenant colonel and his uncle, Major General Vesey John Dawson, another Coldstream officer, had recently retired from the army after a career that saw active service with the Nile Expedition of 1884, and command of the newly raised Irish Guards in 1900. In 1906 he commanded 15 Infantry Brigade at Belfast and later the 2nd London Division of the Territorial Force. Dawson's father, Hon Richard Maitland Westenra Dawson, who was a captain in the 92nd Highlanders, once served as ADC to the Governor of South Australia, Sir James Fergusson. In 1872 Fergusson named a new township supposedly after Lady Jean Maitland, the wife of the First Lord of Kilkerran, it remains some coincidence that his ADC was also called Maitland. Today Maitland remains an isolated settlement that still struggles to raise its population above 1,000.

Like many of his generation of officers, Richard Dawson fought in the South African War and after returning to England was promoted to captain in 1903. Towards the end of 1906 'Dick' Dawson was in Egypt on the Mounted Infantry Course which kept him away from home for over four months. On his return to London he resigned his commission in March 1907 to devote more time to running the family estate at Holne Park in Devon after his father became ill. Today Holne Park House is a hotel and sits in 90 acres of grounds and gardens on the southern slopes of Dartmoor with the scenic River Dart running through it but in 1914, the Dawson family lived very comfortably on the estate with eleven servants attending to their needs. The youngest of the household servants was Arthur Pearce who is described on the 1911 Census as a Hall Boy.[5] He later joined the Devonshire Regiment and sometime afterwards transferred to the Army Service Corps.

Receiving his orders to mobilize, Captain Richard Dawson was ordered to report to the 4th (Reserve) Battalion of the Coldstream which was being formed at Windsor. The barracks at Windsor, built to house 750 men of all ranks, was now expected to provide accommodation for well over 2,000 men returning from the reserve list. The role of the reserve battalion was to supply replacement drafts to the regular Coldstream battalions when the need arose, but convinced the war would be over before Christmas, Dawson and his fellow officers did not expect to be called upon. The adjutant of the 4th Battalion,

Major Sir George Arthur Crichton, himself a reservist, was an old friend of Richard Dawson and since June 1913, a relation through marriage when he married Lady Mary Dawson. George Crichton and Richard Dawson fought together with the Coldstream Guards in South Africa where Crichton was wounded. Aware that his father was a sick man, Richard Dawson was nevertheless shaken by the news of his death which reached him at Windsor on 7 August. Richard Maitland Dawson, had hung onto life long enough to see his only son return to active service.

There was no doubt in Lance Corporal James William Whitfield's mind that once the BEF had landed in France and sorted out the German Army he would soon be back in London on palace guard duty. After leaving school in 1907 James had followed his father, William, underground at the Medomsley Busty Pit Colliery, his younger brother Frederick joining them in 1910. The family home at Medomsley Edge, County Durham was desperately overcrowded; the small terraced house on the Corbridge Road being home to six adults and one child. Apart from his father and mother and younger brother, two married daughters and a 12-year-old child also lived at home which must have put the family accommodation under considerable pressure. Small wonder then that James travelled to Newcastle-upon-Tyne and enlisted in the Coldstream Guards in January 1912 on a three year term of service.

A month later he began his basic training at Caterham and from all accounts proved to be an able soldier who quickly adapted to the discipline of army life. Subsequently on the successful completion of basic training, he was posted to the 2nd Battalion Coldstream Guards (2/Coldstream Guards). As far as James was concerned he was not planning to return to the colliery in the foreseeable future as in August 1912 he extended his term of service to seven years. He was promoted to lance corporal four months before the battalion was mobilized for war in 1914.

Watching the BEF leave for war was a very disappointed William Petersen. He had received the news his territorial unit would not be included in the BEF and having been commissioned into the Essex Field Artillery four months previously he immediately applied for an attachment to 2/Life Guards. There is no doubt that this was helped along by his father's extensive political and social connections, as in late September he was seconded with the rank of second lieutenant and ordered to report to 3rd Cavalry Division. He had a lot to live up to; one of his three sisters was married to Douglas Reynolds who had been awarded the VC for his bravery at Le Cateau only a few days previously on 26 August. Captain Reynolds was serving with the 37th Battery, Royal Field Artillery, and won his VC while extricating what was left of his battery of howitzers under the noses of the enemy. He later died of gas poisoning in 1916.[6]

The right connections were also apparent in enabling the Baron Alexis de Gunzburg to obtain a commission in the 11th Prince Albert's Own Hussars

(11/Hussars). Alexis de Gunzburg, although born in Paris in 1887, was a Russian national who was educated at Eton from 1901 to 1904 and had lived permanently in England since 1907. When war was declared de Gunzburg volunteered as an intelligence officer and was commissioned into 11/Hussars. Having been sent down to Ludgershall to join 3rd Cavalry Division, he was almost immediately sent back to London after it was discovered he was not a British subject. Returning home to Bute House in the exclusive South Audley Street in Mayfair, he made his application to the Home Office. Bute House was the London residence of one of de Gunzburg's relations, Clarissa Bischoffsheim, whose husband, Henry, was related to Nathan Rothschild.

The family business was banking and with Henry Bischoffsheim a director of the well known Jewish banking house of Bischoffsheim and Goldschmidt, the process of naturalization was fast-tracked through official channels. The completed papers were delivered to the Home Office on 13 August with an accompanying note on Foreign Office notepaper from Henry Moore, the Earl of Drogheda, asking that they be 'rushed through'. Just so that the urgency of the matter was fully appreciated, Moore added a final paragraph to his letter:

> '*I will of course vouch absolutely for the applicant and I know that Winston [Churchill] has promised to help as regards the military part afterwards.*'

The mere mention of the First Sea Lord's name was enough to sufficiently oil the wheels of officialdom and four days later Alexis de Gunzburg was granted British nationality.

Apart from the men of the part-time Territorial Force who were mobilized for home defence, the officers and men of the Special Reserve were also mobilized in early August for overseas duty. The Special Reserve was, in some respects, similar to the Territorial Force in that they both consisted of part-time soldiers but there the similarity ended. While soldiers of the Territorial Force were not obliged to serve overseas in 1914, the men of the Special Reserve had to accept the possibility of being called up to reinforce the active units of the regular army in the event of national mobilization. Many of the special reservists had previously served in the Militia and certainly in Ireland, where there was no Territorial Force, all part-time soldering was through the Special Reserve. Alfred Schuster had joined the Kerry Militia as a second lieutenant a year before he was called to the Bar in 1906 and after two years service he was promoted to lieutenant in August 1908. When the Militia was disbanded in 1908 Alfred transferred to the 4th (Queen's Own) Hussars Special Reserve.

4/Hussars had been stationed in South Africa before arriving home in 1908 to their new quarters at the Curragh in Ireland. Situated opposite the racecourse, the Curragh was a sprawling military base near Kildare in central Ireland and the scene of the so called Curragh Incident in March 1914 when the officers of 3 Cavalry Brigade demanded a guarantee that they would not be required to force Ulster into accepting the controversial Home Rule Bill. Their mobilization was completed by 10 August and five days later 4/Hussars embarked on the SS *Atlantian* for Le Havre. Much to his disappointment and frustration Alfred was not with the regiment when they left for the docks at Dublin to join 2nd Cavalry Division. Despite being mobilized early in August, Alfred remained impatiently at the regimental depot in Dublin until September when he and Lieutenant Francis Levita were ordered to join the regiment in France as replacements.

*   *   *

At Chelsea Barracks in London the 2/Grenadier Guards reservists were queuing from early morning on the 5 August. Many had arrived the previous evening and the battalion orderly room was in full swing processing the long line of men back into Guardsmen. The men of the Grenadier Guards were drawn from a wide cross section of the lower classes of society all undoubtedly attracted by the regiment's reputation and status within the army. Service with the Colours had changed significantly since the nineteenth century when a man taking the Queen's shilling would sign away most of his useful life. There was now an option to serve as little as three years with a commitment of nine years on the reserve list and many, like Walter Siewertsen, took advantage of this. Three years service with the Guards provided a man with a reputation for discipline and reliability and could open up later employment possibilities in civilian life.

After Walter Siewertsen enlisted in the Grenadier Guards in April 1913, he was sent down to the Guards Depot at Caterham to begin his fourteen weeks of recruit training. Whilst at Caterham he passed his second class certificate in basic writing and arithmetic and having successfully passed out he was posted to the 2nd Battalion. Despite this promising start, less than a year later, in March 1914 he appeared before a court-martial and was sentenced to 112 days detention for desertion, 'losing by neglect his clothing and equipment' and, 'refusing to obey an order given by his superior officer'. There is no indication in his service file as to the reason why he went absent without leave but the sentence was later reduced to fifty-six days. There is another note in his file written by Lieutenant Ian McDougall in May 1914 to the effect that Walter's sentence was further reduced for 'good conduct to duty.' McDougall was adjutant of the 2nd Battalion at the time and was later killed in action in September 1914.

By early May Walter, having served his sentence, was back with the battalion unaware that in the same month the Austrian and German Chiefs of Staff, von Hotzendorf and von Moltke, had met and agreed a timetable for war.

Consequently when the Archduke Franz Ferdinand was assassinated on 28 June 1914 and Austria's attack on Serbia began one month later, the timetable was activated, launching a chain of events that led to Walter Siewertsen and the officers and men of the 2nd Battalion embarking for France on the SS *Cawdor Castle* as part of 4 (Guards) Brigade, 2nd Division.

The twenty-nine officers of the 2nd Battalion, in common with other British Army regiments, were largely all regular soldiers and many of the officers with the rank of captain and above had seen war service in South Africa. Major Lord Bernard Gordon Lennox, commanding Number 2 Company in August 1914, saw action against the Boers as a young subaltern with the battalion soon after being promoted to lieutenant in 1899. His arrival in the Orange Free State in late April 1900 was the beginning of an arduous tour of twenty-five months during which time the battalion was frequently on the move and often engaged with their elusive enemy. Gordon Lennox's first experience of a major action was at Biddulphsberg Hill in May 1900 when the battalion had first hand experience of the accuracy and firepower of the Boers. It must have been a sobering experience for a regular battalion to lose a fight against an enemy that they had great difficulty in locating. To make matters worse many of the Grenadiers wounded were burned to death in a veld fire when the dry grass was set alight behind them.

Lord Bernard was not the only member of his distinguished family serving in South Africa at the turn of the century. His brother Charles was ADC to Field Marshal Sir Frederick Roberts and his father, the 7th Duke of Richmond and the 2nd Duke of Gordon, was also present commanding the Royal Sussex Militia. Lord Charles Henry, who was described after his death in 1928 as one of the 'quietly great' Victorians, was mentioned in despatches for his services during the campaign and made a Companion Order of the Bath. Another brother, Lord Esme Gordon Lennox, who was three years older than Bernard and an officer in the Scots Guards, served as a staff officer with GHQ.

Returning to England with the battalion after the South African War, Bernard was seconded to the Chinese Regiment at Wei-Hai-Wei in 1904. Wei-Hai-Wei was a British naval coaling station on the northeast coast of what is now the Chinese Shandong peninsular where Britain held exclusive military rights and in the terms of the lease, had the right to station troops and effect fortifications. It was also the base for a native Chinese regiment organized, funded and led by British officers. Although the Chinese regiment was disbanded in 1906, Britain did not finally hand back the territory until 1930.

Esme Gordon Lennox was best man at Bernard's wedding at the Guards Chapel when he married the Hon Evelyn Loch in July 1907. The wedding was a grand affair with the band of the Grenadier Guards in attendance and officers and NCOs lining the porch when the bride arrived with her brother, Lord Loch. The service was officiated by the Archbishop of Canterbury and after the ceremony the reception was held at Lord and Lady Loch's residence in Montague Square. In 1908 George Charles was born, followed three years later by Alexander Henry.

With the experience of the South African campaign behind him, Bernard Gordon Lennox was under no illusions about the reality of war which awaited him on mainland Europe. Undoubtedly fighting the Boers was one thing, going up against the huge conscript German Army and their formidable artillery was yet another. Of course, many of the young officers in the battalion had seen no active service at all. Typical of these was Lieutenant Michael Stocks who had only been with the battalion for just over two years having entered Sandhurst after leaving Eton in 1910. He passed out just before Christmas in 1911 and was commissioned into the Grenadiers at the beginning of February 1912. He wouldn't have long to wait before his baptism of fire.

*   *   *

The BEF which left the shores of England for France in August 1914 was under the command of Field Marshal Sir John French, himself a veteran of the South African War. His force of four infantry divisions was divided into two Corps, I Corps (1st and 2nd Divisions) under Lieutenant General Sir Douglas Haig, and II Corps (3rd and 5th Divisions) under Lieutenant General Sir Horace Smith-Dorrien. In addition there were the two divisions of the Cavalry Corps under Major General Sir Edmund Allenby. Substantial reinforcements would not arrive until the appearance of III Corps (4th and 6th Divisions) which was formed in France on 31 August 1914 and was commanded by Major General William Pulteney. By then, however, the strategic picture had changed dramatically.

Once in Belgium the BEF moved into position in front of Mons and formed a line along the Mons-Condé Canal, just to the left of the French Fifth Army. The first skirmish with the Germans came early on 23 August 1914 when the advance guard of von Kluck's First Army, arrived at Casteau, a small village along the Chausée de Bruxelles on the edge of Mons. In this cavalry encounter between the 4th Dragoon Guards (4/Dragoon Guards) and the German 4th Cuirassiers, Captain Charles Hornby became the first BEF soldier to kill a German, which he did with his cavalry sword, and Corporal Ernest Thomas fired the first British shots of the war. The Battle of Mons had begun.

Sir John deployed his two infantry corps east and west of Mons across a twenty-five mile front, the eastern flank in touch with the French Fifth Army under General Lanrezac, some eight miles away. Allenby's cavalry division was held in reserve in case of need. It quickly became apparent that the British were heavily outnumbered, but despite the odds, von Kluck's offensive against Smith-Dorrien's II Corps began disastrously, the British riflemen exacting heavy losses from the advancing German infantry. Indeed, by mid-afternoon von Kluck had no progress to show for the offensive and drafted in reinforcements. Yet in spite of the successes of the first day, the BEF's intention to stand and fight was thwarted and by the rather surprising news that Lanrezac's Fifth Army was retiring. Given the circumstances Sir John French now found himself in, he had little choice but to conform. With the French in retreat and the Belgian Army also falling back, the BEF was now in advance of the Allied line and if it remained so, would be outflanked. The historic retreat from Mons was underway.

The brunt of the retirement fell on the already battered II Corps which had suffered over 1,600 casualties on 23 August and now, on the left flank of the BEF, was fighting an almost continuous rearguard action. BEF casualties on 24 August were some 2,500 and the majority of these were from Major General Sir Charles Fergusson's 5th Division. The fact that the bulk of II Corps managed to escape and was able to turn successfully and fight at Le Cateau again on 26 August is largely down to Smith-Dorrien's ability and the maverick nature of his style of command. History would repeat itself twenty-six years later when John Standish Vereker, the 6thViscount Gort, succeeded in extracting another BEF and began a retreat with a very different outcome, this time to Dunkirk. Lord Gort was no stranger to Flanders, in 1914 he was a captain serving with the Grenadiers, four years later he had been promoted to temporary Lieutenant Colonel in command of the 1st Battalion and had been awarded the VC, DSO and two bars and the MC. His cousin, Robert Humphrey Vereker, was serving as a company officer with Bernard Gordon Lennox in the 2nd Battalion.

The retreat was probably one of the most testing periods for the troops of the BEF. They were unaccustomed to retiring and quite frankly did not understand why they were in retreat after what they saw as a successful encounter with the enemy the previous day. Apart from the orders to retire, very few had any idea what was going on strategically, creating a general sense of frustration which was not helped by the hot August weather. This only added to the discomfort of the infantry which marched on average some seventeen miles each day over the two weeks of the retreat.

Despite the testing conditions on the march the Grenadiers lost few opportunities to compare their performance to the Coldstream Guards, noting on numerous occasions that the Grenadiers march discipline was 'much superior' to that of the Coldstream. Rivalry between the two regiments had been in existence since the Coldstream were created as a regiment by Cromwell in 1650 and dubbed the Second Regiment of Foot Guards. A dilemma arose when Charles II formed the First Regiment of Foot Guards in 1665, renamed after Waterloo as the Grenadier Regiment of Foot Guards. The Coldstream regimental motto *Nulli Secundus* was adopted as a permanent reminder to the Grenadiers that despite the regimental numbering, they consider themselves to

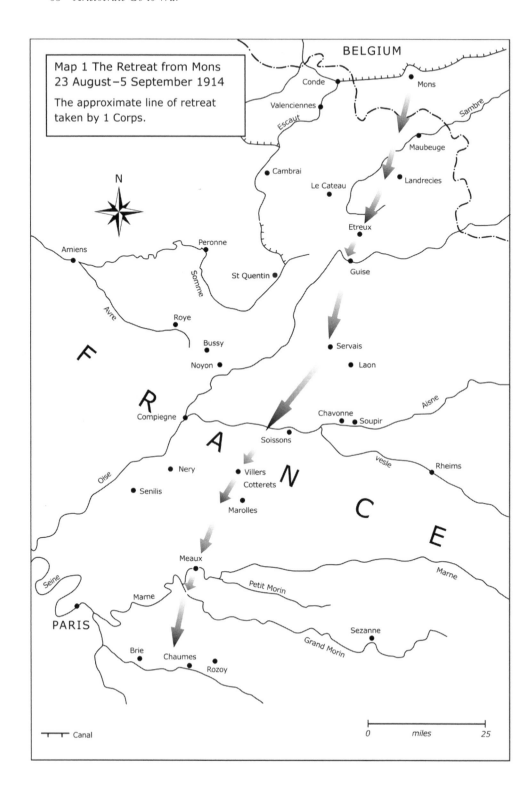

Map 1 The Retreat from Mons
23 August–5 September 1914

The approximate line of retreat
taken by 1 Corps.

be the oldest Guards regiment. No doubt this regimental rivalry provided an occasional much needed boost to morale to the men of both regiments as they marched south towards the Marne.

We are fortunate that Bernard Gordon Lennox kept a remarkable diary of events and continued writing it until shortly before his death. His notes of 24 August give some impression of the uncertainty that prevailed amongst the officers of 2/Grenadier Guards who were retreating with I Corps:

> '*Owing to the absolute secrecy which pervaded everything, no one knew what was going on anywhere: this has been maintained to date and is most disheartening. No one knows what one is driving at, where anyone is, what we have got against us, or anything at all, and what is told us generally turns out to be entirely wrong.*'

The next evening 4 (Guards) Brigade arrived at Landrecies after a long and hot march but there was to be little rest. Gordon Lennox recorded what he described as 'one of the longest nights' he had ever had:

> '*We were in the middle of our dinner about 8.30 when the alarm went and we rushed out to hear heavy firing-musketry-going on outside our end of town. Everyone fell in hurriedly and there was a good deal of scurry but no disorder when the word came down that the Coldstream Guards outposts were being driven back: the remainder of the battalion was sent up to where the firing was going on, in support.*

Unbeknown to I Corps, pursuing German forces of IX Army Corps had penetrated the Forest of Mormal to the north of Landrecies using motorized transport and launched a surprise night attack which fell mainly on 3/Coldstream Guards which had outposts at the north of the town. A simultaneous attack also fell on 1/Gloucesters which was at Le Favil some two miles further east and although the main attack was brought to a standstill, sporadic fighting went on for most of the night both in Landrecies and around Le Favil. In their first encounter with the Germans since landing in France, the Gloucesters lost five men killed including Captain Guy Shipway, together with thirty men wounded.[7] In Number 2 Company of the Grenadiers their casualties were surprisingly light given the intensity of the fighting around the town's railway station:

> '*The moment [they] tried to advance a deadly rapid fire was poured into them. They charged pluckily three or four times, but each time they were mown down. Then we got word they were getting round towards us. We waited quietly, and saw a couple of dull red glows which were no doubt the lamps of the leading officers. We opened a salvo of rapid fire and one of the lights disappeared to be followed shortly*

after by the other one. Bullets began to whisk past us and it was just about this time
that poor young Vereker [Second Lieutenant Robert Humphrey Vereker] was shot
through the head. I also had two corporals wounded at the same time.[8]

On 26 August the relentless march resumed. The Gloucesters were fortunate
that the fighting around Le Favil was the last they would see until the Battle of
the Marne reversed Allied fortunes; turning retreat into pursuit and forcing the
Germans to retreat north towards the Aisne valley. But for 4 Brigade there
would be more fighting. Ordered to cover the retirement of the 2nd Division
with a rearguard action on 30 August, the Guards made a stand in the forest
surrounding Villers-Cotterets and in the desperate hand-to-hand fighting that
followed the Germans were driven back at the point of the bayonet until the
order was given to retire. It was at Villers-Cotterets that Brigadier General
Robert Scott-Kerr was badly wounded and command of the brigade passed
temporarily to Colonel Corry who had been commanding 2/Grenadier Guards.
Little did the Grenadiers know that the fighting in the thickly wooded area
around Villers-Cotterets would be a rehearsal for the fighting in the numerous
woods south-east of Ypres that would become a feature of the defence around
Klein Zillebeke during October and November 1914.

*   *   *

4/Hussars had received no reinforcements since leaving Dublin in August even
though they had been in almost constant contact with German infantry and
cavalry since the retreat began and had suffered twenty-nine casualties of whom
seven were killed. The casualties included their commanding officer,
Lieutenant Colonel Ian Hogg, whose father was the educational philanthropist
Quintin Hogg. By the time Alfred Schuster made contact with the regiment
along with Lieutenant Francis Levita and ninety reinforcements, the regiment
had been billeted at Braine for four days and were enjoying a well deserved rest.
Schuster's journey from England had taken them all over the country in a series
of frustrating efforts to locate a regiment that was constantly on the move. It
was just as well he was an experienced horseman; he would need his rough-
riding experience gained with the Quorn and Devon and Somerset Staghounds
over the coming weeks. Even with the new arrivals the regiment was still very
much below strength and at roll call on the evening of 24 September 1914, the
regiment could only muster 312 all ranks and was still 150 horses short despite
the addition of the 129 fresh mounts Alfred had brought with him.

    When Francis Levita joined his regiment at Braine he had little idea that his
cousin, Lieutenant Michael Stocks, was only some six miles further north at
Chavonne. He had last seen his cousin shortly before war was declared and both
boys had expressed a wish that their regiments would be quickly deployed with

the BEF. They both got their wish; Francis arrived in France just in time to take part in the struggle along the Aisne valley and as a cavalryman would have a different front line experience to Michael. Despite their close proximity, however, the two grandchildren of Major Michael Stocks would never have the opportunity to compare notes.

Michael Stocks, along with the rest of Sir John French's expeditionary force, was now dug in on the British front line and on the receiving end of some very heavy shell fire. The German retreat from the Marne had come to a halt on the northern heights of the Aisne valley. From this commanding position along the Chemin des Dames ridge, which overlooked the whole of the British area of operations, the Germans initiated a strategy and subsequent chain of consequences that would dominate the nature of warfare for the next three years: concentrated artillery barrages, entrenched positions and heavy casualties. As both sides entrenched themselves ever deeper, the constant shelling began to dominate the lives of everyone, Bernard Gordon Lennox wrote on 18 September:

> *'We were subject to a hell of a bombardment all day with shrapnel and Black Maria. So far this has been an unequal contest, as our guns have practically not come into action yet, being unable to find a position or a target, and whenever they do open fire from the valley below, it only draws a hail of shrapnel and high explosive on it at once: and the Dutchmen [Germans] seem to know exactly where they are. The place must be full of spies. Throughout the day shrapnel was bursting right over us and on us, but I have only one man wounded in the arm.'*

Casualties amongst 4 Brigade officers and men had been steadily increasing since 1 September 1914. The 3rd Coldstream had suffered considerably in their positions around Soupir Farm, losing a number of valuable officers and NCOs. On 18 September Richard Dawson arrived at the battalion with a small draft of reinforcements and was immediately given command of Number 2 Company. 2 / Grenadier Guards had also suffered badly, the battalion war diary recorded fourteen officers and 375 NCOs and men killed or wounded in the first nineteen days of September, and although some reinforcements had joined up with the battalion, the continual German shelling was taking its toll. On the evening of 19 September Lieutenants Harry Parnell and Carleton Tufnell arrived with the battalion's new commanding officer, Lieutenant Colonel Wilfred Smith.

Carleton Tufnell, or 'Laddie' as he was known in the battalion, was already a very popular officer and had been devastated when he was detailed to remain behind in August when the battalion left for France. Sport still occupied a large proportion of his spare time as it had done at Eton. At Sandhurst as a cadet he captained the Cricket and Football XIs as well as the athletics team against the RMA Woolwich and his final accolade before being commissioned was the award of the prestigious Physical Training Prize in July 1912.

He was appointed to the Grenadier Guards in September 1912 and quickly established himself in the regiment as a class cricketer. He had represented Surrey in 1911 in the Minor Counties Championship while he was still at Sandhurst and became a regular in the Household Brigade Cricket XI playing alongside other good cricketers such as Bernard Gordon Lennox and Cholmeley Symes-Thompson. His last game had been a month before being mobilized when the Household Brigade drew with the Royal Green Jackets in a close run match at Burton Court. Shortly before he left for France he had become engaged to be married.

For the two new subalterns there was little if any time to adapt to their new surroundings, on the day they arrived the battalion lost another two men killed and five wounded from shellfire. Predictably Gordon Lennox neglects to mention in his diary his own near escapes from German shellfire. With casualties a daily occurrence, there were inevitable occasions when he and others had close encounters. On the same morning that Harry Parnell had a lucky escape from an 8-inch shell, Gordon Lennox had a similar experience. Taking advantage of the sunshine he had spread his greatcoat on the back of the trench to dry out and had not gone more than two or three paces up the trench when 'there was a terrific explosion.'[9] As he wrote later that day:

> '*My coat had the right arm taken off at the shoulder and the left sleeve cut to bits and it was only a yard off me, but I am thankful to say I was not inside the coat at the time.*'

As the fighting on the Aisne became increasingly bogged down in stalemate, the German and Allied forces began extending the line northwards in an attempt to outflank each other in what became known as 'the race to the sea'. Early in October the race had had reached a line between St Omer and Hazebrouck and Sir John French had decided that the BEF should be moved to the extreme left of the Allied line. On the Aisne his three army corps were hemmed in, a situation in which he could not use his cavalry effectively, added to which the British IV Corps were about to land at Zeebrugge. Accordingly, after consultation with Churchill and Joffre, the decision was made that the British should move from their positions on the Aisne and concentrate in Belgium on the left flank of the Allied line.

As usual the cavalry being the most mobile were the first to move. 3 Cavalry Brigade, which included 4/Hussars, was one of the first British units to arrive in the area and was soon providing advanced patrols. Ordered to take the Mont des Cats to the west of Boeschepe on 12 October, C Squadron under the command of Captain John Gatacre came under fire on the southern slopes of the hill. Gatacre was killed and in a brave attempt to go to his squadron commander's aid, Francis Levita also lost his life.[10]

Waiting impatiently in the Aisne trenches for their turn to move, I Corps were the last to leave for Flanders, Bernard Gordon Lennox recorded the handover of the Grenadiers trenches at Chavonne to their French allies on 12 October:

> *'They turned up at 11.40 pm and took a long time to carry out the relief. They only brought 150 men and one officer – all there were of a company of Terriers [Territorials]. The officer was very funny. One thing they would find hard and that is to fire out of our loopholes, as they were not of Guardsmen stature.'*

* * *

By the time the final units of I Corps had detrained at Hazebrouck on 19 October, the last British Army formation to leave England in 1914 had already been deployed by Sir John French east of Ypres along a line that straddled the main Ypres to Menin Road. IV Corps under the command of Lieutenant General Sir Henry Rawlinson, had landed at Zeebrugge in the first week of October to assist in the defence of Antwerp. However, events overtook them and by the time they arrived in Belgium the city was already falling into German hands and IV Corps was instead ordered to assist the westward retirement of the Belgian army. IV Corps was different in composition, in that it only hosted one infantry division, the 7th Division, which was commanded by Major General Thompson Capper. The 'Immortal 7th' as the division came to be known, was formed by mobilizing regular army units from their scattered locations around the Empire, some of which had not arrived in England until late in September. The other half of IV Corps was the 3rd Cavalry Division which assembled with their infantry counterparts in the New Forest at Ludgershall during August and September 1914.

It was at Ludgershall that Second Lieutenant William Petersen and 2/Life Guards joined Lieutenant Regy Wyndham and 1/Life Guards in 7 Cavalry Brigade. Also serving in 1/Life Guards was Second Lieutenant Howard St George. Howard's brother, George, had joined his grandfather in America in 1913 and was working for J P Morgan, leaving his sister and younger brother in England. Howard St George was Gazetted to 1/Life Guards as a probationary officer in January 1914 having left Eton the year before and had only been with the regiment a mere six months before it was mobilized. He had been a member of Eton College OTC but as a probationary officer who had received no formal military training at Sandhurst or in the Militia, he would effectively be learning the trade of soldiering 'on the job' and over the remaining five weeks of his life Howard would be learning a great deal about soldiering.

The 3rd Cavalry Division consisted of 6 and 7 Cavalry Brigades, each composed of three cavalry regiments. 7 Cavalry Brigade, which, to all intents and purposes, was the Household Brigade, consisted of 1/ and 2 /Life Guards and the Royal Horse Guards, their brigade commander was Brigadier General Charles Kavanagh, a cavalryman of some pedigree having commanded the 10th Royal Hussars for two years between 1904 and 1906. His choice of Brigade Major fell on Norman Neill a 34–year-old captain in the 13th Hussars who had just completed the Army Staff College course and had been held back from rejoining his regiment at Meerut in India when war was declared. Neill was another regular officer who had been commissioned from the Militia; he first saw active service in 1902 in the South African War and in 1910 was briefly adjutant of his regiment before being promoted to captain in July of that year. Neill was an interesting character in that after leaving Harrow in 1897 he began life as an artist and studied at the Slade School of Art in London. Yet by 1901 he was a lieutenant in the 5th Militia Battalion, Lancashire Fusiliers and by March 1902 he had clearly decided upon a career in the army as he was Gazetted into the 19th Hussars during his service in South Africa.

Also at Ludgershall was Alexis de Gunzburg. Having received notification that his British nationality papers had been accepted, he had now rejoined the Royal Horse Guards as an interpreter. Each regiment in 7 Cavalry Brigade had at least one official interpreter on its strength and despite the fact that many of the officers, and indeed one or two of the men, spoke French, de Gunzburg's fluency in both French and German would clearly have been an asset. De Gunzburg was appointed as a non–combatant officer; he had received no military training and consequently was not expected to bear arms. In many ways he was typical of the mood of the time, determined not to miss this great adventure and anxious to play his part before it was all over.

Another fluent French and German speaker was Lieutenant Colonel Gordon Wilson who was making his last minute preparations to leave London to join the Royal Horse Guards. With him was his brother Herbert 'Bertie' Wilson, now serving as a captain in the regiment. Lady Sarah was already in France running her volunteer hospital, the Hotel Christol, in Bolougne which was one of a number of such hospitals established and funded by society ladies in the early months of the war when every bed was of value. What she could not have known is that her departure to France in September 1914 marked the last occasion she would see her husband alive. In a short letter to her before he left their Mayfair residence he gave her news of his impending embarkation:

'We are probably off within the next few days from Southampton. I expect we shall leave camp for that place either tomorrow or Monday. I hope everything is satisfactorily settled at your hospital.'

He wasn't too far out in his estimation; in actual fact it was Tuesday, 5 October when IV Corps left Ludgershall for Belgium, an occasion that was recorded by

Regy Wyndham in his diary which he began writing after boarding the SS *Indore* early on the Wednesday morning:

> '*Received orders to march to the quay and embark at 1.30pm. Tremendous cheering in the town. Cigarettes and food and flowers given to the men as they passed.*'

Five days later they first heard the rumour from retreating Belgian soldiers that Antwerp had fallen and then came the news that they were to join the main BEF force which was assembling at Ypres. Their place in the First Battle of Ypres was thus assured.

* * *

Posted initially to 3/Grenadier Guards, 19- year-old Second Lieutenant John Lee Steere finally left England on 16 October sailing on the SS *Normania*. Landing at Le Havre, he spent the next thirty-eight hours on a 'painfully slow train that stopped at every station'. Their destination was Number 2 Infantry Base at St Nazaire which, John noted in one of his first letters home, now placed him 'further from the front now than we were in England.' His arrival at St Nazaire reunited him with the previous draft of officers and men that had left for France before him and whom he noted, with some dismay, had been there for three weeks already. Initially their quarters were in tents some three miles outside the town but later on the 23 October, he wrote home to say:

> '*I am now living in the town, in a real house with a real roof over my head, an absolute luxury after living in a tent. Hot water is available and an excellent café for one's meals exactly opposite.*'

Their quarters were now in the Place du Basin away from the main camp, but this splendid isolation did not relieve them from the daily route march which he described as 'wearisome, we use the same old road every day and with heavy kit.' His frustration at what he saw as 'sitting around doing very little' was soon to pass. On 29 October, much to his delight, John was given notice that he would be now be going to 2/Grenadier Guards, which had the added bonus of being the same battalion as his cousin, Captain Cholmeley Symes-Thompson. John Lee Steere had three cousins on his mother's side who were then serving in the BEF. The eldest, 33-year-old Symes-Thompson, was at St Nazaire collecting a draft of men for the battalion when John arrived from England and despite his imminent return to the front they had both managed to catch up on family news.

Symes-Thompson had been in the army since 1899 when, as an 18-year-old, he joined the 3rd Militia Battalion of the Yorkshire Light Infantry after leaving

Harrow School. Securing a permanent commission in 1901, he was appointed second lieutenant in 1/Grenadier Guards. His father, Edmund, was an eminent Victorian physician and academic and it was his grandfather, Theophilus Symes-Thompson, who introduced the stethoscope into English medical practice in 1828. Symes-Thompson had fought with the 2nd Battalion since they had landed in France in August and had only relatively recently married Grace Churchill in January 1912 at the Guards Chapel, Wellington Barracks. She and their thirteen-month-old daughter Sibil were still living at 43, Argyll Street in South Kensington, no doubt anxious for his safe return.

Having marched in the retreat from Mons and spent several weeks fighting on the Aisne, Symes-Thompson was already war weary. What he privately thought about the obvious impatience of his younger cousin to get to the front line is anyone's guess, but what he couldn't know was that in less than three weeks he and John Lee Steere would be the only officers left in Number 2 Company. There is a hint in John's last letter home to his mother before leaving St Nazaire that he was now focusing on the task ahead of him:

> *'There is a detachment of 200 men rejoining from hospital so we've heard a certain amount of horrid stories about what faces us. Apparently if one is captured without a sword he is treated by the Germans as a private soldier and protests are useless, so I'm keeping my sword but having a web equipment like the men so as not to be easily picked out.'*

The next day, on 30 October 1914, he and Lieutenant Hervy Tudway left St Nazaire with a draft of men for the front line.[11] As they boarded the train before dawn that morning, the First Battle of Ypres was already reaching its most critical point and John Lee Steere had only eighteen days left to live.

Chapter 5

Ypres – The Clash of Arms

The First Battle of Ypres in 1914 was the first of four battles that focused on the ancient walled city. The first battle was, in all probability, the most significant in that had the Allied forces not been successful in their defence of the Ypres Salient, the BEF would have had to retreat to the channel ports, as it did in 1940, and leave France to the invading German forces. If the unthinkable had happened in 1914, then modern European history would have taken a different course and the twentieth century possibly altered beyond recognition.

It was not until 1920 that the War Office's Battles Nomenclature Committee met to standardise the names of the Great War battles and campaigns for the purpose of awarding battle honours. The Great War posed a considerable challenge for the committee, as battles in the sense of previous wars, such as the South African War, were much harder to define. The committee eventually decided to divide the Great War into a series of campaigns and the campaigns into battles. In some cases battles were further subdivided into actions. In the case of the fighting that centred on Ypres they identified four separate engagements that took place during October and November 1914:

The Battle of La Bassée from 10 October until 2 November
The Battle of Armentières from 13 October until 2 November
The Battle of Messines from 12 October until 2 November
The Battle of Ypres from 19 October until 22 November

The Battle of Ypres itself has been further separated into three major actions giving, perhaps, the impression that the periods between were somewhat free of fighting. This was far from the case; in reality there was almost continual fighting, punctuated by the three key actions of Langemarck from 21 to 24 October, Gheluvelt from 29 to 31 October and Nonne Bosschen on 11 November. In addition, German artillery poured a daily and generally very accurate bombardment on Allied positions. By comparison British artillery units in particular were handicapped by an acute shell shortage which inevitably significantly reduced the effectiveness of counter-battery engagements and the vital role of supporting the infantry.

What is also perhaps not fully appreciated is that the battle was very much a coalition of French, Belgian and British Commonwealth forces and that the British contribution alone would not have won the battle. Although the city of Ypres was in many ways the centrepiece of the struggle, the battle was fought along a front that stretched from Nieuport in the north, down to La Bassée in the south. The importance of the II Corps front, which ran south of the river Lys to La Bassée, is often sidelined in accounts of the First Battle of Ypres; yet it was a vital piece of the jigsaw of defence. Had the II Corps front given way, Allied forces further north in the more immediate vicinity of Ypres would have been outflanked and caught in a pocket with their backs to the sea.

The human cost of the battle was enormous. BEF casualties between 14 October and 30 November were estimated to be 58,155, of whom 7,960 were killed. However appalling these figures might be, they would be eclipsed by future battles. On 1 July 1916 alone the casualties after one day of fighting amounted to 57,470 of which 19,240 were killed. Nevertheless in 1914, before the great battles of the Somme, Arras and Third Ypres, the rate of attrition amongst the battalions of I Corps and the 7th Division in particular was extremely high and in many cases battalions were left with little more that one or two officers and a handful of men. Casualties on this scale could only mean one thing: the baseline of experienced officers and NCOs that had landed with the BEF in August 1914 had been practically wiped out. Indeed by 1 November, before the final German assaults of 11 and 17 November, the state of the BEF's original eighty-four infantry battalions can only be described as pitiful:

Number of battalions below 100 all ranks	18
Number of battalions with 100–200 all ranks	31
Number of battalions with 200–300 all ranks	26
Number of battalions with 300–450 all ranks	9

German losses are more difficult to estimate but numerous sources place these in excess of 130,000 of which at least 19,600 were killed. French casualty figures are again difficult to estimate as there is only a total figure of 104,000 for the whole of the Western Front for the period of October and November 1914. However, their casualties around Ypres are thought to have been somewhere between 50,000 and 85,000. For the Belgian forces, fighting in the north of Salient, casualty figures are estimated at around 20,000.

In the series of battles that marked the first Ypres engagement the odds were very much in Germany's favour. Overall her forces had at least a two to one advantage in men and at times this rose to at least six or seven to one. Moreover, the German field commanders had the advantage of continually replacing their front line units with fresh troops, a luxury that was not available to Allied commanders as their meagre and exhausted forces were continually being eroded. Those six weeks, during which twelve VC were won between 22 October and 20 November, witnessed some of the most desperate fighting of the war and on more than one occasion a successful outcome for the Allies hung very much in the balance. It is quite remarkable that the thin, ragged lines of Allied troops held on at all, let alone brought the might of the German Army to a halt.

An overview of the Ypres fighting: 8 October to 20 November.

8 Oct • Apart from the Cavalry, Sir Horace Smith-Dorrien's II Corps are the first to leave the Aisne and move to Flanders and consequently are amongst the first to be deployed against the Germans. They begin to detrain at Abbeville and go into the line west of La Bassée and north of the La Bassée Canal on 10 October and begin advancing towards the Béthune-Lillers line.

11 Oct • Major General Henry Rawlinson and IV Corps begin to assemble in the Ypres area. The 7th Division (GOC Major General Thompson Capper) deploy east of Ypres to a line taking in the villages of Zonnebeke-Kruiseke-Zandvoorde.[1] The 3rd Cavalry Division (GOC Major General Julian Byng) is deployed to the north of Ypres between Zonnebeke and the Fôret d'Houthulst – filling in the gap between the French cavalry to the north and the 7th Division to the south.

• Overnight on 11/12 October, German forces move into Lille.

12 Oct • News reaches the British that the Germans have occupied Lille. This is a serious blow to the overall British strategy, which is to advance to the north east of Lille. Sir John French remains convinced that the Germans are only present in small numbers on his front, a conviction that he retains despite growing evidence to the contrary.

• Further bad news is received when the French lose Vermelles, the results of which leave Smith-Dorrien and II Corps in a dilemma. His orders are to advance to the line of the Estaires-Lorgies Road but at the same time to maintain contact with General Maud'huy at all costs. He now has two choices, move his forces north of the canal to attempt a north easterly advance as ordered, or move south to close the gap left by the French withdrawal and attempt to advance eastwards. He chooses the latter. Givenchy is reached by nightfall.

- Units of the 2nd Cavalry Division (GOC Major General Hubert Gough) reconnoitre Mont des Cats.[2]

- The newly arrived III Corps, under Lieutenant General William Pulteney, are deployed to advance and secure the Ypres-Armentières road between Wytschaete and Le Bizet, the present day N365.

13 Oct
- III Corps advance along a five mile front but are held up by strongly fortified enemy positions at Meteren and Fontaine Houck which are not taken until that evening.

- II Corps make little further progress in the face of a determined German counter-attack. British losses are heavy, particularly amongst the 1st Battalion Bedfordshire Regiment during a heavy German bombardment of Givenchy. Givenchy is lost when the Bedfords withdraw, which in turn isolates the 1st Battalion Dorsetshire Regiment at Pont Fixe, forcing the surrender of a large body of 1st Battalion Cheshire Regiment at Chapelle St Roche.

- There is more success on the cavalry front: Mont Noir is secured by the 2nd Cavalry Division by dusk and patrols sent on to Mont Kemmel. The 1st Cavalry Division (GOC Major General Henry de Lisle) reconnoitre the Neuve Eglise Spur. These cavalry actions convince the German IV Cavalry Corps commander, General von Hollen, to withdraw from Bailleul as the main road back to Armentières is now in danger of being cut off by the British cavalry

14 Oct
- The British Cavalry Corps (GOC Major General Sir Edmund Allenby) reach Messines and the next day clear through Mont Kemmel to establish a link with the right flank of IV Corps at Wytschaete. The so called 'race to the sea' is now effectively ended with the link up of the British Cavalry Corps advancing from the west and the 3rd Cavalry Division moving south west around Ypres. There is now a continuous, albeit tenuous, Allied line from the North Sea coast to the Swiss border.

- Major General Hubert Hamilton (GOC 3rd Division) is killed near Richebourg by shellfire. Command passes to Major General Colin MacKenzie.

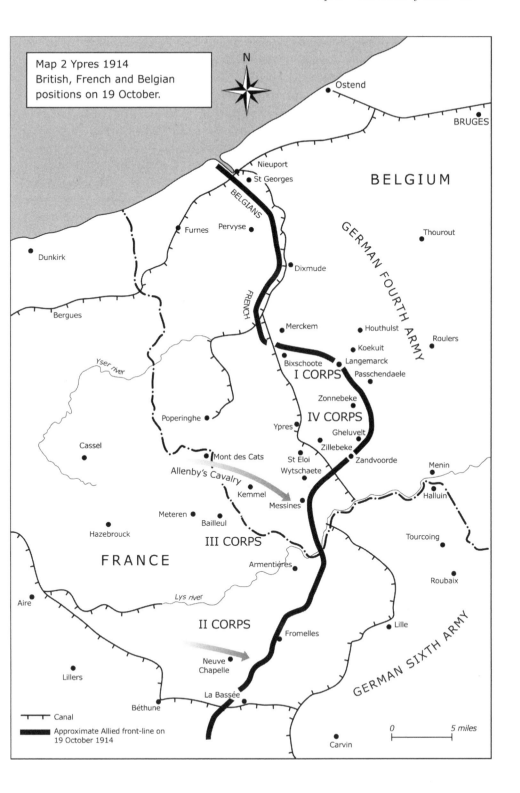

Map 2 Ypres 1914
British, French and Belgian
positions on 19 October.

N

Ostend

BRUGES

Nieuport

St Georges

BELGIANS

BELGIUM

Furnes

Pervyse

GERMAN FOURTH ARMY

Thourout

Dunkirk

Dixmude

FRENCH

Bergues

Merckem

Houthulst

Roulers

Yser river

Koekuit

Bixschoote

Langemarck

I CORPS

Passchendaele

Zonnebeke

Poperinghe

IV CORPS

Ypres

Gheluvelt

Cassel

Mont des Cats

Zillebeke

Zandvoorde

Menin

Allenby's Cavalry

St Eloi

Wytschaete

Halluin

Kemmel

Messines

Meteren

Bailleul

III CORPS

Hazebrouck

Tourcoing

FRANCE

Armentières

Roubaix

Lys river

Aire

II CORPS

Lille

Fromelles

GERMAN SIXTH ARMY

Neuve
Chapelle

Lillers

La Bassée

Béthune

Canal

Approximate Allied front-line on
19 October 1914

0   5 miles

Carvin

15 Oct • Seemingly completely unaware of the build up of German forces in front of him, Sir John French continues to issue ambitious orders for the advance east. It is now becoming quite obvious to the cavalry commanders on the ground that they are encountering German forces in locations that the British infantry were supposed to have reached. However, limited advances continue on all British fronts and some losses are inflicted on enemy formations.

• Having reached Bailleul on 14 October, III Corps are ordered to capture Armentières, repair the bridges over the Lys and prepare for the advance towards Lille. Armentières is occupied on 17 October after the Germans retire east to the Perenchies Ridge.

16 Oct • Givenchy is recaptured by II Corps and held after three days of continuous fighting on both sides of the La Bassée Canal. British losses are significant, although heavy losses are inflicted on the enemy, particularly near Cuinchy. By the end of this period, the British have only advanced the line some six miles in four days.

• GHQ orders III Corps to move down the banks of the Lys and attack the enemy 'on contact'.

• IV Corps is ordered to 'move on Menin', but not to move 'much in advance of the left of III Corps'. 9 Brigade (GOC Brigadier General Frederick Shaw) manages to gain a foothold on the Aubers Ridge.

18 Oct • III Corps attack towards Lille but meet units of the German Sixth Army.

• IV Corps advance some 4,000 yards to a line running through Kortewilde – Terhand – Waterdamhoek with the left flank covered by the 3rd Cavalry Division. At midday Captain Llewellyn Price-Davies, GSO2 with GHQ, arrives at 7th Division Headquarters to enquire why the division is not further along the road to Menin.[3] The vagueness of GHQ's orders and the inference that the division should attack Menin without support and in the knowledge that there are an unknown number of hostile forces ahead, gives Rawlinson food for thought while composing his reply to GHQ!

• Major General Sir Charles Fergusson (GOC 5th Division) is replaced by Major General Thomas Moreland.[4]

- With the suspected troop concentrations at Courtrai and Wevelgem dismissed by Sir John French as nothing more than 'Landwehr', he issues orders for an attack on Menin the following day.[5]

- Von Beseler opens his offensive against the Belgians.

- The German shelling of Ypres begins.[6]

19 Oct
- The First Battle of Ypres officially begins. At 6.30 am IV Corps advances east from Zonnebeke in the direction of the Menin–Roulers road to a point three miles north of Menin, the present day N32. However, it is the Germans who take the initiative on 19 October with a general offensive that begins on the Yser and spreads south along the line as far as Arras. Nevertheless, Sir John French holds firmly to his strategy, apparently failing to realise the whole Allied line is now coming under a sustained attack by both the Fourth and Sixth German Armies.[7] Later that morning aerial reconnaissance gives Rawlinson advance warning of the coming attack on his front.

- 7 Cavalry Brigade are heavily engaged on the Roulers-Menin Road at 9 am and are forced to retire in the face of increasingly strong resistance. At 11.45 am Rawlinson issues orders to IV Corps cancelling the attack on Menin. These orders reach the forward troops at 1.05 pm, just as they are coming under attack from the flanks. General Byng's cavalry and the 7th Division are forced to pull back as far as Zonnebeke, effectively occupying the very positions they had advanced from twenty-four hours earlier.

20 Oct
- I Corps, under Sir Douglas Haig, having arrived from the Aisne the previous day, are ordered to advance northeast of Ypres towards Bruges.

- The Indian Corps detrain at Hazebrouck under the command of Lieutenant General Sir James Willcocks and are deployed on the II Corps front.

- III Corps suffer reverses at Ennetieres. Units of 18 Brigade (GOC Brigadier General Walter Congreve VC) are overwhelmed by the German 25th and 26th Reserve Divisions, the brigade suffering over 1,000 casualties. A little to the north, 17 Brigade (GOC Brigadier General Walter Doran) are also forced back from Premesques.

- On the IV Corps front the German counter-offensive attacks begin early. The retirement of the French on the IV Corps right prompts Byng's 3rd Cavalry Division to fall back, putting pressure on 22 Brigades, (GOC Brigadier General Sidney Lawford). They hold their positions losing five officers and some 130 other ranks. Captain Norman Neill, Brigade Major 7 Cavalry Brigade, is wounded and evacuated to the Casino Hospital, Boulogne.

21 Oct • The 1st Division advances on Poelcapelle and the 2nd Division on Passchendaele. Some progress is made, before the advancing British begin to encounter an increasing number of German Fourth Army troops also advancing to the attack. On the left flank of the 1st Division the French cavalry corps under de Mitry give way and retire west of the Ypres–Comines Canal, having previously abandoned the Fôret d'Houthulst.

- At 3 pm Haig cancels the advance and orders his units to hold their positions. The new front line is only 1,000 yards beyond Langemarck. The fighting leaves the 1st Division badly stretched west of Langemarck and the 2nd Division just beyond Zonnebeke.

- Heavy and accurate German artillery attacks continue along the IV Corps front where the poor location of forward trenches contributes to the retirement of 22 Brigade during the afternoon. The resulting casualties are high, the 1st Battalion Welch Regiment losing seventy-five per cent of its strength.

- III Corps units are becoming increasingly hard pressed by an estimated two German corps along its twelve mile frontage. 11 Brigade (GOC Brigadier General Aylmer Hunter-Weston) is dispersed and held in reserve. Late in the afternoon the 2nd Battalion Inniskilling Fusiliers are forced out of Le Gheer, their positions only regained by counter-attack some hours later.

- The struggle for the Messines Ridge begins in earnest. The 1st Cavalry Division hold the eastern slopes and the 2nd Cavalry Division hold Kortewilde and Houthem. General Allenby is uncomfortably aware that his cavalry is holding one of the most strategically important pieces of ground on the British front.

22 Oct • Lawford's 22 Brigade are reinforced by units from the 1st Division. Infantry and artillery assaults continue through the night on the 7th Division positions.

- Reinforcements arrive to strengthen Allenby's Cavalry Corps in the form of the Indian Cavalry of the Ferozepore Brigade, 1st Battalion Connaught Rangers, 2nd Battalion Essex Regiment and 57th Wilde's Rifles.

- II Corps retire to a new position running from the La Bassée Canal to Fauquissart.

- A German attack is launched along a large stretch of the British line against the 1st, 2nd and 7th Divisions. The Langemarck legend of the 'Massacre of the Innocents' is born. The attack is repulsed along most of the British line, apart from in the centre of the 1st Division. At the Kortekeer crossroads the 1st Battalion Queen's Own Cameron Highlanders are holding a semi-circular position, late in the afternoon the Germans penetrate the northwest sector of the line. At 6.00 pm the Camerons retreat leaving a potential gap in the British line.

23 Oct • Haig responds quickly to the Kortekeer situation by creating a reserve force and the position is recaptured by 2 Brigade with French assistance. At the same time a major German attack against Langemarck is defeated. North of Langemarck, men of the 1/Gloucesters, commanded by Captain Robert Rising, successfully defend the Koekuit road against heavy German attacks. Both battles are over by late afternoon. The same day also sees a French counter-attack, launched by the 17th Division of IX Corps with the intention of taking Passchendaele. The attack, launched from the front held by the 2nd Division, is unsuccessful.

- The 21 Brigade line is overwhelmed and only restored with a costly counter-attack.

- The IX French Army Corps relieves British forces at Pilckem.

- Major General Julian Byng's 3rd Cavalry Division is placed under the command of Allenby's Cavalry Corps.

- De Maud'huy sends three infantry battalions and three artillery batteries to take over the defence of Givenchy.

24 Oct • The British I Corps is relieved by elements of the French IX Corps. I Corps begins its move to the Menin Road area.

- At 9.30 am German infantry break through 21 Brigade (GOC Brigadier General Herbert Watts) lines at Reutel situated on the eastern edge of Polygon Wood. Three companies of 2nd Battalion Wiltshire Regiment surrender. The position is restored by units of the 2nd Division by noon but another breakthrough on 20 Brigade's (GOC Brigadier General Harold Ruggles-Brise) frontage takes until evening to restore.

- Units of the 2nd Division begin to move south to take over 22 Brigade lines, reducing IV Corps frontage to four miles.

- The German Fourth Army begins a major assault on Dixmude, French marines hold their positions through repeated artillery bombardments and infantry attacks.

- Shell shortages result in GHQ issuing orders to restrict the expenditure of ammunition to thirty rounds per day for 18-pounders and fifteen rounds per day for 4.5-inch howitzers.

25 Oct • The German 43rd Reserve Division breaks through the Dixmude defences. Desperate hand-to-hand fighting ensues before they are finally driven out.

- The German XXVII Corps begins its assault on the 7th Division's positions north and south of the Menin Road. 20 Brigade positions around Kruiseke suffer from a sustained German artillery bombardment lasting some thirty-six hours; the forward trenches are rushed at 8.30 pm forcing a retirement.

- North of the Menin Road, sometime after 6.30 am the remaining 2nd Wiltshires are almost totally annihilated during a German counter-attack on the Reutel positions by elements of the German 244 Reserve Regiment. What is not apparent to the German commander on the ground is that his troops have broken through the British line. A potential disaster is averted by the quick response organised by General Capper. The gap is hurriedly filled by a scratch force of reserves and German forces are pushed out of Polygon Wood. The situation remains critical for the remainder of the day.

26 Oct • The abandoned British trenches at Kruiseke are retaken in a costly counter-attack but by 3.00 pm all the surviving British troops of 20

Brigade have retired from the village in the face of the continuing artillery bombardment.

- The Royal Horse Guards make a demonstration of force on the Kruiseke Ridge in support of 20 Brigade. General Capper spends the night of 26/27 re-establishing the line between Zandvoorde and Veldhoek.

- A prolonged and heavy bombardment of the II Corps lines further south is followed at 4.00 pm by a massive infantry assault. On this occasion the German VII Corps breaks through the line held by the 2nd Battalion Royal Irish Rifles to capture Neuve Chapelle. Despite several counter-attacks it is not possible to regain the whole village and the line is adjusted around it.

27 Oct • Von Falkenhayn completes his review of operations in Flanders resulting in the formation of a new army group to be inserted between the Fourth and Sixth Armies, comprising of: II Bavarian Corps, XV Corps, 48th Reserve Division and the 6th Bavarian Reserve Division. There are now twenty-three German divisions facing eleven Allied divisions. Army Group Fabeck will operate independently of the Fourth and Sixth Armies, answerable only to Supreme Headquarters. The front selected for von Fabeck's assault runs from Ploegsteert Wood to Gheluvelt.

- The 7th Division is transferred to I Corps. Rawlinson and his staff return to England. The 7th Division now hold the line from Zandvoorde to the Menin Road, the 1st Division from the Menin Road to Reutel and the 2nd Division from Reutel to the Moorslede-Zonnebeke road.

- Sir John French reports to Kitchener that the enemy are 'quite incapable of making any strong sustained attack'.

28 Oct • With units of the German Fourth Army now across the Yser, the Belgian centre gives way. Belgian engineers succeed in their second attempt to open the weir and sluice gates at Noovdvaart to let in the sea. The Germans renew their attack and manage to breach the Belgian line at Ramscapelle. Fortunately the rising floodwaters, assisted by a very high tide on the 29 October, force their retirement. The crisis on the Yser is averted and the coastal zone from Nieuport to Dixmude remains flooded until after the war.

- II Corps are unsuccessful in their attempts to regain Neuve Chapelle, the attack on the 28 October results in 65 officers and 1,466 other ranks becoming casualties.

- A German wireless message is intercepted from the Fourth Army to the XXVII Reserve Corps ordering an attack on the British positions on 30 October. British intelligence suggests that units in the line from Kruiseke to Polygon Wood in the north should expect to be attacked.

- Joffre authorises Foch to begin construction of a fortified zone to protect the Channel ports.

29 Oct
- With no preliminary bombardment, the first German troops appear punctually at 5.30 am advancing along a front that straddles the Menin Road from Becelaere in the north, to Epines in the south. Initially cloaked by the early morning fog, the massed German infantry units soon overwhelm the forward British positions, reducing a number of the defending battalions to little more than cadre strength. 1/Coldstream Guards is left with 1 officer and less than 100 men and 1/Grenadier Guards with 2 officers and 250 men. At 3.00 pm the line is restored 500 yards east of the crossroads.

- I Corps Headquarters moves to Hooge Chateâu from the Chateâu Biebuyck (White Chateâu).

- The French IX Corps continues offensive action in the north and recaptures Zonnebeke and Kortekeer.

30 Oct
- Messines Ridge again comes under pressure with a heavy bombardment and infantry attacks from the 3rd and 4th Bavarian Divisions. Under increasing enemy pressure the 2nd and 3rd Cavalry Divisions fall back to the Canal and Hollebeke is abandoned.

- Northeast of Ypres the German XXIII Reserve Corps attack de Mitry's 87th Territorials at Bixschoote and Langemarck. Bixschoote is lost but the attack on Langemarck fails.

- Polygon Wood comes under fire and is attacked in force. French and British units successfully defend their positions. The attack is, in all probability, a feint designed to draw British forces away from Gheluvelt.

- At Gheluvelt the German 54th Reserve Division together with the 30th Division attack north of the Menin Road. Their advance fails in the face of British rifle fire. A second attack an hour later is equally unsuccessful.

- Further south the artillery bombardment that fell on Gheluvelt between 6.45 am and 8.00 am is replicated at Zandvoorde where 7 Cavalry Brigade (1/ and 2/Life Guards and Royal Horse Guards) are dug in on the forward slopes of the village. On their left flank are the 1st Battalion Royal Welch Fusiliers. At 8.00 am the German 39th Division attacks in force and two squadrons of Life Guards and the Royal Horse Guards (Blues) machine-gun section are killed or captured. The Royal Welch, now being attacked on their right flank as well as their front, fight on until every officer has been killed or wounded, less than 100 men rejoin the brigade. The Germans are now in possession of the entire Zandvoorde Ridge.

- With Klein Zillebeke now threatened, 6 Cavalry Brigade (Brigadier General Ernest Makins), are reinforced by the Royal Scots Greys, 3/(King's Own) Hussars and 4/Hussars. Together with French reserves, under the command of General Moussy, they manage to hold the line until they are relieved that evening by Lord Cavan and 4 Guards Brigade.

31 Oct
- Heavy fighting on the Messines front continues but the arrival of 2nd Battalion King's Own Scottish Borderers and 2nd Battalion King's Own Yorkshire Light Infantry from II Corps, goes some way to strengthening the British line. Later that evening the London Scottish (1/14th Battalion London Regiment) arrive from Wytschaete. The battalion immediately counter-attacks on the northern edge of Messines. The line is temporarily stabilised.

- Kaiser Wilhelm II arrives at Courtrai to celebrate what is assumed will be a triumphant entry through the gates of Ypres.

- At 8.00 am Haig orders the 3rd Cavalry Division north to support British positions astride the Menin Road.

- The attack on Gheluvelt continues at 6.00 am. The 16th Bavarian and 246 Regiments attack along the Menin Road. Met by intense and accurate British rifle fire the assault is brought to a halt. At 8.00 am the bombardment begins as a prelude to the massed assault of von

Fabeck's divisions advancing north and south of the Menin Road. British battalions fight a desperate and very costly action during the morning. By midday, Gheluvelt is taken by the Germans.

- North of the Menin Road the remnants of the 1st Battalion South Wales Borderers and the 1st Battalion Scots Guards are still in touch with their right flank until they are thrown back through the grounds of Gheluvelt Château. Realising they will soon be surrounded they decide to make a stand on the south-eastern edge and fight to the last man. The grounds of the château are now in German hands and the British line is effectively wide open at this point.

- At 1.00 pm the I Corps divisional staffs meet in the annex of Hooge Château to discuss the severity of the situation. At 1.15 pm a shell hits the room in which they are meeting and almost every officer present is either killed or wounded. Major General Samuel Lomax (GOC 1st Division) is severely wounded and incapacitated and Major General Charles Monro (GOC 2nd Division) is concussed.[8] Brigadier General Herman Landon (GOC 3rd Brigade) takes temporary command of the 1st Division.

- Brigadier General Charles FitzClarence (GOC 1st Infantry Brigade), orders the 2nd Worcesters to advance on the château from their positions at Polygon Wood. At 1.45 pm three companies of the Worcesters famously advance into British Army legend and retake the château grounds. The gap is closed.

- South of the Menin Road the 7th Division battalions are overwhelmed and those units that survive are gradually pushed back by the dense mass of German troops. At 4.15 pm Brigadier General Edward Bulfin (GOC 2 Infantry Brigade), now in danger of being outflanked, realises his only course of action is to attack. He gathers together his limited reserves and counter-attacks through the trees of the Shrewsbury Forest with the remnants of the 2nd Battalion Gordon Highlanders (2/Gordon Highlanders).[9] The Gordons' charge is joined by the 1st Battalion Northamptonshire Regiment (1/Northants) and 2nd Battalion Royal Sussex Regiment (2/Royal Sussex). In the face of this offensive action the mass of the German 39th Division is gradually turned. By 5.30 pm, as other units of the division lend support, they recover much of the ground lost during the day.

- At around the same time as Bulfin is counter-attacking through Shrewsbury Forest, British troops, under the command of Lieutenant Colonel Lovett of 1/Gloucesters, are defending the Menin Road at the Veldhoek crossroads. This small force of Gloucesters, together with what remains of the 1st Battalion Queen's (Royal West Surrey) Regiment, 2nd Welch and 2nd Battalion King's Royal Rifle Corps (60th Rifles) await the arrival of 105th Saxon Regiment. British rifle fire together with artillery support breaks the Saxon advance and forces them to retire.

- That evening the French XVI Corps arrive on General Bulfin's right, effectively shortening the I Corps frontage.

1 Nov • Further reinforcements arrive from the French XX Corps and Conneau's II Corps to reinforce positions to the north and south of the I Corps line.

- The French Cavalry Corps take over part of the line held by Allenby's cavalry. Messines Ridge again attacked in force by the 6th Bavarian Reserve Division drawing to a conclusion a struggle that saw the ground between Messines and Wytschaete captured and recaptured until finally the Germans secure the ridge. Messines is evacuated.

- The battle continues sporadically along the III Corps front from Hill 63 along the eastern edge of Ploegsteert Wood to Le Touquet and the outskirts of Armentières.

- Generals Bulfin and Ruggles-Brise are both wounded and evacuated. Lord Cavan assumes command of Bulfin's 2 Brigade.

- Lord Kitchener meets with the French including Joffre and Foch at Dunkirk. He offers to replace Sir John French with Sir Ian Hamilton. Joffre declines.

3 Nov • Second Lieutenant John Lee Steere joins 2/Grenadier Guards at Klein Zillebeke.

5 Nov • On the II Corps front the Indian Corps take over the Givenchy-Neuve Chapelle line releasing a composite force of two brigades to begin to relieve the exhausted 7th Division.

6 Nov • A German attack along the 2nd Division front at Zwarteleen pushes back the French and Irish Guards leaving the right flank of 2/Grenadier Guards exposed. The gap is quickly exploited and German troops are only driven back after the timely intervention of 7 Cavalry Brigade which has been held in reserve. The brigade counter-attacks in what must be one of the finest dismounted actions by the cavalry in 1914. A new line is established in front of and parallel to the Brown Road. During the action Lieutenant William Reginald Wyndham, Lieutenant Colonel Gordon Chesney Wilson, Lieutenant Carleton Wyndham Tufnell, Lieutenant William Sinclair Petersen, Captain Norman Neill and Baron Alexis George de Gunzburg are killed.

• At 10.00 pm 22 Brigade arrives at Zillebeke and 3 Brigade relieves 7 Cavalry Brigade in the trenches, consolidating the eastern end of Zwarteleen and the woods further to the north.

7 Nov • At 5.00 am 22 Brigade counter-attack in an attempt to regain some of the lost ground. The attack, led personally by General Lawford, is only partially successful leaving the brigade with only 4 officers and 700 men on roll.

• Advancing after the attack, 3 Brigade units, including 1/Gloucesters, come under heavy rifle and machine-gun fire from the eastern end of Zwarteleen. By nightfall the line is consolidated but amongst those killed is Captain Robert Rising. Included in 2/Grenadier Guards casualty list (19 killed, 46 wounded and 3 missing) is Private Walter Siewertsen.

• German attacks on le Touquet, Ploegsteert, Herenthage Woods and Broodseinde are all repulsed.

8 Nov • Von Falkenhayn creates a new army group to press home an attack along the line of the Menin Road with three divisions to the south and one to the north. Army Group Linsingen is comprised of: XV Corps, 4th Pomeranian Division and Winkler's Guard Division.

10 Nov • A heavy bombardment on both sides of the Menin Road for much of the day reduces many of the established trenches. There is no subsequent infantry attack but casualties are reported to be high. 2/Grenadier Guards, holding the line near Zwarteleen, suffer very badly. Amongst the dead are Lieutenant Michael Stocks, Lieutenant

Henry Parnell (Lord Congleton) and Major Lord Bernard Gordon Lennox.

11 Nov • At dawn the German Fourth and Sixth Armies open fire again on the Allied line to deliver the heaviest bombardment of the war to date. Twelve German battalions attack along a nine mile front between Messines and Reutel. German infantry rapidly close on British and French positions. The attackers meet with little success except astride the Menin Road where British and French troops are driven back 500 yards. Fighting alongside the 2nd Battalion Royal Munster Fusiliers and the 2nd Royal Welch at Zillebeke, Private William Gibson of the London Scottish is killed.

• A more critical situation soon develops to the north of the road where lightly held British defences are quickly overrun by elements of the German 2nd Guard Grenadiers who break through the weakened British 1 Brigade southwest of Polygon Wood, forcing a near 1,000 yard gap in the line. By 10.00 am German infantry are exploiting the breach. Despite being hampered by broken ground and intense rifle fire from isolated strong points, attacking groups pass into and through the undefended Nonne Boschen Wood. A potentially disastrous situation is only averted by yet another hastily assembled counter-attack, this time by the 2nd Battalion Oxford and Bucks Light Infantry, which successfully expels German forces from Nonne Boschen, and with it, all hopes the German high command have of a breakthrough.

• General FitzClarence, known affectionately as 'GOC Menin Road' by the troops, is killed late in the afternoon near Polygon Wood while attempting to organize another counter-attack.

• Further to the north Dubois' IX Corps together with Bidon's Territorials and Mitry's 1st Cavalry Corps are holding the line from Zonnebeke to Bixschoote. Large scale German attacks fail to advance beyond the ruins of Bixschoote and Langemarck remains in Allied hands.

15 Nov • Second Lieutenant Howard Avenel Bligh St George is killed while serving with 1/Life Guards at Zwarteleen.

17 Nov • The last serious attempt to break through the Allied lines is made south of the Menin Road by the German XV Corps on 17 November. 4 (Guards) Brigade come under heavy shellfire but are able to drive

the enemy infantry back inflicting heavy losses. The positions are held until the Guards are relieved by the French on the 20 November. Losses amongst the Grenadier and Coldstream Guards include: Lance Corporal James Whitfield, Captain Cholmeley Symes-Thompson and Second Lieutenant John Lee Steere on 17 November and Captain Richard Dawson on 20 November. Lieutenant Alfred Schuster is killed on the same day, serving with 4/Hussars at Hooge.

Chapter 6

A Very Gallant Officer

In March 1914, on the anniversary of the regiment's action at Alexandria in 1801, Captain Robert Rising assembled with the officers of 1/Gloucesters for an official photograph to be taken with Brigadier General Herman Landon, GOC 3 Infantry Brigade, and the Mayor of Gloucester.[1] Absent from the line-up at Bordon was Rising's great friend and colleague, Captain Harold Richmond, who was completing his secondment at the Camberley Staff College.[2] A little over seven months later both officers would find themselves at Ypres in October 1914 but serving in different capacities; Harold Richmond as a Staff Captain at Sir John French's GHQ, and Robert Rising as a company commander. Their friendship, which began when Harold Richmond joined the regiment in 1900 from the Militia, had developed during the battalion's service in India and Robert had been Harold's best man in December 1909 when he married Mabel Cadell at the church of St John the Evangelist in the Bombay cantonment of Colaba.

Born on 23 May 1871 at Reading, Robert was the son of Thomas and Kate Rising, who, in 1914 were living at the Manor House at Great Ormesby in Norfolk. Robert was the eldest of four children who were brought up in comfortable surroundings with all the privileges of wealth and status. After leaving Charterhouse he entered Sandhurst in September 1891, where his exemplary performance resulted in promotion to Under Officer. In November 1892 he was commissioned into the Gloucestershire Regiment. He was 25-years-old when he married his first wife Amy Worship, the daughter of one of his father's business partners, and tragically less than a year after the couple arrived in India with the 1st Battalion, she succumbed to peritonitis at Pachmirbi and died.

Sickness and even death was not uncommon amongst the European white families in India. During the two months of July and August 1897 for example, there were eighteen European deaths recorded at Pachmirbi from dysentery, enteric fever, (typhoid as it is known today) diarrhoea and peritonitis. Sadly six of these were children of serving soldiers' families. Worse still, although confined to the poorer parts of the city, 1897 also saw an outbreak of Bubonic plague in Bombay; the severity of which even prompted questions being asked at Westminster by the Hackney MP, Sir Andrew Scoble.

Shortly before the British Empire went to war against the Boers in October 1899, four infantry battalions including the Gloucesters were mobilized in India and despatched to South Africa. Within weeks of the outbreak of hostilities the British Army found itself besieged in the townships of Kimberley, Mafeking and Ladysmith by a Boer force that was better armed in terms of artillery and far more tactically adept. On receiving the news at home of this embarrassing turn for the worse, the seriousness of the situation in South Africa was finally realized and Lord Roberts was sent out from England with a large force to recover the credibility of the army. Caught up in the initial blundering by British Army commanders was 1/Gloucesters which had arrived two days after war was declared at Durban on 13 October. They were immediately marched up to Ladysmith and were soon in action at Rietfontein on 24 October as part of Sir George White's column.

Coming under hostile rifle fire from a range of hills skirting the road the Gloucesters were ordered to advance towards the Boer positions. The British column had been successfully ambushed by their shrewd adversaries and despite their gallantry in advancing over the veld in the face of the all too accurate Mauser fire the British soldiers found themselves pinned down and unable to move without attracting a further hail of fire. When the order finally did come to retire, Colonel Wilford, the Gloucester's commanding officer, was killed directing the battalion's withdrawal. For Robert Rising and the majority of the officers and men of the battalion it had not only been their first taste of action but the first occasion the battalion had been under hostile fire for fifty years; one which left five men dead and fifty-eight wounded. This sobering experience had been a severe and sharp baptism of fire but worse was to befall the battalion in their next clash with the Boers.

On 29 October 1899, Lieutenant Robert Rising was on outpost duty and consequently was one of the five battalion officers who remained behind at Ladysmith, while four companies of the Gloucesters with six companies of the 1st Royal Irish Fusiliers were sent out from Ladysmith under the cover of darkness to take control of a ridge known as Nicholson's Nek. Commanded by Lieutenant Colonel Carleton of the Fusiliers, the ill-fated expedition was a catalogue of disasters and poor command decisions which served to further highlight inept leadership. Taking full advantage of British misfortune, which included the pack mules stampeding with most of the ammunition, guns and water, the Boer forces won a splendid victory which resulted in the humiliating surrender of the surviving British infantrymen. Nearly 400 of the Gloucesters, including eighteen officers, were marched off into an eight month long captivity at Pretoria. The battalion's casualties were seventy-five men wounded,

bove: Zillebeke churchyard cemetery.

Above: One of the two bells donated by the de Gunzburg family in memory of Alexis George de Gunzburg.

Left: The church window donated by Mrs Evelyn St George in memory of her son, Howard Avenel Bligh St George.

Left: Richard Long Dawson, killed in action on 20 November 1914.

Above: The original metal nameplate that was placed on Dawson's cross at Zillebeke churchyard. Note the bullet hole and the incorrect date of death.

Dawson's grave at Zillebeke in 1919. The ruins of the church are in the background.

Baron Alexis George de Gunzburg who was killed in action on 6 November 1914. His naturalization papers were rushed through to enable him to go to war with the 3rd Cavalry Division.

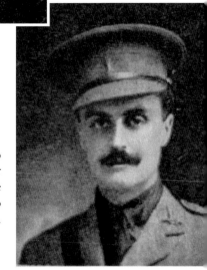

The ruins of Zillebeke
Church 1919. After
four years of fighting
the church and village
were reduced to rubble.

The interior of
Zillebeke Church
November 1914.

John Lee Steere's grave marker at
Zillebeke 1920.

The plaque erected in memory of Alfred
Felix Schuster.

IN MEMORY OF LIEUTENANT
ALFRED F. SCHUSTER. 4TH
:QUEEN'S OWN: HUSSARS
BORN 30TH JULY 1883 ✝
KILLED NEAR LA HOOGHE
20TH NOVEMBER 1914
ΟΥ ΔΕ ΤΕΘΝΑΣΙ ΘΑΝΟΝΤΕΣ

The Household Brigade Memorial at Zandvoorde in the final stages of its construction in 1924.

Above: Howard Avenel Bligh St George in the dress uniform of the 1st Life Guards. He was killed by a sniper on 15 November 1914.

Sarah T. Wilson

Right: Gordon Chesney Wilson, taken at Windsor in 1911. Wilson commanded the Royal Horse Guards until his death on 6 November 1914.

Left: Lady Sarah Wilson who was running a hospital at Boulogne at the time of her husband's death.

Men of the 1st Battalion The Gloucestershire Regiment.

Caricature of Robert Rising drawn while the regiment was stationed in India.

The Gloucestershire Regiment Memorial at Clapham Junction, Ypres.

1st Battalion The Gloucestershire Regiment at Bordon in 1914

Back Row: (L-R): 2/Lt.R Grazebrook, Capt.W Temple, 2/Lt D Baxter, Lt.J Caunter, Middle Row: 7th from left, 2/Lt.W S Yalland,
Front Row: ANO, Capt.R Gardner, ANO, Capt.J O'D.Ingram, ANO, Lt.Col.A C Lovett, Brig.Gen.H Landon, ANO, Maj.A J .Menzies,
ANO, Capt.R E Rising, ANO, Capt.G M Shipway.

Sandhurst 1901. Cadets under instruction at the Riding School. This was the last year that cadets at the RMC would wear the blue serge uniform and forage cap. The author's grandfather is in the second row, second from right.

Old Etonians at Sandhurst in 1913. John Lee Steere is standing third from the left in the front row, leaning against the wall with his arms folded.

His Majesty the King reviewing Sandhurst cadets in July 1913. Present amongst the invited guests are the parents of John Lee Steere.

Grenadier Guards of the 1st Battalion parade prior to leaving for France with the BEF in August 1914. The battalion was all but wiped out at Ypres in October 1914.

Left: William Sinclair Petersen. Killed on 6 November 1914.

Right: Norman Neill, the Brigade Major of 7 Cavalry Brigade. Killed on 6 November 1914.

The memorial to the 157 Glenalmond old boys who were killed in the Great War. Petersen's name is amongst them.

Carleton Wyndham Tufnell.

John Henry Gordon Lee Steere.

Left: Postcard written by John Lee Steere from the Zillebeke trenches ten days before he was killed in action on 17 November 1914.

John Lee Steere's cousin Cholmeley Symes-Thompson.

Left: Harry Parnell, the 5th Lord Congleton, at New College Oxford in 1911.

Right: Harry in the dress uniform of the Grenadier Guards in 1913.

One of the less serious student pranks that Harry Parnell was involved in during his time at New College.

The gentleman whose trousers were found at the bottom of the drain in Garden Quad on Thursday morning, may recover them on application to the Bursary.

Dec. 2. 1910.

L.Q.W.L.

Above left: Walter Frederick Siewertsen.

Above right: Michael George Stocks.

Left: L-R Major Lord Bernard Gordon Lennox standing with his brother-in-law Major Beckwith and his elder brother Lord Esme Gordon Lennox. Bernard was killed on 10 November 1914, the same day Michael Stocks was killed serving with Number 4 Company. Esme was wounded at Zandvoorde but survived the war, as did Major Beckwith.

Left: Alfred Felix Schuster at New College Oxford, pictured sitting in front of Frederick Murray Hicks. Hicks was commissioned in 1914 and survived. Alfred was killed on 20 November 1914 at Hooge.

Right: William Gibson in London Scottish dress uniform. Gibson was a territorial soldier from Ilford who lost his life on 11 November 1914.

The Brown Road today, looking much the same as it did over ninety years ago. It was along this road that the Grenadier Guards held the line on 6 November 1914.

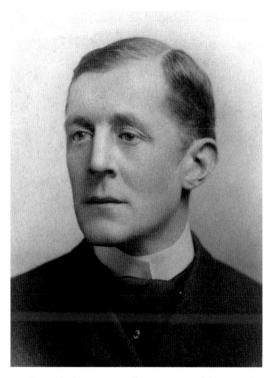

Above left: Hon William Reginald Wyndham circa 1912.

Above right: Second Lieutenant Wyndham at Fulford Barracks, York in 1897 soon after being commissioned into the 17th Lancers.

Mounted on Wengy, one of the two horses he took with him to France in October 1914.

The memorial to the war dead of the London Scottish in the drill hall at Horseferry Road, London. William Gibson's name is amongst them.

The Menin Gate at Ypres shortly after its inauguration in 1927.

MAJOR ROBERT E. RISING, D.S.O.
MAJOR SIDNEY J. B. LACON.
PRIVATE FRED ALLEN.
FREDERICK A. J. BECK.
REBA BRISTOW.
GEORGE W. CROW.
ROBERT C. DERRY.

Robert Rising's name on the village war memorial at Ormesby St Margaret, Norfolk.

The memorial to Cholmeley Symes-Thompson at St Michael's Church, in the Oxfordshire village of Finmere.

TO·THE·LOVED·MEMORY·OF
CHOLMELEY·SYMES·THOMPSON
CAPTAIN·1ST·BATT·GRENADIER·GUARDS
BORN·16·APRIL·1881·GAVE·HIS·LIFE·FOR
THE·HONOUR·OF·HIS·COUNTRY·IN·THE
BATTLE·OF·17·NOVEMBER·1914·NEAR·YPRES

BE·THOU·FAITHFUL·UNTO·DEATH·AND
I·WILL·GIVE·THEE·A·CROWN·OF·LIFE

HOWARD AVENEL BLIGH ST. GEORGE,
2ND LIEUT 1ST LIFE GUARDS
15. NOV. 1914.
HARRY BALDWIN,
SERGT OXON & BUCKS L.I.
19. FEB 1917
AARON PAIN,
PTE R. WARWICKS
4. OCT. 1917
WILLIAM KING,
A.B. R.N.DIVN
1. APRIL 1918.

TO THE GLORY OF GOD AND IN UNDYING MEMORY OF THE MEN OF THIS PARISH WHO GAVE THEIR LIVES FOR THEIR COUNTRY IN THE GREAT WAR 1914-1918.

AND 1938-1945.
C. JOHN H. BRAGGS
DVR R.A.S.C.
20. MAY 1944
FRANK H. CRUNDWELL
A/C.1. R.A.F.
9. AUG. 1940.
WILLIAM TARVER
PTE R. WARWICKS
14 AUG 1940
C. JOHN WRIGHT
CON. GRENADIER GDS
7. NOV 1943

WE FORGET.

The name of Howard St George commemorated on the Newbold Pacey war memorial in Warwickshire.

The Ivan Mestrovic wood carving 'Descent from the Cross' bought by Evelyn St George in memory of her son.

most of whom went into captivity, and thirty-three men dead who were later buried on the battlefield.[3] It had been an unmitigated debacle.

Although he had volunteered to march with the column, when news of the outcome of the fight at Nicholson's Nek reached Ladysmith, Robert Rising was probably thankful he had been left behind. Those of the battalion who had not been with Carleton fought on and suffered in Ladysmith until the siege was raised in February 1900. Casualties from long range shell fire continued to deplete the battalion. On 22 December, at the Gloucesters' outpost positions at Railway Cutting, they had the misfortune to lose eight killed and nine wounded to a single 6-inch shell. After the relief of Ladysmith the battalion took little active part in the campaign. In June 1900 they were reunited with the officers and men who had been held captive at Pretoria and on 21 August 1900 they embarked for Ceylon to guard Boer prisoners.

In early 1901 Robert married again; this time to Constance Elizabeth Edis, the 23-year-old daughter of Lieutenant Colonel Robert William Edis. Having taken his accumulated leave after the battalion returned to India, he returned home to England where he and Constance were married in London. Robert Edis was a well known Victorian architect and writer whose designs included, amongst others, the Marylebone and Liverpool Street Station hotels and the ballroom at Sandringham Park. The Edis family, apart from their London residence, had a family home at Great Ormsby and were neighbours of Thomas and Kate Rising. The recently widowed Robert would have had little difficulty in finding his second wife from the five Edis daughters; no doubt encouraged by Robert Edis who would have approved of a military son-in-law. Edis was commanding officer of the Artist's Rifles at the time of Robert and Constance's marriage and was knighted in 1919. He died in 1927 at the family home in Norfolk.

Although 1/Gloucesters returned to England in 1910 after seventeen years foreign service, Robert came home with a pregnant Constance in late 1905 having been appointed Adjutant to the 3rd Territorial Battalion based at Horfield Barracks, Bristol. During this period Constance gave birth to two children, Robert Edis, who was born shortly after they arrived home, and Elsie Mary Elizabeth, born in September 1909. It must have been with some relief that Constance was able to give birth to both her children at home in England and once the battalion arrived back in England, the family moved from Bristol and were able to settle down to the comfortable existence of home service at Bordon. August 1914 brought an end to any plans the Rising family may have made for themselves or their children when the battalion was ordered to mobilize. 1/Gloucesters were one of the four infantry battalions that formed 3 Infantry Brigade along with the 1st Battalion South Wales Borderers (1/South Wales Borderers), 2nd Battalion Welch Regiment (2/Welch) and the 1st

Battalion Queen's (Royal West Surrey) Regiment (1/Queen's). Eight days later they landed at Le Havre.

The events in France and Flanders were closely followed by Robert's parents at their home in Norfolk. Thomas Rising was a self-made man who had begun his legal career as a solicitor's clerk in Reading. Through hard work and diligence he eventually qualified as a solicitor and became a senior partner in the local Yarmouth firm of Messrs Worship, Rising and Frederick. In 1914 the firm also employed Robert's younger brother Arthur, who had graduated from Trinity College Cambridge in 1891. Constance and the children moved back to her father's home at Ormesby St Margaret soon after Robert had embarked with his battalion on the SS *Gloucester Castle*, but the family was not unduly concerned, after all, with any luck Robert would be back in time to see the children opening their Christmas presents.

*   *   *

Until their arrival at Poperinghe on Tuesday 20 October 1914, the Gloucesters' battlefield casualties had been relatively small in number but their entrance into the ancient city of Ypres marked the beginning of a period of intense and desperate fighting that would leave a permanent mark on the officers and men of the battalion. Of the 26 officers and 970 other ranks that marched past the cheering crowds which lined the Grote Markt and the Meensestraat the next morning, only 2 officers and some 100 men returned through the Menin Gate four weeks later.

What the Gloucesters were not aware of, as they marched out of Ypres, was that their Commander-in-Chief, Sir John French, had still not fully appreciated the full extent of the huge German troop concentrations that were now moving from Antwerp towards the BEF. His optimistic orders for a general advance, which he stubbornly clung to for several days, were never going to be realized. It was to be only a matter of hours before the military strategy that would determine the nature of the fighting over the next few weeks would begin to unravel as the Allies were forced into a series of defensive actions by a numerically superior opposition.

To be fair, when Sir Douglas Haig and I Corps arrived at St Omer from the Aisne on 17 October, Sir John French could easily have taken the most obvious course of action and deployed Haig to bolster the numerical weakness of the cavalry corps holding the Wytschate-Messines line. Instead, recognizing the danger to the Allied left flank by the sudden arrival of fresh German troops, he sent Haig's army corps to the northeast of Ypres. Although he was then unaware of the build up of German forces in the area, his instinct was fortunately well timed. Just after midday on Wednesday, 21 October the Gloucesters, along with the rest of I Corps, collided head on with the German Fourth Army.

That all was not going to plan must have become apparent as the Gloucesters arrived on the outskirts of Langemarck. Almost immediately they ran into heavy shellfire and the forward units of the Fourth Army cavalry screen. Behind them German infantry of the 51st Reserve Division were moving en-masse from the north and, as the French on the British left retreated, the 3 Brigade battalions were becoming increasingly exposed. Advancing on the extreme left of the British line, Lieutenant Colonel Lovett, mindful of the danger of an exposed flank, deployed B Company to Langemarck railway station to provide an emergency flank guard while C and D Company pressed on through the town towards Koekuit. Wary of committing all his available forces at once, Lovett held A Company, which was under the command of Robert Rising, in reserve just south of Langemarck. Sometime after 10.00 am C and D Companies occupied Koekuit village and dug in.

German cavalry patrols had been apparent all morning and one or two had even been shot down as they galloped across the Gloucesters' field of fire; but it was not long before the main German thrust came from the direction of Mangalaere.

Around 100 German infantry attacked in short rushes but were quickly repulsed by Lieutenant Wetherall's platoon before they could close on the Gloucesters who were using a drainage ditch as their fire base. Clearly this was no skirmish as there was now sustained enemy shell fire from the direction of Poelcapelle registering along the whole 3 Brigade frontage; 1/Queen's in particular were taking numerous casualties in their hastily prepared scrape holes. Another attack at 2.00 pm by 200 grey clad infantry advancing four abreast was again brought to a standstill by the disciplined C Company rifle fire. Two hours later the final half-hearted attack was broken up very quickly with three bursts of rapid fire.

Despite this very effective defensive fire, the situation was becoming a little tense with enemy formations now threatening both flanks of the Gloucesters' positions, which had taken the shape of a pronounced salient around Koekuit. However, there they remained in their rather precarious positions until after dark when they were relieved and sent back to a farm east of Langemarck. The Gloucesters dubbed it Varna Farm, after the camp of the same name the old 28th of Foot had shared with the French in the Crimea sixty years previously. Shortly after they arrived at their new billet, the awkward defensive position at Koekuit was abandoned and the line pulled back to a new line north of Langemarck.

It was at Langemarck, where the German Reserve Corps died in such large numbers, that the legend of 'the massacre of the innocents' was born. German casualties on the British I Corps front were enormous, with some units losing up to seventy per cent of their effective fighting strength. There are numerous British accounts of German units marching into battle singing their battle anthem *'Die Wacht am Rhein'*. One of these accounts was written in 1922 by

Robert Grazebrook who was a lieutenant with the Gloucesters in 1914. He recalled Germans of the 46th Reserve Division singing patriotic songs as they attacked the Gloucesters' positions around Koekuit on 21 October. The vast majority of these reserve troops were young inexperienced men; many of them students flushed with patriotism who hurled themselves against the British and French positions and died in their thousands. The sombre German military cemetery at Langemarck serves as a dreadful testament to their sacrifice. Strictly speaking the Langemarck cemetery contains more than just the 1914 dead; but what immediately strikes the visitor are the bronze panels in the gatehouse commemorating the thousands of young students who died during the First Battle of Ypres.

Regardless of the losses, the seemingly endless numbers of German infantry and the intensive artillery barrages had brought an end to any hopes that Sir John French might have had of continuing his advance in the northeast. By and large the I Corps attack on Poelcapelle and Passchendaele had lost its impetus but the news was not all bad. Some progress had been made, Langemarck was still firmly in British hands and the 2nd Division had secured Zonnebeke. However, the fight for Langemarck was not over yet. German forces were consolidating for another attack and it would be Robert Rising's men that would take the brunt of the German infantry attack along the Koekuit Road.

A little before dawn on 23 October Rising was directed to take two platoons of A Company to the northern outskirts of Langemarck to fill a gap that had developed between 2/Welch and 1/Coldstream Guards. Langemarck was now almost unrecognisable; in just a few days the German artillery had reduced much of the small town to ruins with 8-inch howitzers and as Rising's men picked their way through the debris and the flickering fires that still burned amongst the rubble, the occasional high explosive shell was still targeting what was left of the church and the chateâu. It took the Gloucesters some forty minutes to march from Varna Farm to the railway line that marked the northern limit of the chateâu grounds. It was at first light when they made contact with the Royal Engineers of 26th Field Company who were in position on the Koekuit Road. Major H L Prichard, who was commanding the small detachment of sappers, quickly appraised Rising of the situation before they set about preparing their defensive positions.

The Gloucesters were in fact digging in along a vital section of the front line that had been left undefended, and only the urgent message sent back to 3 Brigade headquarters by Major Prichard had alerted anyone to the situation. The break in the line was the result of the capture of the Kortekeer Cabaret salient by the Germans the day before which resulted in 1/Coldstream Guards drawing in its companies and creating a 400 yards wide gap between them and 2/Welch. Rising's men, assisted by Major Pritchard's sappers, dug-in some 500 yards north of the village on the Langemarck to Koekuit Road. On the right was

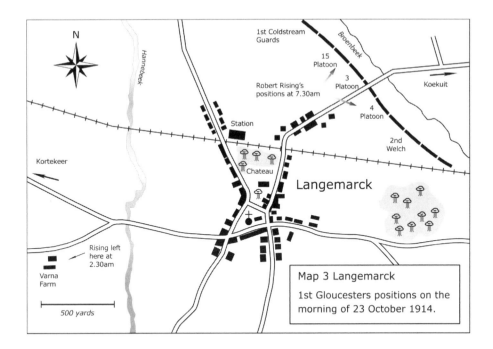

Map 3 Langemarck

1st Gloucesters positions on the morning of 23 October 1914.

Lieutenant Hippisley and 4 Platoon, while Lieutenant Baxter's men of 5 Platoon dug-in across the road itself.[4] In discussion with Major Pritchard, Rising agreed that their positions were probably going to take the full force of the enemy attack from Koekuit and diverted 15 Platoon and Lieutenant Yalland from D Company to dig-in on the left of the road.

25-year-old William Yalland was an accomplished rugby player and regularly featured in the battalion XV. He was also well known in cricketing circles having made an appearance for Gloucestershire in 1910. In 1910 the battalion won the hotly contested Army Rugby Football Cup and in 1913 Yalland scored in the semi-final of the cup, playing again two weeks later in the battalion side that lost 9–3 to 2/Welch at Twickenham. Any friendly rivalry that still existed between the two battalions had been put aside that morning as the men of both regiments strained their eyes in the early morning mist for signs of movement that would signal the approaching enemy.

In common with the other company commanders in his battalion, Robert Rising knew his NCOs well and despite the fact that a large proportion of his company was made up of reservists, many of his NCOs had been with the battalion for a number of years. Individuals such as Lance Sergeant Thomas Knight, who would be awarded the DCM for his bravery later that day, were the backbone of the company and had been instrumental in shaping up the reservists since the battalion landed in France.[5] Good NCOs provided a depth of experience that would be essential in the coming weeks if the company's discipline under fire was to be maintained. The famed discipline under fire, that would forever be associated with the men of the BEF, created soldiers who could maintain a rate of fire of between fifteen and twenty aimed rounds per minute with the Short Magazine Lee Enfield rifle. The effect of such firepower could be devastating against closely packed advancing infantry. Good shooting was not just the preserve of the men. Rising himself held the extra certificate in musketry and was acknowledged in the battalion as an accomplished shot. They did not have to wait long to demonstrate their skills. Private J S Barton was fighting with 4 Platoon:

> *'Shortly after 9.00 am German cavalry were seen coming towards us down the Koekuit road, which ran in a straight line for about a mile. At a point 350 yards from us they turned to their right down a lane to a farm 325 yards from our position. They were going at a full gallop and although we fired on them I did not observe any casualties. A large body of enemy infantry was then seen to be coming down the Koekuit road led by mounted officers.'*

Having successfully halted this initial advance with rifle and machine-gun fire, the attacking German troops were forced into cover. Yet it wasn't long before the German infantry managed to outflank the trenches occupied by Number 2 Company of 1/Coldstream Guards by using the high banks of the Broenbeek to screen their movements. The Coldstream soon found themselves attacked on two sides; a situation that immediately put the British line under severe pressure. With characteristic orderliness the surviving Guardsmen retired to a fresh position where, supported by the three platoons of Gloucesters and 2/Welch with covering fire, they dug-in in a turnip field.

With the Guards' former positions overrun, the Gloucesters now found themselves dangerously exposed on one flank. Taking the full force of the German attack, Rising's men directed their fire into the seemingly endless wall of enemy infantry as they continued to advance shoulder to shoulder down the Koekuit road. Private Barton again:

> *'Ammunition was becoming scarce. All the wounded and killed were searched for ammunition. The attack from the farm direction was again pushed and reached a point 75 yards from us where it was pinned down. The fire from the ditch was so intense that many of our bayonets were broken by bullets. When hit they snapped like glass and the flying fragments were responsible for seven head and neck wounds, two of them very serious.'*

By mid-afternoon the fight was over. It had been an astonishing victory and served to illustrate sharply the effectiveness of sustained and accurate rifle-fire against close-packed infantry. The Gloucesters had fired an average of 500 rounds per man, the evidence of their defiant resistance now lying in heaps in front of their positions. But the cost to Rising's command had been a heavy one: two of the three platoon commanders, Lieutenant Yalland and Lieutenant Harold Hippesley, had been killed; Lieutenant Baxter had been wounded and fifty-one other ranks killed or wounded. Despite these losses the exhausted Gloucesters had borne the full weight of the attack and forced a much larger force to retire. For his leadership during that intense and sustained fire-fight Robert Rising was awarded the DSO which was Gazetted on 9 November 1914, two days after his death:

> *[He] 'Went up with supports and conspicuously controlled the defence of the battalion's trenches against a determined attack by the enemy. But for this stout defence the line must have been penetrated.'*

As for the positions abandoned by 1/Coldstream Guards, a combined counter-attack made by the remainder of A Company under Captain McLeod and Number 2 Company of the Coldstream, regained the lost trenches by 7.00 pm that evening. The German official account of the Langemarck encounter of 22 to 23 October shows how completely their plans were frustrated by I Corps:

> *'With the failure of the 46th Reserve Division to gain a decisive victory between Bixschoote and Langemarck, the fate of the XXVI and XXVII Reserve Corps was also settled. For the time being any further thought of a breakthrough was out of the question.'*

*   *   *

On the 24 October, I Corps was relieved by the French IX Army Corps, the 1st Division handing over their positions to the 87th Territorial Division. As the Gloucesters marched from their billets near Pilckem to Bellewaarde Farm, the next critical phase of the battle for Ypres was about to begin. For the Gloucesters it began with a night in the open; fortunately the weather was kind and the battalion moved the next morning to the wooded area around Hooge Chateâu on the Menin Road. Here they dug new trenches only to abandon them later that evening on receipt of fresh orders from the brigade commander, Brigadier General Herman Landon, to occupy a new position north of Veldhoek. The bulk of the battalion dug in again along the road leading north from the village to Polygon Wood. A small detachment of sixty riflemen were deployed under Lieutenant Wetherall, along with Lieutenant Duncan and the machine-gun section, to reinforce the Coldstream Guards who were holding the Kruiseke crossroads.

The village of Kruiseke had already been lost and 1/Grenadier Guards had lost a significant number of men in its defence on the 26 October. One of John Lee Steere's cousins, 27-year-old Lieutenant Philip Van Neck was one of the officers of the battalion who was killed when two platoons were overwhelmed during 20 Brigade's retirement from the village.[6] The Van Neck family was already in mourning when news of Philip's death reached them. Six days earlier, on 20 October, 21-year-old Second Lieutenant Charles Hylton Van Neck had been killed by a sniper on the II Corps front line near La Bassée serving with the 1st Battalion Northumberland Fusiliers.[7]

Punctually at 5.30 am on the morning of 29 October the German attack began in earnest and almost immediately overwhelmed the units holding the line on both sides of the Menin Road at the Kruiseke crossroads. Peering through the early morning fog the men of the Coldstream Guards and Black Watch, who were entrenched north of the road, were practically annihilated as the first wave of the 6th Bavarian Reserve Division stormed their trenches. It was a similar story with the remnants of 1/Grenadier Guards and 2/Gordon Highlanders who were south of the road. An officer of the Grenadiers later described the attacking German formations as rather like a crowd leaving a football match:

'Shoulder to shoulder they advanced much in the same way as their ancestors fought under Frederick the Great, and though for spectacular purposes at Grand Manoeuvres their mass formations were very effective, in actual warfare against modern weapons they proved to be a costly failure.'

Costly failure it might have been in terms of casualties, but for the riflemen of the British battalions, the difficulty was to shoot the advancing infantry down rapidly enough to avoid being overrun. At the Kruiseke crossroads their combined firepower was not enough to prevent disaster.

At around 7.00 am the Gloucesters were ordered to advance towards Gheluvelt and counter-attack in support of the shattered remnants 1 and 20 Brigades. With the Germans pouring men through the breach in the line north of the Menin Road, the remaining men of 3 Brigade were moved up at noon enabling the 1/South Wales Borderers to reach the eastern edge of the Gheluvelt Chateâu, while 2/Welch and 1/Queen's pushed through Gheluvelt to occupy the eastern outskirts and the cemetery to the south of the Menin Road. The situation was already looking grim for the beleaguered British troops.

Meanwhile, the Gloucesters had been taking heavy casualties all morning in their various contacts with the enemy. At 7.00 am Lieutenant Colonel Lovett ordered A Company to advance north of the Menin Road to assist the Black Watch and the Scots Guards, thereafter, in the confused events of the day, all four companies of Gloucesters became detached from each other, each fighting wherever they found the enemy. Robert Rising and his men, along with D Company got to within 300 yards of the Kruiseke crossroads where they helped rally the 1 Brigade survivors. Attacked again from the northeast, Rising and his men gradually fell back while covering the retirement of Major Robert Gardner and D Company to make a stand on the outskirts of the village. There was a slight advantage here. Gheluvelt is situated on relatively high ground and the attacking enemy forces were obliged to advance uphill from the crossroads, giving a commanding field of fire to the British battalions. Even so, by the time the remaining 3 Brigade battalions reached the Gloucesters in the late afternoon to stabilise the line temporarily the battalion had taken heavy casualties. 7 officers and 160 other ranks were either killed, wounded or were missing. Of these, 3 officers and 14 NCOs had been killed. As dusk fell the shell-battered and burning Gheluvelt was still in British hands but no-one was under any illusion that the battle was over.

The night of 29 October was cold and wet, but it provided a brief respite for the surviving Gloucesters who, by now, had been withdrawn to the Veldhoek trenches. The rain did little to mask the noise of troop movement coming from behind the German lines; a rumbling that announced the continuing build-up of Army Group Fabeck. Much to the surprise of the British troops, dawn on the 30 October was relatively quiet on the Gheluvelt front. German artillery continued to reduce the village to ruins but the German effort was being concentrated around the hilltop village of Zandvoorde further to the south where 7 Cavalry Brigade and 22 Infantry Brigade were dug in on the southeast facing ridge. The Gloucesters remained at Veldhoek, losing another seven men killed and five wounded by shell fire, with orders to standby to assist if the enemy broke through the thin line of defence in front of Gheluvelt. That line was to be severely tested the next day.

* * *

The German attack on the morning of the 31 October began just after 6.00 am when the defensive line of the 1st Division was attacked in force by the 16th Barvarian and 246th Regiments. The British riflemen opened a devastating fire at medium range bringing the attack to a juddering halt as the first and second waves of enemy infantry were brought down. By 7.30 am the initial German infantry attack had dwindled away and there was a pause before an hour-long artillery bombardment began at 8.00 am.

The method adopted by the enemy forces in their attacks on British positions along the Menin Road nearly always ran to the same tactical plan. All the batteries in the area would concentrate their fire on the road itself and the trenches to the left and right, completely destroying these forward positions. While the surviving troops were still recovering from the inferno of shell fire, a dense mass of infantry would be poured through the gap created in the line. Enemy infantry would then surround the trenches that were still being defended to the left and right of the gap. In this manner whole companies of men who had survived the shell fire were often completely overwhelmed and annihilated.

Soon after 9.00 am, the 1/Queen's and 2/Welch, which were in positions south of the Menin Road, had lost most of their officers and NCOs killed or wounded. The remnants of those battalions began to fall back through the village in the face of the ever advancing wall of infantry. In the confusion of this withdrawal, men of different battalions and even different brigades found themselves fighting together, often commanded by an officer or NCO who had collected groups of stragglers. It was in this chaos of battle that a little piece of history was made. For the first time in the long history of the Queen's, both regular battalions found themselves fighting side-by-side.

To the north of the road, four battalions of the German 54th Reserve Division were held by 130 men of 2/Welch until around 11.45 am when only thirty-seven men were left standing. This dogged determination not to bend under the onslaught was not an isolated event. The men of 1/South Wales Borderers and 1/Scots Guards, who were fighting close to the chateâu grounds, were putting up a similar defence as several companies of German infantry penetrated the village and brought fire to bear onto the rear of some British units. But it was the beginning of the end and by midday the battle for Gheluvelt was all but over. Five weak battalions, which could barely muster 1,000 men between them, were no match for the thirteen German battalions they faced. The situation was now critical and the British line showed every sign of breaking down under the pressure.

But worse was still to come, while the I Corps divisional staffs were meeting in the annexe of Hooge Chateâu at lunchtime to discuss the severity of the situation, the room in which they were gathered was hit by a shell and almost every officer present was either killed or wounded. Major General Samuel Lomax (GOC 1st Division) was severely wounded and incapacitated and Major General Charles Monro (GOC 2nd Division) was badly concussed. Yet this incident, which delivered a potentially devastating blow to the command structure of I Corps, served to illustrate the professionalism and depth of leadership that still existed amongst the brigade and battalion commanders. An element that was no better illustrated by the events that followed.

At 2.00 pm another German attack wiped out the right flank of 1/South Wales Borderers and the remaining men of the battalion fell back through the grounds of the Gheluvelt Chateâu. Germans were now advancing in force up the Menin Road, Gheluvelt was in flames and a gap had opened up in the line. In a desperate but futile counter-attack, Major Gardner and D Company of the Gloucesters were sent into the village. Some eighty-strong when they set off, they were reduced to just fifteen men left standing by the time they met the advance parties

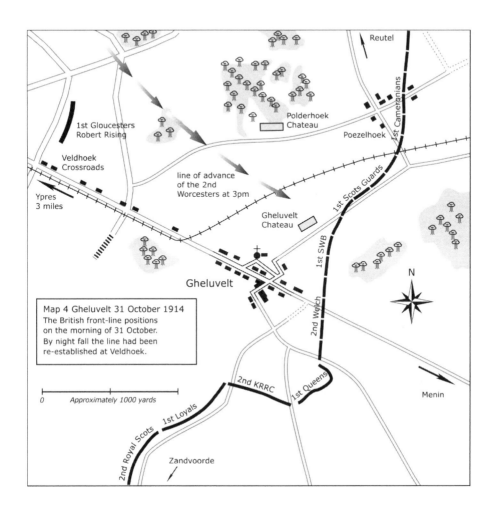

Map 4 Gheluvelt 31 October 1914
The British front-line positions on the morning of 31 October. By night fall the line had been re-established at Veldhoek.

of the 54th Reserve Division. Gardner died at the head of his men and the handful that remained held out until they were overwhelmed and taken prisoner.

Just when it looked as though the day was lost and the road to Ypres was wide open, Brigadier General Charles FitzClarence, GOC 1 Guards Brigade, threw in the only reserves left to fight, the 2nd Battalion Worcestershire Regiment (2/Worcesters). Desperately below strength they were now ordered to advance from Polygon Wood on the chateâu, where the Scots Guards and South Wales Borderers still clung onto their positions. It was a last desperate effort to plug the gap in the line. In theory the situation looked hopeless; how could a severely understrength battalion possibly alter the course of events in the face of such overwhelming odds? Nevertheless at 3.00 pm, 370 men led by Major Edward Hankey, ran at the double across a mile of open ground before they charged with fixed bayonets into the mass of well over 1,000 German infantrymen.

More than 100 of the Worcesters had fallen before they reached the woods in front of the chateâu but the ferocity and surprise of their attack routed the German force, which fled abandoning much of their arms and equipment. It is probably going a little too far to suggest that the Worcesters' charge saved the day, but crucially, it did enable the men of the 1st Division to rally, reform and restore the integrity of the front line north of the Menin Road. It also allowed the British line to be redrawn further east without the inevitable casualties of a fighting withdrawal.

Later that afternoon, a similar counter-attack to stabilize the right of the I Corps line, took place south of the Menin Road in Shrewsbury Forest under the leadership of Brigadier General Edward Bulfin. It was almost as if it had become a prerequisite that counter-attacks should only be carried out in the face of overwhelming odds with as few men as possible. In reality of course, many such attacks during the First Battle of Ypres were usually the last desperate throws of the dice, carried out by anyone that was still upright and could hold a rifle and bayonet. Possibly the prospect of the failure to hold the line and the image of German troops entering Ypres en-masse were enough to provide the determination and energy to drive the Germans back time after time. A more probable explanation was the degree of panic that an unexpected body of charging, shouting men with fixed bayonets could wreak on an enemy force.

Unquestionably the courage and battlefield discipline of the British soldier had won the respect of their adversaries. An officer of the German General Staff was reported to have said that:

> *'The Englishman is cool and indifferent to danger … he stays where he is commanded … he shoots magnificently, extraordinarily well. He is good at bayonet attack … and it is during these bayonet attacks when luck is against him that he is at his very best.*[8]

By mid-afternoon, south of Gheluvelt, the 105th (Saxon) Regiment had cleared the last of the British defence and was now in a position to advance up the Menin Road. Ahead of them lay Veldhoek and three understrength companies of the Gloucesters reinforced by a collection of stragglers from other 3 Brigade units. From the cover of a barricade across the road at the Veldhoek crossroads, the battalion's rifles stemmed any further advance towards Ypres. Lieutenant Robert Grazebrook's account still survives:

> *'The barricade across the Menin Road at Veldhoek and the houses on either side provided excellent cover for snipers to pick off the Huns advancing up the road or amongst the ruins of Gheluvelt. Sgt Major Long and CQMS Mayell did excellent work from one of the houses and accounted for many of the enemy as they attempted to cross the road from the south.'*

At 6.00 pm that evening the British troops north of the Menin Road were withdrawn to a fresh line stretching from the Gloucesters' position at Veldhoek, past the Polderhoek Chateâu and up to Polygon Wood. The Germans' near breakthrough at Gheluvelt would remain one of the closest they came to breaking the Allied lines around Ypres until 1918.

The Gloucesters were by now unrecognisable from the battalion that marched out of Ypres earlier in the month. They had been fighting almost continuously since their first contact with the enemy at Langemarck and were now badly in need of a rest. In fact, a roll call on 2 November at Inverness Copse revealed their fighting strength was less than 240 all ranks. That morning the whole of 3 Brigade could only muster some 800 men of all ranks as it marched to Sanctuary Wood for what the men imagined was to be a period of rest away from the front line. It was not to be. By 1.00 pm on 3 November, they were back on the Menin Road near Clapham Junction to counter the German attacks south of the road at Herenthage Wood. A few hours before, 200 reinforcements had arrived at Sanctuary Wood to bring the battalion strength up to a little over 400 men. They were going to be needed in the next few days.

The route through Gheluvelt was now being used to move enemy forces in the battle for the wooded area south of the Menin Road around Klein Zillebeke. Predictably it drew in the 3 Brigade infantrymen who were close at hand. As the Gloucesters left the cover of Railway Wood northwest of Bellewaarde Farm in the late afternoon of 6 November 1914 and marched southeast over the Menin Road towards Zwarteleen, Robert Rising effectively crossed his Rubicon: he had twenty-four hours left to live.

Chapter 7

Holding on at all costs

The 2nd Division was one of the last BEF units to arrive in Flanders. For the officers and men of 4 (Guards) Brigade the journey from the trenches of the Aisne to Flanders was long and tedious. Having entrained at Fismes at 4.00 am on 14 October 1914, they eventually arrived at Hazebrouck some twenty-seven hours later. As usual the men travelled in cattle trucks while the officers were more fortunate in having the comfort of what was described as 'some pretty poor third class accommodation.' Despite the discomfort, the brigade was delighted to have left their trenches at Chavonne and the daily shell fire that had become such a deadly feature of that sector. Typically, shortly before they left, the Grenadier and the Coldstream Guards were on the receiving end of a bombardment while in billets at Chavonne village, this time in retaliation for an earlier action, Bernard Gordon Lennox described the episode:

'*Back to billets: singularly quiet day up to 3.00 pm. From then for about one and a half hours the [Germans] subjected us to a terrific bombardment in the village, shrapnel and high explosive. It was quite like old times at Soupir and we couldn't work out what had woke the beggars up, they simply plastered the village and some came so close we got orders to be ready to move out of the village at once. Luckily this did not happen. Result: three transport horses killed and a lot of tiles and roofs not looking their best Strolled up to the Coldstream Guards [3rd Battalion] billets about 6.30 and saw Tony [possibly Lieutenant A F Smith, Adjutant]who told me the reason of their peevishness. They apparently have a big trench 500 yards in front of the Coldstream with a lot of men in it. The Coldstream Guards got up an RA officer to have a look at it. He telephoned down to the big howitzers and they planted their very first shot right into the middle of the trench. Tony tells me he never heard such a squealing and sqorking (sic) and howling and moaning which went on for the best part of an hour ... the result was the [Germans] became very peevish and let us have it for all they were worth. One of our transport men had a lucky escape. He was standing beside a horse when a high explosive took the horse's head clean off : man untouched.'*

At Hazebrouck the Grenadiers were met by four new officers and a new draft of NCOs and men, some of whom were returning from base hospitals having been casualties in the August fighting. Carleton Tufnell had taken over as the battalion machine-gun officer, Michael Stocks was by now a seasoned platoon commander in Number 4 Company, Harry Parnell commanded a platoon in Number 3 Company and Cholmeley Symes-Thompson was second-in-command of Number 1 Company. Bernard Gordon Lennox, the senior major in the battalion, remained in command of his Number 2 Company. Fortunately the battalion was not deployed immediately and after a short rest period, early on 20 October they marched to St Jean, a small village to the north of Ypres. Here they assembled with the remaining Guards battalions of 4 Brigade. Brigadier General the Earl of Cavan, himself an old Grenadier, had been in command of 4 Brigade since 19 September and was now commanding operations as the brigade received its orders to advance northeast towards Passchendaele.

Advancing across the flat, featureless fields in open artillery formation, 4 Brigade passed over the Zonnebeke – Langemarck road where the ground rises slightly towards Hill 32. Progress was slow over a landscape that was intersected by numerous streams and hedgerows and dotted with small farms and cottages; nevertheless, the leading formation of 3/Coldstream Guards was in sight of the church spire at Passchendaele before any significant resistance was experienced. Observing as part of the cavalry screen, Regy Wyndham's diary recorded the Guards' advance:

'Saw the Guards attacking today. They advanced in open order with men dropping, but no one turned or stopped. They went on steadily in spite of a heavy fire.'

Captain Richard Dawson, who was commanding the advance company of the Coldstream Guards, came under fire soon after reaching a wooded area near Aviatik Farm running east-west on the ridge ahead. Aware that he had probably advanced too far ahead of the battalion, and unsure of the strength of the enemy forces in front of him, he sent a runner back to report his situation and ask for support. His company was not alone in losing touch, by this stage in the afternoon the remaining companies of the 3rd Battalion had also lost touch with 5 Brigade on their left and 2/Coldstream Guards on the right, and although Lord Cavan took immediate steps to support 3/Coldstream Guards' right flank, contact with increasing numbers of German Fourth Army units had effectively brought the advance to a halt. This was the first real indication of the large numbers of German forces that were advancing through the Fôret d'Houthulst on a wide front towards them, certainly in greater numbers than the single German corps that Sir John French believed was in the vicinity.

Having dug in along a line that ran roughly parallel to the Stroombeek, the brigade was attacked on several occasions during the night. Bernard Gordon Lennox's diary recorded an attack on the Grenadiers' positions by 'about 200 Germans who got it in the neck about 70 yds off, and retired precipitately.' The next morning there were no further infantry assaults but they were heavily shelled; the German gunners keeping up their harassing fire for most of the next two days with the inevitable casualties. On 23 October, the same day that Robert Rising and the Gloucesters were fighting on the outskirts of Langemarck, Bernard Gordon Lennox recorded the death of 22-year-old Lieutenant Frederick Miller who had been with the battalion since landing in France and had fought all through the retreat from Mons and at Chavonne on the Aisne:[1]

> *'With great grief I had to record the death of poor old 'Donald' Miller this evening in the advanced trenches. He was blown to bits by a shell, poor lad: a most excellent officer and a real good friend and companion.'*

It was becoming increasingly obvious that the I Corps advance had been stopped in its tracks by the weight of the German Fourth Army and as more and more units became engaged with the enemy, so the list of friends from other regiments that had been killed and wounded began to filter through. One of these was Bernard's elder brother Major Esme Gordon Lennox, who had been badly wounded by shell fire while serving with 2/Scots Guards at Zandvoorde on 21 October.

Further advance by British troops in this sector was now checked and on 24 October the brigade was relieved by units of the French Sixth Army and moved into reserve at Eksternest. There was to be little respite; the following morning the 2nd Division received orders to advance on Reutel. The attack began with the usual artillery bombardment on German positions in the village and despite the rather late start and stiff resistance, the Irish Guards made enough progress to gain a foothold on the Passchendaele-Becelaere Ridge. 4 Brigade had been ready to move at 6.00 am, Bernard Gordon Lennox noting with some disgust that:

> *'We did not move until about 9am when we advanced towards Reutel. On the way saw Gerry Ruthven [Major Hon W Hore-Ruthven, Brigade Major, 4 Brigade] who gave me very encouraging news of Esme. We got to a big wood [Polygon Wood] and remained there until midday when we got the usual orders to be prepared to resume the offensive. The idea was that the Irish Guards were to go for Reutel from the north-west while we should work up a small stream*

[Reutelbeek] through a big wood and come at it from the south-east … we managed to get about 150 yards along the stream when we came under a heavy cross fire which luckily did remarkably little harm. We stopped where we were and Dowling [Lieutenant C M Dowling] came in to report the situation to me. The situation was my company was attacking a strongly fortified position on a one man front which didn't seem quite sound'

The brigade came under a very heavy fire after leaving the shelter of the wood towards Reutel, a position which was strongly held by the enemy posted in force on the high ground north of the village. At 5.00 pm the Irish Guards on the left, with 3/Coldstream Guards in support, had succeeded in getting within 200 yards of the northern exits of the village, but came under heavy rifle fire from concealed enemy trenches on the right. Night fell before any further progress was made and the Grenadiers found themselves occupying a line formed by the edge of the grounds of Polderhoek Chateâu. Their situation was not improved by strong winds and torrential rain; Bernard Gordon Lennox recalled:

'A fearfully dark night, raining and blowing also and I don't think I have spent such an unpleasant night for a long time. Feet absolutely wet through and I have not had my boots off since leaving Boescheppe on the 21st.'

Their overnight positions were in the woodland to the southeast of Polygon Wood. In 1914 the area of woodland west of Reutel was more extensive than it is today and punctuated by sections of open ground and wide rides. The dense woodland prevented the Grenadiers from pinpointing exactly where the enemy trenches were situated and for that matter, exactly where the remainder of the brigade was. But from the volume of fire being directed at them, they had a notion of how strongly the German trenches in front of them were held. During the night they were attacked three times:

'At about 9.00 pm, 12 midnight, and 3.00 am, (sounds like a prescription on a medicine bottle.) Very heavy firing each time, but I don't think they really meant to come on. The last attack however was so strong that I felt justified in sending back to Headquarters suggesting a [company] being sent up in support … as they would probably come on again at dawn if at all.'

Fortunately there was no dawn attack on the 26th and 4 Brigade consolidated its line with 2/Coldstream Guards moving into position between the Grenadiers and the Irish Guards and later 3/Coldstream Guards taking up new positions on the right of the Grenadiers. This gave them some respite from the fighting of the previous twenty-four hours enabling Gordon Lennox to comment in his diary on the performance of other battalions:

'Same position all day, a lot of sniping on both sides, and the chateâu heavily shelled and knocked about. We improved our trenches, but this difficult as the ground low lying and wet ... digging like mad to improve them. Can't make out why every battalion doesn't dig itself in properly. If they did they might never be turned out of their trenches like some of them have been lately.'

The final line of the 4 Brigade advance, which allowed the 2nd Division to close up with the hard pressed units of the 7th Division, became home for the two battalions of Coldstream Guards for the next three weeks. For Captain Richard Dawson and Lance Corporal James Whitfield the next twenty-two days would be spent in waterlogged trenches, often up to their knees in water, under ceaseless shell fire and continual sniping. 3/Coldstream Guards' trenches zig-zagged along the extreme eastern edge of Polygon Wood, which in places was little more than 300 yards from the outskirts of Reutel; while those occupied by James Whitfield and 2/Coldstream ran through the wood itself. To add to the general unpleasantness, the woods in front of their lines were thick with unburied German infantrymen. In describing the conditions in which the battalion found itself, 2/Coldstream Guards war diary inadvertently provided a glimpse of the future of warfare on the Western Front:

'Throughout this period innumerable attacks and demonstrations were made against the line and a great deal of annoyance and loss was caused by the enemy's snipers and rifle bombs, as well as their artillery. The position was improved from day to day, elaborate rifle pits and communication trenches were constructed, wire entanglements and other obstacles erected and so forth ... the enemy continually sapped closer to us and in two places their trenches were eventually scarcely 20 yards from our own ... The composition of the line was frequently altered, the troops on either flank being moved repeatedly, but the line held by the battalion remained unaltered throughout this period.'

On 30 October the battle for Gheluvelt was one day away from its nail-biting climax and the four battalions of 4 Brigade found themselves temporarily broken up. Responding to an urgent request for support, Lord Cavan took the Grenadiers and the Irish Guards to Klein Zillebeke to protect the right flank of General Bulfin's 2 Brigade in order to reinforce the cavalry who were holding the line north of Hollebeke. The remaining two battalions of Coldstream Guards were destined to occupy the Polygon Wood positions under the command of Lieutenant Colonel Cecil Pereira. Pereira would soon be joined by the shattered remnants of the 1st Battalion which had suffered enormously at the Kruiseke crossroads and the subsequent fighting on the outskirts of Gheluvelt, leaving just eighty men standing and able to bear arms.

In spite of the bitter fighting of the previous day on the Menin Road, the morning of 30 October was relatively quiet on the Gheluvelt front. The Grenadier Guards were in their reserve positions at Nonne Bosschen Wood and although they had not been involved in the desperate fighting at the Kruiseke crossroads the previous day, they had witnessed the storm of German shell fire that was gradually reducing Gheluvelt to rubble and fully expected to be moved up in support of the 1st Division who were now in hastily dug trenches on the outskirts of the village. However, the anticipated resumption of the German attack did not fall on Gheluvelt that morning; instead von Fabeck focused his attentions on Zandvoorde.

From Nonne Bosschen Wood the German artillery attack on the Zandvoorde Ridge would have been all too obvious and it came as no surprise when the orders arrived later in the afternoon for the Grenadiers to be ready to move. Their route took them past 1/Gloucesters' reserve trenches at Veldhoek, over the Menin Road and south towards Klein Zillebeke. By 5.00 am Cavan's half brigade of Grenadier and Irish Guards had relieved the Royal Horse Guards and were astride the Klein Zillebeke-Zandvoorde road. The Grenadiers were on the right and in touch with 4/Hussars on the opposite bank of the Ypres-Comines Canal while the Irish Guards took up positions on the left. Bernard Gordon Lennox described the move south:

'We got our orders to move in support of the 7th Division. We started off about 4.00 pm blobbing towards Hollebeke and arrived there after dusk and proceeded to take over the cavalry trenches and the junction of canal and railway. The first person I saw was Harold Brassey: delighted to see each other. The cavalry had been hard pressed and the Irish Guards and ourselves came up to support them … We proceeded to dig in, the Royals being ahead of us about 300 yards. It started raining hard which did not improve matters, but we eventually got it done just before daylight.'[2]

Captain Harold Ernest Brassey was an old friend.[3] The two men had first met as boys at Eton in 1891 and after passing through Sandhurst together continued their friendship. More recently, Bernard's brother, Charles, had married Harold's sister, Hilda Madeline Brassey. One of the last occasions they had seen each other was at the Household Brigade Steeplechases at Hawthorn Hill in April 1914. This annual event was one of the foremost social highlights of the year and was widely reported in the society pages. The weather had been unusually good that April and the event had been well attended by officers and their ladies from the Household Brigade and the Brigade of Guards. Sadly many of the individuals who had enjoyed the April sunshine at Hawthorn Hill, including Harold Brassey, Harry Parnell and Bernard Gordon Lennox, would soon feature in the casualty lists.

On 31 October the German attack on Gheluvelt recommenced. Flushed with the success of taking Zandvoorde from the cavalry the previous day, von Fabeck launched his attack north and south of the Menin Road with a massive artillery bombardment. At Klein Zillebeke 4 Brigade trenches were heavily shelled. Bernard Gordon Lennox again:

'As soon as daylight came we were subjected to a terrific shelling: the enemy's captive balloon was observing and I regret to say they got the range of No. 2 Company's trenches which were in the open. Ivor Rose [Lieutenant Ivor St C Rose] had a wonderful escape, a high explosive landed absolutely in his trench and buried the whole lot. He was dug out just in time and dreadfully shaken, with cracked ear-drum. 2 or 3 men killed and others buried. Shortly after another one arrived & demolished another of my trenches ... To the left our centre had to give way a bit and I received a message saying "our centre has been driven in: the safety of the Army depends on the Irish Guards and the Grenadier Guards holding on at all costs." That was all right. The Germans advanced and came into a wood in our front, but No. 1 Company took tea with them and they didn't advance any further. I have established my own Headquarters in a trench immediately next to the railway, a spot they hammered at incessantly all day and towards evening brought up a couple of field guns and fired point blank at me.'

The original plan for 31 October was to retake the lost cavalry trenches on the Zandvoorde Ridge but von Fabeck's attack rendered this quite impossible and the Guards were forced to remain on the defensive in their Klein Zillebeke positions. On the other hand, events on 2 Brigade's front were being dictated by the battle raging in Gheluvelt. When Gheluvelt was taken towards midday, the left flank of General Bulfin's 2 Brigade became dangerously exposed, forcing him to order his beleaguered men to retire to the Zillebeke crossroads. While 2/Royal Sussex was able to complete its retirement relatively unscathed, 1/Northants and 2/Gordon Highlanders dug in along the Brown Road, (so called after its colour on the 1914 maps), suffered considerably and, in retiring, had to cross an exposed area of open ground. But as was recounted above, all was not lost and when news filtered through that the Worcesters had closed the gap at Gheluvelt Chateâu, Bulfin, with characteristic dash, counter-attacked through Shrewsbury Forest and regained much of the lost ground. Bulfin attacked again after dark in an attempt to re-establish the line they had held that morning and although this second counter-attack was successful, 22 Brigade on their left were unable to match the advance and the battalions of 2 Brigade had to fall back once more.

Nightfall on 31 October 1914 ended a day of desperate fighting; the British line had been pushed back practically everywhere except at Klein Zillebeke and Zonnebeke. The recapture of Gheluvelt Chateâu by the Worcesters had been neutralized to some extent by the retirement south of the Menin Road by 22 Brigade, resulting in Gheluvelt being abandoned and the line pulled back to Veldhoek. Although Gheluvelt was considered to be of little material importance, its loss and the subsequent readjustment of the front line now pushed Klein Zillebeke into the limelight in the form of a sharp salient. German interest would now be focussed on the vulnerability of this sector. As for 4 Brigade, the Irish Guards were ordered to remain in their trenches for another night; they had taken 400 casualties during the fighting of the previous two days. Included amongst the eleven officer casualties was the commanding officer, Lieutenant Colonel Reginald Brabazon, the Lord Ardee. The Grenadiers were relieved after dark by the French XI Corps for what they hoped would be at least a few hours sleep and moved back to a larch plantation (probably Battle Wood) by the railway.

All they got was a couple of hours before they were sent to assist the Irish Guards who were retiring in the face of a furious bombardment that by 3.00 pm had reduced the battalion to a mere 200 men. It appeared the German effort was now focussed on breaking the line held by the Irish Guards; a hail of very accurate high explosive rained down on their trenches, blowing in the earthworks and knocking out machine-gun positions. With instructions from Cavan to hold a new line in the wood behind them, the Irish Guards, with the French supporting on their right, managed to hold off any further attack and the position was stabilized for the time being.

The situation was once again reaching a critical stage and German infantry were close to breaking through at a number of points along the line. Fortunately the French XI Corps held firm despite the fact that the Irish Guards had withdrawn and exposed the French left flank. But there was to be no time to relax; further to the east close to the Menin Road the relentless probing of the British front line had forced 1/Northants to retire and German infantry were reported to be advancing in numbers through the woods southeast of the Menin Road at Herenthage. Cavan responded quickly by plugging the gap that had developed as a result of the Northamptons' retirement with 2/Grenadier Guards. Aware that the line to the left of the Northamptons was still held by the Royal Sussex, standing firm under the command of Captain Villiers despite its losses, he ordered the Grenadiers to clear the wood at the point of the bayonet.

'Off again after a couple of hours, being well shelled on the way, to support the 5th Brigade [sic] further to the east. Arrived with a few losses from high explosives. No. 2 Company was in support: blobbed in sections and lay down in a field. Unfortunately one section thought they were better off under a hedge and had no sooner got there than a high explosive burst almost in them, killing two and wounding four. We waited for an hour or so then got the order to advance in line through a wood and clear it of any Germans we might find.'

The woods around Ypres in 1914 were very similar to English copses, and even today there is a striking similarity with English woodland. Bernard Gordon Lennox does not mention in his account of the action that the woods were full of pheasants and these startled birds rose up ahead of the lines of Grenadiers as they pushed their way though the undergrowth:

> 'We advanced in line with fixed bayonets and reached our objective without encountering any [Germans] in the wood actually, but a platoon which emerged on the other side of the wood came under enfilade fire and had to remain under cover of a bank till dark … We then dug ourselves in. It is curious the different ideas one gets out here. Ever since one has been a soldier and sited trenches one has always been given to believe the main object is to get a good field of fire: out here we have never had one, and in this case our field of fire is about 15 to 20 yards in a thick wood.'

The Guards' advance through the woods had restored confidence along the British line and the Northamptons were able to re-occupy their trenches. They barely had time to repair the damage before the Germans attacked again on the same sector of the line, no doubt hoping for a repeat of their success of the morning. This time the Northamptons withheld their fire until the enemy infantry were within fifty yards of their positions. The war diary tells us that not a single enemy soldier reached the Northamptons' trenches and over 200 German dead were counted.

General Bulfin's evacuation after being wounded on 1 November had resulted in Lord Cavan taking command of the whole British front line from the Menin Road to the French left flank. Cavan found himself taking over a composite force of units from the 1st and 2nd Divisions at a decisive point in the battle. Arriving at Bulfin's head quarters with his Brigade Major, Major Gerry Hore-Ruthven, he was confronted by a disorganized staff unsure of the next move without direction from the now absent Bulfin. German forces were breaking through the line and to make matters worse high explosive shells were bursting all around:

> 'Very slowly Lord Cavan drew out his cigar case, and having carefully selected a cigar, proceeded to light it, turning it round to see that it was evenly lighted. This had a wonderful effect on all present, for it not only enabled Lord Cavan himself to concentrate his thoughts upon the problem and to see clearly the pressing needs of the moment, but it also inspired all the officers with confidence. As a staff officer said afterwards, that cigar saved the situation.'[4]

It was the stuff of story books and Cavan's response to the urgency of the situation could easily have been plucked straight out of the pages of a John Buchan novel.

With Lord Cavan in command, the front line situation on the morning of Monday, 2 November saw the Northamptons in touch with the 7th Division on the left, 2/Grenadier Guards and the Oxfords in the centre, and the Irish Guards on the right. In addition he had 22 Brigade in reserve. German pressure was maintained by four infantry attacks during the day, each preceded by intense shelling. Bernard Gordon Lennox takes up the story of Number 2 Company:

'In the same trenches. 450 yards in our front and facing away from us the Germans advanced. Tuffy's [Lieutenant Carleton Tufnell] machine gun and No. 2 got them in enfilade and killed quite a nice lot. The remainder returned, and a few stopped to dig in. We improved out defences during the day which passed off fairly quietly but a continual sniping on both sides was carried on. At night there was a lot of firing but we could not see anything much although we gave them moral support by sharp bursts of fire: there was a yowl just ahead of us, so some bullet found its mark. Remainder of the night passed off without incident as far as we were concerned, but the Oxfords on our left had a merry fusillade on more than one occasion. Bright moonlight and very cold.'

On the morning of 2 November there was a renewal of the attacks along the Menin Road. This time it was the barricade across the road at Veldhoek that was on the receiving end of a high explosive bombardment. Once the barricade had been demolished German infantry attacked units of 1 Brigade, which after some desperate hand-to-hand fighting eventually had to yield some 300 yards after falling back to the next line of trenches. With Brigadier Landon's promotion to GOC 1st Division after General Lomax had been injured at Hooge Chateâu on 31 October, command of 3 Brigade fell temporarily to Colonel Lovett of the Gloucesters. Lovett found brigade command almost a step too far and by early November 1914 he was clearly finding the pressure too much. However, by nightfall on 2 November the British line was once again intact and largely occupied the ridge of high ground that runs from the corner of the canal at Hollebeke to Zonnebeke in the north; it was a line that remained in British hands until the end of the battle.

3 November was comparatively quiet, which was just as well as Second Lieutenant John Lee Steere arrived that day at Klein Zillebeke with Lieutenant Hervy Tudway and the draft of men they had brought up from St Nazaire. It had taken five days to reach the battalion, the last few miles being completed on foot from Ypres. For John Lee Steere it was not the first occasion that he had visited Ypres; his arrival in November 1914 at the gates of the shell-torn city would have been in huge contrast to the walled medieval city he had visited with his mother as an 8-year-old in August 1903.

The battalion would have been very glad to see them and John was soon sent up to Number 2 Company just in time to receive his first experience of German shelling as both sides began an artillery duel. His first letter home from the trenches of Number 2 Company was dated 4 November and in it he tried hard not to betray any signs of nervousness:

'Just a hurried note, no time for more. I've reached the battalion, I may mention no places. Having my first experience of the horrors of assault shelling, they are giving us pretty fair hell today. Saw Warren yesterday and heard from him the awful tale of the way the 1st Battalion has been cut up. [1/Grenadier Guards was reduced to 4 Officers and 250 men after Gheluvelt on 31 October] You've heard of course of poor Phil [Lieutenant Philip Van Neck] being killed. How awful for Aunt Grace and all of them ... forgive disjointed letter, but I must confess to being rather jumpy at the moment. Hope it will pass off. Don't know when I shall get this posted as one can't move from the trenches. There are forward trenches ahead of us, sounds if they are pretty badly hit.'

He had no need to worry about feeling jumpy, even Bernard Gordon Lennox thought it to be a most 'disagreeable' day:

'A German aeroplane came over about 3.00 am and discovered us and shortly after the worst shelling we have had was administered to us: it went on all day unceasingly and we had many casualties. Poor old Mary – Noel's horse got one in the head and was killed: also 4 or 5 other horses. I had two men killed and 7 wounded, some of them being the draft of 10 who had just joined the company ... The shelling subsided at nightfall and we were all thankful to get some relief from the eternal din. It came on to rain just after nightfall and poured in torrents: altogether a most disagreeable ending to a most disagreeable day ... but there is a certain amount of satisfaction in knowing things are equally if not more disagreeable for the Dutchmen [Germans].'

John Lee Steere was now positioned at the junction of De Moussy's French Division and the four battalions commanded by Lord Cavan. Over the next week the full weight of the German attack would fall on that thinly held line.

Chapter 8

The Fire Brigade

For the moment we must leave John Lee Steere and the Grenadier Guards at Klein Zillebeke and return to the whereabouts of Regy Wyndham and 7 Cavalry Brigade. Sir Henry Rawlinson and IV Corps began arriving in the Ypres area on 11 October 1914 and were quickly deployed on the offensive by Sir John French. The 7th Division's orders were to advance east to occupy a line from Zonnebeke, through Kruiseke and down to Zandvoorde. The 3rd Cavalry Division was initially deployed to screen the infantry and gather intelligence before being withdrawn to the northeast side of Ypres where they filled the gap between the 7th Division and the French cavalry to the north. But before we follow the part played by 7 Cavalry Brigade, the background to exactly why IV Corps was at Ypres in 1914 requires some explanation.

Under the initial mobilization plan in August 1914 a composite regiment composed of a headquarters squadron and one squadron from each of the three regiments of the Household Brigade had been in France and Belgium with the BEF since 16 August. Commanded by Lieutenant Colonel Edwin Cook of 1/Life Guards, the composite regiment fought with 4 Cavalry Brigade at Mons and had taken part in the retreat and subsequent advance to the Aisne before arriving at Kemmel on 17 October. Up until 11 November, when the regiment was broken up and absorbed back into their parent units, they fought in the desperate battle for the Messines Ridge. It was a battle in which the British cavalry, outnumbered and outgunned, held their positions resolutely until 31 October when they were forced to retire. Sadly their casualties were heavy; Colonel Cook died on 4 November1914 of wounds received on 22 October, his place being taken by Lord Henry Crichton who himself was killed in action on 31 October.[1]

The composite regiment's departure for France in August 1914 was witnessed with some gloom by those remaining behind. The campaign was expected to be short and as the politicians were predicting, would be over in a matter of months. The 1st, 2nd, 3rd and 5th Infantry Divisions that left England with the first wave of the BEF were shortly reinforced by the 4th

Division which arrived just in time to take part in the Battle of Le Cateau on 26 August 1914. Although the 6th Division followed before too long to join up with the BEF as they advanced across the Aisne, it was becoming apparent to some observers that perhaps the initial estimate that the war would be over by Christmas, might have been a little on the optimistic side.

Even so, preparations were underway for the formation of two further divisions, one of infantry and a second of cavalry. As early as 17 August the three commanding officers of the Household Cavalry regiments, the Duke of Teck (1/Life Guards), Lieutenant Colonel Algernon Ferguson (2/Life Guards), and Lieutenant Colonel Gordon Wilson (Royal Horse Guards or the Blues as they were more commonly called) were summoned to the War Office to discuss the Household Cavalry's deployment as 7 Cavalry Brigade should it be required.[2] 6 Cavalry Brigade under the command of Brigadier General Ernest Makins, had already been put together on paper and consisted of three regiments, the 3rd Dragoon Guards (3/Dragoon Guards) from the home establishment and two regiments that had been summoned from South Africa, the 10th Hussars (10/Hussars) and the Royal Dragoons (Royals). By late September 7 Cavalry Brigade had assembled at Ludgershall and was almost up to war strength despite the initial shortage of junior officers, but 6 Cavalry Brigade lacked 10/Hussars and the Royals who were still at sea and would not arrive until 4 October.

Events in Belgium now forced the pace. As the Allied and German Armies began the 'race to the sea' in an attempt to outflank each other, the position of the Belgian Army at Antwerp became more and more precarious. German artillery began its bombardment of Antwerp on 28 September, a bombardment so fierce that preparations for a retreat to Ostend by the Belgian government were communicated to the British and French governments. This prompted an undertaking on 1 October by the British War Cabinet to send 7 Infantry Division providing the French contributed to the proposed relief force.

On 2 October, after the Belgian government evacuated from Antwerp, Kitchener wrote to Sir John French advising him of the situation at Antwerp and the impact that the fall of the city would have on the Allied war effort in respect to the Channel ports. What appeared to be a degree of panic prompted the British government to send immediate reinforcements in the form of two naval brigades and a marine battalion to Antwerp, a decision that saw Winston Churchill offering to resign as First Sea Lord and take personal command of the British forces at Antwerp! The Antwerp affair served only to highlight the fate that befalls ill-equipped and hastily conceived expeditionary forces. Fortunately the naval brigades were spared annihilation and for many of them their war ended with surrender and internment.

While all this was taking place, 7 Infantry Division and 3 Cavalry Division were landing at Zeebrugge and Ostend. By 8 October Antwerp had fallen to the

Germans and with it the primary objective of Rawlinson's IV Corps. It would be another two days before the news became official but Regy Wyndham, now with D Squadron of 1/Life Guards, had advance warning of the fate that had befallen the city:

> *'About midday they ordered us to move, and we marched to Bernen. On the way we met a lot of Belgian artillery at Oostcamp returning, they came from Antwerp and Ghent. They said Antwerp had fallen and was in flames. They looked very tired and said they had been fighting 5 days hard and wanted rest'*

On 10 October they were told officially that Antwerp had fallen and 3 Cavalry Division would be retiring to cover the retreat of the Belgian Army. Rather surprisingly rumour still abounded that the war was practically won and their stay in Belgium would be a short one. Nevertheless, William Petersen serving with 2/Life Guards had finally got his wish to be part of the great adventure, as had Alexis de Gunzburg who was now on the strength of the Royal Horse Guards. Serving with 1/Life Guards was 19-year-old Second Lieutenant Howard St George, who, at half the age of Regy Wyndham, must have been one of the youngest officers in his regiment.

1/Life Guards clattered through Ypres on Tuesday 13 October 1914 having bivouacked the previous night on the racecourse at Rumbeke. Both regiments of Life Guards pressed on down the Menin Road; 2/Life Guards actually getting into the outskirts of Menin before encountering German forces. In the early days before the two sides clashed, cavalry patrols were being deployed to gather intelligence and on occasions it was sometimes difficult to differentiate between friend and foe immediately. Ordered to retire at dusk on 13 October, 1/Life Guards stumbled upon 6 Cavalry Brigade. Regy Wyndham's diary recorded the confusion that followed:

> *'While retiring we mistook the Royals and the 10th [Hussars] for enemy, which created much confusion. Teck [Lieutenant Colonel The Duke of Teck] recalled Sutton's [Captain Sir R Sutton] troop at a gallop, drew swords, and prepared to charge. Clowes [Captain St George Clowes] and self with my troop were coming in from the left, and thought everyone had gone mad. Kearsley [10/Hussars] restored order and we marched ... to Iseghem where we arrived about 9.30pm.'*

This episode of mistaken identity served to illustrate the situation east of Ypres at the time. Marauding patrols of British and German cavalry were clashing frequently as the German Fourth Army began their advance to contact with the British. In the fading light of the day the men of 6 Cavalry Brigade could easily have been Uhlans but fortunately the error was recognised before any casualties occurred.

The Brigade returned to Ypres on 14 October but not before there had been reports of several more exchanges with German cavalry:

'Met Roxburgh [Lieutenant the Duke of Roxburgh, RHG] near Gheluvelt, he was flank guard, and while waiting by the road an Uhlan patrol came up to them. They killed one and captured another ... Hugh Grosvenor [Captain Lord Hugh Grosvenor] came up and told me that on flank patrol he had surprised about 16 Uhlans in Gheluwe. They had come from Menin by the light railway. They surprised the Germans, killed three, captured one and wounded several, but were afraid to hunt them out of the houses in case they managed to fire at his horses.'

On 16 October the Brigade began running into the outer fringe of German infantry that Regy Wyndham felt were 'marching northwest to Dunkirk.' One of the squadrons of 2/Life Guards, commanded by Captain Hon Arthur O'Neill, came under fire from a farm southwest of Oostnieuwkerke that was strongly held by German infantry and Lieutenant Sir Robin Duff was killed as the squadron approached the farm buildings. Finding themselves being shot at from three directions, O'Neill waited until his squadron was reinforced by Captain Lord Belper's squadron before attacking in force and reportedly killing twenty of the enemy, including the man who had killed Robin Duff.

The Hon Arthur Edward Bruce O'Neill was the second son of Baron O'Neill and was the first MP to be killed in the Great War. After Arthur's elder brother William died in 1882, he became heir presumptive to the title while he was still a schoolboy at Eton. Attending Eton from 1890 until 1895 he shared his school career with Bernard Gordon Lennox and Richard Dawson. He was commissioned in 1897 into 2/Life Guards and six years later married Lady Annabel Crewe-Milnes. His entry into Irish politics as the Unionist MP for Mid-Antrim in 1910 saw him leaving the army to pursue his new career, a career that was cut short by the outbreak of war in 1914. Arthur O'Neill and Annabel had five children together, one of whom, Terence Marne O'Neill, became Prime Minister of Northern Ireland in 1963. Rejoining his old regiment in August 1914 Arthur was now in command of a squadron.

By 19 October 1914 the advanced units of 3 Cavalry Division, unlike their commander-in-chief, had no illusions as to the strength of the German forces confronting them. Leaving their overnight billets near Passchendaele at 6.00 am 7 Cavalry Brigade ran into a strong force of German infantry and cyclists as they approached the Hooglede-Staden-Roulers cross roads. Two squadrons of 2/Life Guards were ordered to advance towards the railway line and immediately drew heavy fire from the direction of the level crossing, forcing the startled troopers to find cover and wait for support. Colonel Ferguson recorded the action in the regiment's war diary:

'In the retirement Captain F Pemberton was killed. Lieutenant Anstruthers tried to get him along but finally had to leave him in a ditch. In the meantime I held the village facing E. with my other two squadrons and endeavoured to cover the retirement by rifle and maxim fire. The latter was very effective and the hostile infantry could be seen scattering. Very soon the enemy brought up some guns and placed their first shot on the precise spot my two maxims had just left. Their fire set some houses on fire and under the cover of the smoke my regiment withdrew.'

With 1/Life Guards on Colonel Ferguson's left flank, the two regiments withdrew from the village under the cover of the burning buildings. It wasn't long before the advancing German infantry occupied the village and despite being shelled by K Battery, Royal Horse Artillery, held onto their new positions. The British counterattack was never going to succeed in the face of such superior numbers but it went ahead regardless. On the right flank Colonel Gordon Wilson commanding the Blues managed to establish a squadron on the outskirts of the village. They occupied a house initially, killing a German officer and ten other ranks which they found inside but were eventually forced to retire in the face of increasing numbers of German infantry. At the same time as the Blues were moving forward 2/Life Guards carried out a mounted attack with two squadrons covered by rifle fire from a dismounted line. The war diary again:

'A tremendous fire opened from the village, and my advanced squadron which had got near enough to hear the German words of command, had to retire. My advance became impossible, and instead I took Belper's squadron up to cover Ashton's [Captain Sam Ashton] retirement ... we had held up a strong force, probably the flank guard of an army corps from 9am until 3.30pm, and I was glad to give the men General Byng's message that they had done exceedingly well.'

Colonel Ferguson's assessment of the engagement was quite correct; they had run into the flank guard of an army corps, in fact six divisions were advancing across the Menin-Thourout Road towards the British and French. 7 Cavalry Brigade had unfortunately come into contact with a battalion of the 52nd Reserve Division at the crossroads, an event they did not expect, as a reconnaissance the previous day had found the area completely clear of German troops. Under heavy shell fire from German batteries the brigade retired to the cover of a small wood on the right of their line in order to reassemble before galloping out of range. The day had not been a complete disaster, however, they had held up a very much larger force of enemy infantry and cyclists for nearly seven hours but the cost had been high. Regy Wyndham's diary gives little away about the events of 19 October but does draw attention to the plight of the Belgian civilian population:

> '*Moved out and met a large force of enemy on Menin-Roulers road. Had a very stiff fight against 10,000 Germans. Pte [Private] Stone of 2nd Troop was killed. Capt. Pemberton of the 2nd [Life Guards] killed, Roxburgh [RHG] wounded. We retired to Zonnebeke where we passed a wet night. It was a pitiable sight to see all the Belgian people flying from the villages with all their children carts and goods. Brocklehurst [Lieutenant Sir Phillip Brocklehurst] was hit today.*'

On the other hand, Gordon Wilson's letter to Lady Sarah, written two days after the skirmish, provides us with more of a flavour of the conditions in which the brigade was operating. His estimation of the number of enemy troops is probably referring to the number engaged along the whole of the IV Corps front:

> '*Poor Bumble [Brocklehurst] was wounded two days ago in another fight we had, when our Division took on 15,000 Germans and held our own all day. The 2nd [Life Guards] lost heavily and 3 officers. Our casualties have been very reasonable so far, and I hope they may continue to be so. A shrapnel has just burst 100 yds, from where I write. I luckily keep fit and well. Our days are long, and our sleep, as a rule, very short. We get into billets or bivouacs after dark and leave in the morning at 5.00 am. The country we have been passing through the last week has been a most difficult one for cavalry to work in, as it is quite flat and intersected with hedges and small woods and twisting roads dotted with innumerable farm buildings, from which we are perpetually sniped ... Our horses poor things, are beginning to show signs of exhaustion. Long hours under the saddle and irregular and insufficient feeds. The musketry has just opened near here and I must close as we may be wanted.*'

By dawn on 20 October, 3 Cavalry Division was up and on the move with orders to entrench and defend the Westroosebeke – Passchendaele Road. The cavalry's ability to move swiftly to support the infantry was of immense value during the battle for Ypres in 1914. However, the number of men actually available for action in the trenches with a rifle and bayonet was limited. Not only were the individual regiments often below strength due to increasing numbers of casualties but one man was required as a horse-holder for every four horses. Consequently a cavalry brigade such as 7 Brigade could possibly only muster 600 men in the firing line at any one time and as the battle for Ypres progressed, this number would fall significantly.

On this particular morning the horses and their holders had been concealed in a wood behind the trench line but as the German shell fire increased the horses were moved further back. The first German infantry appeared just before noon and were soon in evidence in greater numbers advancing towards the road. On the 7 Cavalry Brigade frontage any attempt to cross the road was checked by rifle fire and for a while the enemy advance was halted. As with any wide frontage held by defending troops, however, each unit must hold its sector without retiring if the line is to remain intact. As soon as any one unit retreats the line is compromised, leaving a gap which an attacking force can exploit.

This is precisely what happened around 2.00 pm on the Passchendaele road. Without warning, the French 79th Territorial Regiment on the extreme left of 6 Brigade began leaving their trenches and retiring, giving the British cavalrymen and the units of the 7th Division on their right no option but to follow suit. Casualties were relatively light but 'Cecil' Rhodes, a 28-year-old Corporal in Regy Wyndham's troop, had to be left behind:

> *'When Corp. Rhodes was hit, Mclean, who was next to him, said "Are you hit Cecil?" Rhodes took his pipe out of his mouth, and laid it on the trench, said "yes", and fell down dead on top of Corporal Dawes.'*[3]

Falling back to a new line running from Zonnebeke to St Julien the brigade finally linked up that evening with Sir Douglas Haig's I Corps which had left Ypres on the previous day.

There was one other casualty on 20 October that impacted across all three regiments of 7 Cavalry Brigade. Captain Norman Neill, the Brigade Major, was wounded by shellfire and evacuated, eventually being admitted to British General Hospital No.13 which had taken over the Casino at Bolougne. A building designed for the more frivolous activity of gambling, it offered its patients rather splendid accommodation in its brilliantly illuminated gaming halls, cafes and ballrooms, the like of which many of the hospital's patients had, in all probability, never experienced before. Norman Neill's wounds were not severe and within two weeks he was back with his brigade. The brigade major was the principle staff officer at brigade headquarters, answerable to the brigade commander and ensuring his orders were clearly interpreted and sent out to all units. He would also accompany his brigadier in the field and as General 'Black Jack' Kavanagh was an individual who liked to direct operations himself, the risk this entailed would, by necessity, be shared by the brigade major. Kavanagh was very popular with the officers and men of his brigade and very much championed the notion of the cavalry corps as an effective fighting arm of the BEF. Standing 6 feet, 4 inches inches tall he is reputed to have once accused a fellow officer, who in 1916 had suggested the abolition of the cavalry corps, of being a traitor to the cavalry. Lloyd met him briefly when brigade headquarters were at Voormezele in October 1914:

'The general was actually shaving. He was in his shirt sleeves, and performed before a small hand mirror stuck on the fall. The other occupants of the billet were the Brigade Major (Captain Kearsey) and Private Tichener ... I was struck by the absence of all the pomp and eyewash one is apt to associate with a general and his suite. Here was one of the finest generals the army had produced up to now, actually sharing quarters, rations and shaving water with a private. What a contrast to many of our junior officers who kept two men eternally running about after them with hot water and other luxuries morning and night.'

The morning of 21 October saw the infantry battalions of I Corps now advancing to the northeast of Ypres, with the 3rd Cavalry Division adopting a protective role in guarding the flanks of I Corps. This soon changed, however, following an urgent call for help received from the 7th Division. At Zonnebeke the advancing 52nd German Reserve Division was putting Brigadier General Lawford's 22 Infantry Brigade under severe pressure and by mid-morning had developed into a serious threat. 7 Cavalry Brigade was quickly despatched to provide much needed support until units of General Cavan's 4 Brigade arrived at 4.00 pm to relieve them. The arrival of the cavalry injected a much needed boost to the flagging infantry and afterwards earned the brigade the personal thanks of General Lawford. Gordon Wilson described the episode in a letter to Lady Sarah:

'We are now joined up with Haig's army [sic] ... Yesterday the infantry had been almost annihilated in some trenches in a position at Zonnebeke ... and our brigade were told off to fill them, which we did and held them till 4.00 pm, with splendid results. Casualties in my regiment, 3, in the other two, considerably higher, especially in the 2nd. [Life Guards] We were thanked especially in an order from the GOC of that particular force [22 Brigade] for not only having saved but turned the situation into a good one. This was most satisfactory to me and my officers.'

Regy Wyndham's recollections of the day were a little different from that of Gordon Wilson. His description of the experience of D Squadron on that afternoon provides a greater insight into the lot of the soldier on the front line:

'Sitting in a wet ditch, unable to see anything, with bullets whizzing over us. Once we retired by mistake, but returned at once. Corporal Tatchell got badly hit by one of our own shells, fired too low over the hill [where] we were sitting.'

However, their appearance had stabilized a critical situation and it was after the events of 21 October that 7 Cavalry Brigade began to be referred to by the infantry as 'Kavanagh's Fire Brigade'. Lloyd, who was also serving in D Squadron, later wrote of the 7 Cavalry Brigade's role at Ypres:

'Whenever any part of the line within a few miles was hard-pressed or in danger of being broken, or whenever the French ran away and left a gap, the reserve brigade was called upon. It straightway galloped to the danger point, dismounted, and going in with the bayonet, put things in order.'

Very often such a call was received on the most inconvenient of occasions; the Wyndham diary has us almost salivating at the prospect of that glorious beefsteak which had to be despatched with some alacrity:

'Spent the morning shaving and changing my clothes. Then, while enjoying the glorious spectacle of a beefsteak being cooked for lunch, came the order to march out … Bolted the steak and started.'

After Norman Neill had been injured the post of brigade major passed to Captain Alexander Kearsey. He had been awarded the DSO in 1901 and, like Norman Neill, had graduated from the Camberley Staff College in 1914. One of the first operational orders he wrote was to direct the brigade to march to Hooge on 22 October. The move south reunited 7 Cavalry Brigade with 6 Cavalry Brigade which had taken over the Scots Guards' positions at Zandvoorde. Three squadrons of 10/Hussars were in the shallow trenches that had been dug on the forward slope of the Zandvoorde Ridge and serving with that regiment was a member of my own family, Second Lieutenant William Sydney Murland, who was still finding it difficult adapting to the wet and cold conditions of Flanders after the heat of South Africa. Late on 23 October 1/ and 2/Life Guards attempted to relieve them:

'Today we were sent to relieve the 10th Hussars in some trenches, but the shell fire was so heavy they decided not to change the garrison of the trench till the evening. While the colonels and squadron leaders were talking it over, two [shrapnel] shells burst over them. Brassey. Tweedale, Colonel Ferguson, two of the 10th were all hit, but none of them badly hurt … In the evening we relieved the 10th. We had great trouble opening the gate out of the village into the field where the trenches were.'

A master of understatement, Regy Wyndham had not realized that Colonel Ferguson had actually been hit in four places. Ferguson signed off the regimental war diary before he left with the words 'lost a piece out of my leg' and 'had to retire to hospital.' Command of 2/Life Guards thus fell to Major Hugh Dawnay.

Inevitably casualties began to increase now the brigade was in the front line trenches. What we need to appreciate about the 1914 trenches is that they were nothing like the elaborate trench systems that came to dominate the Western

Front. These trenches were little more than a series of unconnected holes and their rather exposed positions at Zandvoorde were heavily shelled both night and day, punctuated only by bursts of heavy rifle and machine-gun fire. Familiar faces were being lost in all three regiments as the intensity of German artillery and infantry attacks began to increase:

> *'We were shelled for two hours this morning, besides the occasional shells all day. No one was hit in my trench, though bits of shell fell into it. In Stanley's trenches Levinge [Sir Richard Levinge] and two men were killed, and in the evening Dick Sutton was hit … The Germans delivered a night attack in a somewhat half hearted way. After a lot of firing they gave up. Later in the night they made another, but did not press it home. On the whole we have had a hard time, but the men in Stanley's [Captain Algernon Stanley] trench said it was worse there, as one could not put one's head over the parapet at all.'*⁴

Behind them the village of Zandvoorde was practically destroyed by German high explosive shell fire. The church where Bernard Gordon Lennox's brother Esme had been wounded the day before had been particularly targeted to prevent the tower being used by the British as an observation point. Regy Wyndham still managed to complete his diary despite the appalling conditions in their waterlogged holes. Sunday 25 October began with sunshine:

> *'A lovely sunny morning, the day went well until the afternoon. Suddenly they began shelling us with big shells shewing [sic] a greenish smoke. They hit our emplacements time after time. Then they shouted to me two men were hit at the other end of the trench. Both men were named Smith. One was hit through both thighs, and the skin of his testicle bag was carried away. His pants and drawers were soaked with blood. The wound in his left thigh, the wound left by the fragment of shell that had been through him, was 5 inches x 3 inches. It was an awful wound to manage, but neither leg was broken … Went to Dawes' trenches and found Lawson was hit through the head. Dawes said the body was warm, but we could see he was dead as his jaw had dropped … While I was bandaging … Smith a big shell fell just where I had been sitting, and one [piece] of it smashed through Groves' water bottle … and fragments fell on Groves.'*⁵

At 6.00 pm in pouring rain the 7th Brigade was relieved by 10/Hussars; the dead were hurriedly buried while spent bullets from the German lines dropped all around them. It was later discovered that Lieutenant Sir Richard Levinge had been buried with the squadron's pay still in his jacket and the next evening after dark a party was sent to retrieve it.

Two days later on 26 October the 7th Division was again under severe pressure at Kruiseke; on this occasion it was the embattled battalions of 20 Brigade. At

2.00 pm an urgent request for help was received at brigade headquarters for assistance in covering the retirement of the remaining 300 men of the 2nd Battalion of the Border Regiment (2/Border Regiment). The battalion had been holding their trenches resolutely since early October with orders to hold their positions until relieved. At the time the only available reserve to answer the call was Gordon Wilson's Royal Horse Guards which were at Klein Zillebeke. They were immediately ordered to make a 'mounted demonstration' towards Kruiseke, in effect a show of force to distract attention away from the embattled Border Regiment.

A squadron of 1/Life Guards under Captain Hugh Grosvenor had been in the Kruiseke trenches with the Border Regiment since the previous day and were no doubt as surprised as the Germans were by the arrival of the Blues just as it was getting dusk. The Blues were quickly into action. One squadron under the command of Alastair Kerr rode straight through 1/Life Guards' trenches and across the frontage of two German cavalry regiments before dismounting and opening fire on the enemy. The remaining squadrons of the Blues dismounted behind Hugh Grosvenor's men and, advancing over the ridge, put down covering fire. Recovering from the initial shock the German trenches opened fire on the galloping horsemen, suspecting the whole British Cavalry Corps was behind them and ready to gallop into their trenches. There is no doubt this bold action by Gordon Wilson's men caught the German cavalry by surprise and during the ensuing mayhem, 20 Brigade was able to complete its withdrawal in the fading light of the day. General Kavanagh is said to have been open mouthed in approval, a view shared by Gordon Wilson:

'Last night the Blues were called upon to make a marked demonstration against the enemy's trenches ... We were promised the support of two batteries, but owing to a mistake they never came into action, the result being that we came under heavy shrapnel fire, plus rifle and maxim, for a quarter of an hour. We had eleven wounded and one killed, and 25 horses laid out. We were able, however, to line the ridge, and so good was our fire that we silenced the enemy, and, having accomplished the demonstration, rode back a mile across country in the dark. The Brigadier thanked me personally for the services rendered by the regiment ... but we should have but half our force if the shells had burst 6 feet lower than they did. Alasdair then had his horse shot, carried a wounded corporal out of action on his back, as did Trooper Nevin. I have recommended them both to the GOC's notice.'

A slightly more blasé diary account was provided by another Blues officer:

'We rode onto the crest between the two trenches held by Hugh Grosvenor's squadron, and here the Germans spotted us and we came in for a hail of shrapnel and bullets. My horse was hit in the shoulder and I got into a trench in which were

> *Hugh Grosvenor and Gerry Ward. They seemed surprised at our selecting this spot for a point-to-point.'*

German pressure on the 7th Division front was increasing steadily. Von Fabeck's Army Corps was getting into position for its assault along the line from Ploegsteert Wood in the south to Gheluvelt which lay astride the Menin Road. Regy Wyndham's diary of 27 October gives an inkling of the patchwork of support that was being employed to strengthen the British front line:

> *'Grosvenor's squadron came in after 72 hours in the trenches. A lovely morning, but it rained a little in the afternoon. In the evening we turned out without horses to take over the trenches [at Zandvoorde]. They sent us up to the trenches on the right where the Royals were. My troop was put in reserve behind Gen. Kavanagh's quarters. Then we were suddenly turned out to relieve the Warwicks in their trenches. The 2nd [Life Guards] came too. When we got there we found the 2nd were sufficient, so they brought us back. The big German shells have dug deep pits in the Zandvoorde street[s].'*

Writing to Lady Sarah on the same day from the relative comfort of the regiment's billets at Hollebeke Chateâu, Gordon Wilson appeared quite relaxed. As commanding officer he would have taken some comfort from the fact that the regiment's casualties were up to now manageable and although 7 Cavalry Brigade was spending more time dismounted in the trenches to the south of the Menin Road, there were periods of respite:

> *'We are all well and at present I write from a Chateâu which is deserted, and have just been able to have a bath and a change of raiment, so feel fit and clean again … I have just received a parcel with a thick khaki coat, which will be very comforting, as the weather is cold and showery. I am so glad that you have at last been able to get what you want done regarding your hospital.'*

Although Sir John French felt the Germans were 'quite incapable of making any strong sustained attack' it is difficult to believe that all the British commanders on the ground shared this perception. If they did then the events of the next few days would have quickly dispelled any misconceptions they might have had. As for 7 Cavalry Brigade, the storm of fire that was about to break on the Zandvoorde Ridge would thrust them forever into British cavalry legend.

Chapter 9

Play Up and Play the Game

With Kruiseke now abandoned by the British, German attention became fixed on the line that ran south from Zandvoorde through Hollebeke and along the Messines Ridge. It was von Fabeck's intention to break through the line between Messines and Zandvoorde in order to seize the high ground at Kemmel. With this in mind, von Fabeck concentrated his divisions on the overstretched positions south of the Menin Road held by the 7th Division and the three cavalry divisions stretched out from Zandvoorde to Messines. Still unsure of the depth of the Allied reserves, von Fabeck planned a diversionary attack at Zonnebeke to draw attention away from his primary objective and draw the reserves north. In this he failed; nowhere north of the Menin Road did German forces break through and as the early morning mist cleared away, the men of the 1st and 2nd Divisions exacted a heavy toll on the attacking forces. South of the Menin Road it was a different story. Numerically there was little on paper to prevent von Fabeck sweeping aside the exhausted troops that still held the key to the channel ports. That he failed to do so was largely down to the indomitable spirit of the British soldier.

At Zandvoorde the positioning of the trenches on the forward facing slope of the ridge had, in retrospect, been an error of judgement. Regy Wyndham described them in his diary as being 'badly placed' and many of the 3rd Cavalry Division whose misfortune it was to occupy them referred to them as 'a death trap'. The trenches followed the contours of the ridge and curved around the southeast side of the village and were in full view of German observers; their strategic value lay in the fact they were on the crest of a prominent ridge that offered a vantage point over the plain below. Their weakness, as far as the British were concerned, lay in the fact the positions were practically surrounded by enemy forces and were open to attack on three sides. Nevertheless, Zandvoorde was still considered to be of strategic importance and on the morning of 30 October the trenches were manned by 1/ and 2/Life Guards and the Royal Horse Guards. On the immediate left of the cavalry positions were the 1st Battalion Royal Welch Fusiliers, their trenches, a succession of muddy holes, curved back from the Zandvoorde trenches and faced almost north.

If the intended rotation of relief had gone according to plan, 6 Cavalry Brigade would have relieved the 7th Brigade in the Zandvoorde trenches at dusk on 29 October and Second Lieutenant William Murland and 10/Hussars would have been fighting for their survival the next morning; a factor which may have altered the path of my family tree had he been killed. But fate played a different card and 6 Cavalry Brigade was called away to support the infantry and did not return to billets at Verbrandenmolen until after dark, leaving the men of the 7th Brigade in the trenches for another night. By that time they had, in fact, been in the trenches for three days and nights under almost continuous shell fire from the south and east and occasionally from the direction of Hollebeke in the west. They were tired, wet, cold and hungry.

Yet the hand of fate was to reach out and interfere further. Just before their relief was about to arrive on 25 October, 1/Life Guards discovered one of the regiment's machine guns had jammed and was to all intents and purposes useless. Recognising the need for the full complement of machine guns in the front line, Captain Kearsey, in his role as brigade major, asked Lieutenant Charles Pelham (Lord Worsley) of the Blues to remain in post with his machine-gun section to provide the necessary fire power. This he apparently did 'most cheerfully', reportedly telling Kearsey it was 'all in the day's work.' On the fateful morning of 30 October 1914, Lord Worsley and his men had just clocked up the start of their seventh day without relief. It was to be their last.

Von Fabek had originally intended to storm Zandvoorde on 29 October to coincide with the attack on the Menin Road but the delay of the German XV Army Corps forced a postponement until the next day. The German attack began at 06.45 am with an artillery bombardment which lasted a little over an hour. The storm of shrapnel and high explosive literally blew 7 Cavalry Brigade's trenches to pieces before the infantry assault by the German 39th Division and three Jaeger battalions got underway at 08.00 am. The bombardment was witnessed by Lloyd who was in reserve with the remainder of D Squadron at Verbrandenmolen:

> '*A hellish bombardment broke out on the Zandvoorde Ridge. It was the hottest we had heard up to then. Its suddenness and intensity caused us to stand still for a moment or two and gape. One idea formed itself immediately in all our minds – this was the expected big German attack ... For upwards of an hour the ground trembled and the air was full of din. Then gradually the shelling subsided and machine gun and rifle fire swelled up into a roar ... Gradually, about 8.30 or 9 am., the rifle fire grew less lively.*'

From all accounts it appears the Zandvoorde Ridge was in enemy hands sometime after 9.00 am. Regy Wyndham and his troop from D Squadron were on the right flank of Worsley's machine gunners:

> *'In the morning they all attacked us. They shelled us hard, and one of the first shells buried Dawes all except his head, and also buried my belt, pillow, glasses and haversack. Then their infantry attacked. We knocked a good few over, but the Maxim on our right ran out of ammunition, and one trench on our right was driven in. We kept on firmly until our ammunition was finished. The spare box of ammunition was buried by the shell which buried Dawes. In the end we had no more ammunition, and they began to enfilade us from our right. Had to order Sergt. Arthurs to retire from the right hand trench, and then ordered my troop to retire.'*

Overwhelmed by sheer weight of numbers and dazed from the initial bombardment, most of the brigade still managed to retire in good order but in the chaos of hand-to-hand fighting and the general pandemonium of combat, the order to retire did not reach all the cavalry positions.

While the squadrons on the right completed their retirement back through the village to 6 Cavalry Brigade's trenches, the machine-gun section of the Blues and one squadron from each regiment of 1/ and 2/Life Guards held their positions and fought to the last man. Regy Wyndham managed to bring the remnants of his troop out of the firing line but in doing so had to leave his sergeant, 'Cabby' Dawes, behind as they fell back through the village:[1]

> *'We ran back to the farm. The Maxim killed Sergt. Arthurs. Then after finding Clowes had left the farm, I went on and found Dawes and Brooks. Dawes was slightly hit. We found Bussey badly wounded, but could not move him. We picked up a man of Arthur's troop and helped him along until he dropped dead. Then when we reached the X roads where Levinge was buried, Dawes had his leg broken by the shell fire. The shells had been bursting just over us all the way. Had to leave Dawes lying where he was … Then set to work to find the [remainder of the] men. Found most of them when we got back to the horses. As we retired down the road, the Germans shelled it and Charlie Fitzmaurice [Lord Charles Petty-Fitzmaurice] was killed. Then found that my troop of 20 had 9 killed and wounded, there were only 7 left of Arthur's troop of 26 men.'*[2-3]

The exact deployment of 7 Cavalry Brigade at Zandvoorde is still unclear. The official history of the Household Cavalry is at variance with the map later drawn by Captain Stuart Menzies in 1923 which was included in a letter to General Kavanagh. Menzies was the Adjutant of 2/Life Guards at the time of the battle and his sketch map (see Map 5) of the positions of the various squadrons of Life Guards is probably the more accurate. The problem was of course that at the end of the war there were few, if any, survivors from the battle who were able to provide any coherent detail of what exactly happened to the squadrons which fought to the end. Although Stuart Menzies' account of the events of 30 October 1914 sheds little further light on the course of the battle, it does raise the question of the fate of the wounded:

'On the 30th the Household Cavalry regiments were in the front line in the order shown on the enclosed sketch. When the German attack was launched the 7th Division on the left was compelled to retire, I believe to conform with the retirement of troops on their right. Beyond the above practically nothing is known of what occurred as the two squadrons and the machine guns of the Blues completely disappeared, and only a few survivors were taken prisoner, and on their return at the end of the war they were unable, I understand, to throw much light on the attack. My regiment had an officer who was on the extreme left who managed to escape with slight wounds. According to his story which was somewhat confused owing to his being dazed, the attack was made by German infantry after a very heavy preliminary bombardment. I can only conclude that the squadrons were cut off owing to their somewhat forward position, and were ultimately all killed, though it is remarkable that there should have been so few wounded taken

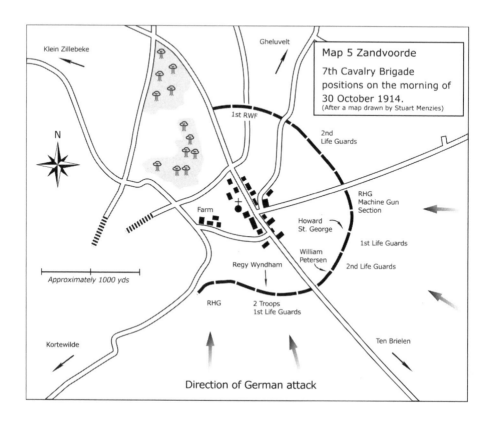

Map 5 Zandvoorde
7th Cavalry Brigade positions on the morning of 30 October 1914.
(After a map drawn by Stuart Menzies)

Direction of German attack

prisoner. I fear that one must assume that the Germans behaved in an ultra-Hunlike manner and gave no quarter.'

Once the cavalry positions had been overrun, the German infantry battalions began moving north round the crest of the Zandvoorde Ridge until they were in a position to enfilade and surround the Welch Fusiliers. From this moment on the Fusiliers' position was a hopeless one; their right flank was unprotected and the trenches little more than muddy holes in the ground. The battalion, which was under the command of Lieutenant Colonel Henry Cadogan, fought on until every officer had been killed or wounded; only eighty-six men survived to rejoin 22 Brigade after the battle. A battalion which had numbered over 1,000 men two weeks earlier had effectively been annihilated and the remnants were absorbed into 2/Queen's.

The loss of an entire squadron of men was undoubtedly a serious setback to both regiments of Life Guards. 2/Life Guards' war diary records only one survivor from Captain Alex Vandeleur's C Squadron, while 1/Life Guards' casualties in Captain Hugh Grosvenor's squadron numbered over 100; barely six survivors rejoining the regiment later that evening.[4] The fate of the Blues machine-gun section and their young section commander, Lord Worsley, is to this day still shrouded by the fog of war.[5] Undoubtedly they fought on until the last round had been fired and were then overwhelmed along with the Life Guards on their left and right. By reputation Worsley was not a man to offer surrender if there was a possibility of fighting on and without orders to retire, he and the others gallantly remained in position and played the game to the final whistle and the inevitable conclusion.

An attempt was made to get a message from D Squadron to Hugh Grosvenor's men and order their retirement. The first two runners were killed before they got halfway and in his book Lloyd relates a reported conversation between a troop officer nicknamed 'Santa' and Driver Tapper:

'Santa, feeling the weight of his responsibility, decided to send a third runner and approached Tapper. It was too late, and Tapper knew it.

"Look here Tapper" Said Santa. "I wonder if you would try to get through with a message to C Squadron?"

"Wot me?" Says Tapper. "Look at them two poor blighters out there! No fear! It's too bloomin' late anyway."

"I say Tapper, your nerves are all in pieces. Have a Morphine tablet."

"Ave a wot? My nerves is all right. Ave a bloomin' jujube [morphine tablet] yourself. I may be a bloody fool, but I 'aint as big a bloody fool as you think."

At that point the argument was terminated by the appearance of a wave of the enemy, and the ensuing ten minutes were hot enough to try the nerves of both Santa and Tapper.'

It had been a terrible day for the brigade and as the survivors limped their way back to the horse lines at Verbrandenmolen, many of them still in a state of shock, Lloyd recalled the moment Regy Wyndham arrived:

'They looked bedraggled and weary to death as they marched in. Sinbad the Sailor, covered in mud, and with a rifle slung over his shoulder like a Tommy, walked alone at the head of what remained of his troop. His troop sergeant, Cabby Dawes, had been wounded in the first bombardment, and as somebody tried to carry him back he had been hit again and killed. Sinbad and Cabby were kindred spirits and inseparable at all times. Neither had any thoughts for himself. Their horses were never short of forage, nor the men of rations. Better soldiers than those two and their troop of scallywags and hard cases did not exist'

There is no official record of whether Howard St George or William Petersen were in the front line trenches at Zandvoorde on 30 October but it is highly likely that they were. In all probability they were positioned on either side of Worsley's machine-gun section and managed to escape unscathed as there is no report of either of them being wounded. As one would expect, once the dust had settled and the reality of the situation was grasped, there was a great deal of uncertainty amongst the men of the brigade as to who had survived and who had not. One Life Guards officer, who was originally reported missing after the battle, was discovered a few weeks later up in a London military hospital with absolutely no recollection of the battle or how he arrived in England. Even by dusk on 30 October, Gordon Wilson was still unsure of the fate of the missing squadrons but had managed to establish that his brother Bertie was amongst the survivors:

'We suffered considerably. 'Pickles [Second Lieutenant Hon Francis Lambton] was first of all buried with ten men, and as he was being extricated shot through the head. We fought a rearguard action to enable the 6th Brigade Cavalry to come up, which they eventually did, and are in action now as I write. I have now only 190 fighting men left in my regiment, so you will see we have suffered a good deal. Bertie was in the trench near Pickles, and hung on to the end and came out unhurt. Our casualties for the day were 65. The 1st have lost an entire squadron, and the 2nd, ditto; at least, they have not yet been heard of; also our machine gun and its men under Worsley ... Many thanks for the your letter received today, and for the little box of cigars, which are most acceptable.'

Three days later the brigade was assuming the inevitable; Gordon Wilson adding a postscript to his letter to Lady Sarah:

'I fear poor Worsley has been killed in our affair at Zandvoorde. A squadron of the 1st under Hugh Grosvenor, and one of the 2nd, under Vandeleur are still missing.'

Once the Zandvoorde Ridge had fallen and 7 Cavalry Brigade had retired to reform behind the 6 Cavalry Brigade and elements of the Blues, there was a lull in the battle which allowed reinforcements to be drawn in from neighbouring infantry brigades. Von Fabeck's attack of 30 October had pushed the British back to a line which now ran from Gheluvelt to the corner of the Ypres-Comines Canal at Hollebeke. Douglas Haig was quick to realize the next few hours would be critical and in reinforcing this line summoned help from Allenby's Cavalry Corps. One of these hastily despatched cavalry regiments was 4/Hussars along with Lieutenant Alfred Schuster.

*   *   *

We last left 4/Hussars at Mont des Cats where Michael Stocks' cousin, Francis Levita, was killed during the morning of 12 October 1914 near the Trappist monastery. Another casualty on 13 October was Lieutenant Raymond Lonsdale who was a school friend of John Lee Steere. The two boys had been in the same house at Eton together and although Raymond was a year older and joined 4/Hussars in 1913, they had kept in contact. Raymond Lonsdale died of his wounds at Boulogne on 29 October 1914, the day before John Lee Steere left St Nazaire for the front line to join his battalion.

On the morning of 30 October the Hussars were at Hollebeke; dug in along a line running south of the village from the Ypres-Comines Canal along the Linde road. From these trenches they were able to observe the attack taking place on the Zandvoorde Ridge and although they initially thought they would also be coming under attack, it soon became apparent that, for the time being, the main assault was directed against Zandvoorde. At 12.00 pm they were relieved by the 129th Duke of Connaught's Own Baluchis and ordered up to Zandvoorde to stand by for a counter-attack with 3/Hussars and the Greys.[6] Even after they had assembled on the Klein Zillebeke road the overall strategic situation in the area was still far from clear. Von Fabeck's attack had torn several gaps in the British front line south of the Menin Road and judging by the succession of contradictory orders that were received by 4/Hussars in the space of an hour, there was some uncertainty at command level as to where exactly the reserves should be dispatched in order to stem the tide of the German advance.

At about midday German artillery on the newly won Zandvoorde Ridge began to direct its fire to support the infantry assault that was being mounted against Hollebeke. By 1.15 pm the Baluchis and the 5th Lancers were being shelled out from their positions just south of Hollebeke and were falling back on the second line trenches along the line of the canal. In receipt of their final set of orders for the day 4/Hussars now found themselves galloping back to Hollebeke to defend the northern side of the canal and by 2.00 pm were installed in the very trenches that they had dug themselves three days earlier. It had been a frustrating day for the regiment thus far, but once the horse lines had been established in the rear, Alfred Schuster and C Squadron took over the trenches on the right of B Squadron, which was between the railway line and the Hollebeke Road.

While the regiment had been up at Zandvoorde 4/Hussars' machine-gun section under Lieutenant Kenneth North had been in action all morning in support of the troops at Hollebeke, holding up the German infantry with his two machine guns for over an hour after the last British troops had left the village. When he eventually received the order to retire at 2.00 pm and rejoin the regiment on the canal, the enemy infantry were just 100 yards away, nevertheless it still gave him sufficient time to make his escape, with the guns being transported in a wheelbarrow. He and his men had effectively held up the best part of a brigade of German infantry for most of the morning, which was just as well, as at midday on 30 October at least a mile of the canal line had been left completely unoccupied by British troops for a good hour or more.

Meanwhile the German gunners had managed to bring several field guns up into Hollebeke itself and were firing on some of the Hussars' positions from a range of 700 yards. Just before it became dark, German infantry began moving up from Hollebeke along the edge of the canal towards the trenches held by B and C Squadrons. While their movements were initially cloaked by the undergrowth, once they lost their cover the Hussars were able to prevent the attack from developing with a very accurate fusillade of rifle and machine-gun fire. At 6.30 pm the bridge over the canal between the two squadrons was partly blown just before orders were received to keep it intact as French troops intended to use it in their attack the next morning!

With the bridge out of commission, the front line positions settled down and the Hussars were serenaded by German bands playing in Hollebeke Chateâu. Alfred Schuster had been with the regiment for just over five weeks and as a troop commander was now well established in C Squadron. Back in England his two brothers had not been slow in volunteering for military service. Edgar was now a second lieutenant in the Wessex (Hants) Royal Garrison Artillery and was about to leave for the front line with his battery. Edgar had married in 1905 and he and his wife Beatrice had settled in Sandown on the Isle of Wight with their two children Aubrey, 5, and Helen, who had just had her first birthday. Beatrice must have hoped that her husband's patriotic zeal had not clouded his judgement; his talents lay in the academic haven of the medical research field, not on the battlefield. At 35-years-old, Edgar was not a particularly strong individual and his hitherto academic lifestyle was poor preparation for the rigours of being a gunner subaltern.

Alfred was best man at his elder brother George's wedding in December 1908 when he married Gwendolen Parker, the daughter of Lord Justice Parker and after resigning as Liberal candidate for North Cumberland, George had been assisted by one of Alfred's university friends, the Hon Arthur Villiers, in obtaining a commission into his local yeomanry regiment, the Oxfordshire Hussars. Arthur Villiers was a lieutenant with the regiment and had been in France since 19 September and had already seen action earlier in the month, the regiment earning the distinction of being the first Territorial Force regiment to be brought into action.

The morning of 31 October opened with a heavy artillery barrage which continued for most of the day and accounted for Alfred's squadron commander Captain Frederick Hunt, who was killed while going to the aid of a badly wounded Kenneth North. The promised French attack at 11.00 am never really got beyond the Hussars' trenches but they nevertheless remained on hand to help repel a much more determined German infantry attack which was launched in mid-afternoon. After dark the regiment, with the exception of A Squadron which remained for a further night, handed over their trenches to the French and 1/Life Guards and departed to St Eloi and billets. Regy Wyndham and his troop of Life Guards arrived amid very heavy shellfire but managed to get into position without casualties. After a very cold night during which they had little sleep the artillery barrage continued next morning:

> *'An awful morning of shellfire during which Brassey and Anderson were hit, and Clowes' haversack smashed, and his gaiter cut by a big shell bursting over them, the French came to relieve us. While we were retiring the Germans in the château opened up on us. Corp. Webb was hit, Barrington was killed.'*

The fight in which 4/Hussars were engaged at the Hollebeke canal turn was one of many local engagements that took place during the last two days of October 1914. However, the strategic significance of the cavalry action at Hollebeke is perhaps not always fully recognized. Had the canal turn been overwhelmed by the repeated German artillery and infantry attacks, the British line at Klein Zillebeke would have inevitably succumbed, putting the integrity of the whole southeastern corner of the Salient in doubt. It is a fitting tribute to the resolve and firepower of the British cavalrymen that they held their positions and with the assistance of their French allies prevented a disaster.

* * *

While Alfred Schuster had been fighting at Hollebeke, General Allenby had been in contact with Sir John French on 30 October with the news that the cavalry corps, which stretched from Hollebeke, south to Wytschaete and Messines, was unlikely to hold its positions for much longer without reinforcements. This rather disquieting communication resulted in four battalions being dispatched from II Corps to bolster the cavalry's positions along the Messines Ridge. Wytschaete itself was held by the 415 men of the Composite Household Cavalry Regiment which included amongst its number two of Regy Wyndham's brothers, Captain Edward Wyndham and Lieutenant Everard Wyndham. Opposite them, and outnumbering them by some twelve to one, were the XXIV and II Bavarian Corps, considered to be some of the best fighting men in the German Army.

The desperate situation on the Messines Ridge and the chronic shortage of troops on the ground was the deciding factor in bringing the London Scottish into action on 31 October 1914. The London Scottish, or correctly, the 14th Battalion, County of London Regiment, had a history reaching back to 1798 when a militia of Scots living in London was formed in response to the Napoleonic threat of invasion. After the South African War, where the regiment fought with distinction, the volunteers became part of the new Territorial Force under the Haldane reforms of 1908. Even before this, the regiment was very much a London organization and essentially Scottish in character with many of the rank and file drawn from the professional classes. After 1914, when the shortage of officers became acute in the Territorial and New Army battalions, the London Scottish supplied a large number of candidates for commissioning. In fact by November 1915 they had provided 1,200 officers for other units.

At the end of July 1914 Private William Gibson arrived at Ludgershall Camp to begin his two week annual camp. It was pouring with rain and the battalion was soaking wet as it arrived at the tented camp that had been prepared for them. Barely fifteen minutes after lights out was sounded, they received orders to return immediately to London to await mobilization, the annual camp was over before it had begun and two days later Britain declared war. Events now moved swiftly for the Scottish. On 12 September the commanding officer, Lieutenant Colonel G A Malcolm, received embarkation orders for the following week. All leave was cancelled and the day before they left for Southampton the battalion was issued with the Mark 1 Lee Enfield rifle.

Expecting to join the BEF who were fighting on the Aisne there was great disappointment when the battalion's eight companies were split up and assigned to 'lines of communication' duties across northern France. William Gibson and F Company were dispatched to Le Mans, arriving after a seventeen-hour rail journey in cattle trucks. Le Mans was the base for a number of stationary British military hospitals and the men of F Company were soon unloading the wounded and dying who arrived daily by train from the front. Many were in a pitiful condition when they arrived at Le Mans after spending several days travelling in overcrowded hospital trains. If the young soldiers of the London Scottish hadn't already considered the reality of war they most certainly would have done after the disconcerting experience of observing it by unloading hospital trains on a daily basis

On 25 October Colonel Malcolm was ordered to reassemble his battalion at St Omer; at last it looked as though they were going to be deployed on the front line. By 29 October the battalion was ready and marched to the outskirts of St Omer in the pouring rain where they were met by a fleet of London buses and their civilian drivers who were to transport them to Ypres. The battalion had no baggage, transport or machine guns and was still armed with the Mark 1 Lee Enfield rifle. Unbelievably the Mark 1 rifle's incompatibility with the new Mark VII ammunition would not be discovered until shortly before the battalion went into action on 31 October. The new ammunition caused the rifle mechanism to jam, forcing the soldier to load the weapon with a single round each time it was fired. The nine-hour journey, particularly for those on the top deck of the open top buses, was a miserable one, but eventually, in the early hours of Friday 30 October, wet, cold and hungry, they reached Ypres.

Just before first light on 31 October 1914, the London Scottish companies paraded on the St Eloi road. Brigadier General Cecil Bingham's 4 Cavalry Brigade, now fighting as dismounted troops, was struggling to hold its positions on the Messines Ridge and the Scottish were hurriedly brought up to reinforce the cavalrymen. As the battalion moved down the road towards Wytschaete the local inhabitants were in full flight, streaming away from the battlefield amid the bursting shells that were reducing the town to ruin. Advancing through the gun lines the battalion initially found shelter in the Bois de l'Enfer before being instructed to move up in support of 4/Dragoon Guards. Their positions were marked by two farms just west of the Wytschaete to Messines road and a prominent windmill on the crest of the ridge. William Gibson and the men of F Company were held in reserve on the high ground east of the Bois de l'Enfer, while the remainder of the battalion dug in along the road.

The German attack began at 9.00 pm accompanied by loud cheering and martial music. The Scottish held their nerve and despite the difficulties experienced with their weapons, poured an accurate and devastating fire into the dense mass of advancing Bavarian infantry. Row upon row were shot down in front of the British lines, which in itself was quite a feat of arms bearing in mind they had no machine guns and a large percentage of the battalion's rifles would only fire one round at a time. German casualties would have been heavier still had the Scottish been able to fire more effectively. The battalion war diary noted afterwards that some fifty per cent of the battalion's rifles were ineffective owing to faulty magazines. At midnight an artillery bombardment announced a second infantry attack. By now the burning farm houses and the blazing outline of the windmill together with a full moon provided the Scottish with enough light to repel rush after rush of German infantrymen with their rifle fire; a magnificent feat given the condition of many of the rifles. Private L Wilkins later recalled how useful the light from the burning buildings was:

'*A blazing barn in their rear enabled us to see them very plainly, so we opened fire, being able to use our sights fairly well. We brought a lot of them down in front of this barn. Soon they began to get very close, for by sheer weight of numbers they had evidently broken through the trench in front. An officer ordered us to cease fire and to wait until the Germans got quite close … Then the order came to fire and we simply poured lead into them.*'

Just when they thought the night's work was over, a determined German attack with the bayonet pushed the forward elements of the Scottish back, opening up a gap in the line between the Scottish and the left flank of the cavalry. It was a critical point in the battle and the Scottish counter-attack was one that propelled it onto the front pages of the nation's newspapers. The counter-attack was the work of the battalion reserve which of course included Private William Gibson who was fighting alongside his comrades in F Company. The war diary recorded the event with little fuss:

'*About 2.00 am the German attack came past and through our trenches and they were driven back by our reserve company in a counter-attack. This counter-attack was assisted by a portion of C Coy [company] who had earlier been withdrawn from the trenches.*'

The Times was a little more enthusiastic:

'*It is a special event because it forms an epoch in the military history of the British Empire, and marks the first time that a complete unit of our Territorial Army has been thrown into the fight alongside its sister units of the Regulars.*'

It was indeed a special event and the Scottish had performed beyond expectations but it was not the end of the fighting. Some time after 3.00 am the Germans broke through again, this time on the Scottish left and with no reserves left to throw into the fight Colonel Malcolm had no choice but to retire to avoid being overwhelmed. By first light large numbers of the enemy had worked round both flanks of the battalion with machine guns and the Scottish retirement was carried out under a murderous crossfire as they pulled back across the Steenbeek valley towards Wulverghem. The regiment had been 'blooded' in what can only be described as a gallant but futile attempt to stabilize the British line clinging to the ridge.

1/Life Guards squadron of the Household Cavalry Composite Regiment was holding positions just north of the crossroads at Wytschaete. They were fortunate in that one of their three machine guns was still serviceable, which helped keep the German infantry at bay until the ammunition began to run out. Forced into a fighting withdrawal they mounted several counter-attacks with the bayonet, each time driving the Bavarian infantry back with the ferocity of their charges. It was during one of these bayonet charges that Regy Wyndham's brother Edward, already wounded once, was wounded for a second time. By first light the Germans had fought their way into the market place at Wytschaete and had effectively outflanked the Composite Regiment, forcing a retirement in the direction of Kemmel.

The Messines Ridge was lost and would not be retaken until June 1917. For William Gibson and the territorial soldiers of the London Scottish their fight on the ridge had been a brutal first engagement involving hard close-quarter fighting made all the more traumatic by defective weapons. As always there had been a price; the full extent of which began to unfold at the roll call of officers and men near Wulverghem later on 1 November. Their casualties amounted to just under fifty percent of their strength; 394 officers and men were listed as killed, missing or wounded. Those that had survived marched back to La Clytte where F Company found some respite from the weather by sheltering in pig-sties before the battalion was ordered to fight alongside Lord Cavan's 4 (Guards) Brigade. The battle for Ypres was reaching its conclusion and the Scottish were about to join John Lee Steere and the Grenadiers in the fight for Zwarteleen.

Chapter 10

The Last Stand

Captain Norman Neill resumed his duties as Brigade Major of 7 Cavalry Brigade on 1 November 1914. Although his absence had been a short one, much had changed since his evacuation to hospital on 20 October. The news of friends in the casualty lists would have probably reached him at Bolougne but the full story of Zandvoorde would not have been unfurled until his return. After his wounding on the Passchendaele Road, the telegram informing his wife, Eleanor, arrived at Yew Tree Cottage in the Surrey village of Merrow, near Guildford. The family had only recently moved there from Hursley where they had lived with their daughter Audrey during Norman's appointment to the Staff College at Camberley. No doubt he soon put Eleanor's mind at rest making light of his wounds and assuring her he would be careful once he was back with the brigade.

His arrival back at brigade headquarters coincided with a spell of good weather during which the officers and men took advantage of a rare opportunity to relax and enjoy the sunshine. Writing to Lady Sarah on the morning of 2 November 1914 Gordon Wilson was in an optimistic mood:

'We are held in reserve today, as yesterday, and will probably be put into the firing line, in the trenches, this evening. Last night I slept in a château near here, out of which General Lomax and his staff were blown by a big shell the previous day, two [sic] being killed. Although a few shells fell during the night, no harm was done to man or horses. This is a glorious day and I write this in the sun, in a wood of pine trees, with a battery of ours in action 50 yards away, over which the enemy are now bursting their shrapnel ... I have had some parcels from Fortnum's which have been acceptable, but chiefly butter and milk tins. I think some preserved plums and Muscatels would be very good ... please ask Fortnum and Mason to send me a pair of their service boots. They can get my size from my boot maker, Tom Hill, opposite Tattersalls, Knightsbridge. They are very soft and comfortable and should be a size bigger than one's ordinary boots.'

Gordon Wilson and the Blues were in Sanctuary Wood as was the remainder of the brigade. The men of 1/Life Guards were also enjoying the sunshine and being out of the firing line; Regy Wyndham in particular enjoying a change from his usual diet of army rations:

> 'Some lovely boxes of food came sent by Phyllis Brooks. We spent the morning sitting in the sun, reading our letters and eating Phyllis Brooks' present.'[1]

Unfortunately the brief morning's sojourn soon came to an abrupt end when a call from the infantry near Gheluvelt had them galloping down the Menin Road under heavy shellfire. The bursting shrapnel was uncomfortably close to the advancing horsemen and before long some of it found its mark on both man and beast. Regy's horse, Wressle, was hit as they crossed some open ground:

> 'In the afternoon we were suddenly galloped off to the Ypres–Menin road. We had to cross a field under heavy shrapnel fire. Wressle whom I was riding went end over end … in the evening after firing ceased, went down to where Wressle lay. He was not killed, and whinnied to me as I came up, but could not get up … took what I could off Wressle and shot the poor horse. It was pitiable to hear him whinny to me.'

Wressle was one of the two horses Regy had brought with him from England at the start of the campaign and the animal had been hit by shrapnel through the shoulder. The regiment suffered one man killed and five more wounded in their short excursion to Gheluvelt and it was only when Regy returned later that evening, having got a lift in a Belgian armoured motor, that his name was removed from the missing list. The regiment was bivouacked east of Zillebeke where they were again shelled during the night, losing four more horses and one man killed. 'Being shelled while one is between blankets' he wrote the next morning, 'is most un-nerving.'

Wednesday, 4 November was another fine, sunny day and 1/Life Guards were back in reserve at Sanctuary Wood finishing off the contents of Phyllis Brooks' hamper. A little further south near Klein Zillebeke, 2/Grenadier Guards were on the receiving end of the usual daily German artillery barrage. In what was the last entry Bernard Gordon Lennox would make in his diary he mourns the loss of friends and reveals his fears for his own survival:

> 'I suppose one gets inured to seeing all one's best friends taken away from one and can only think one is lucky enough to be here oneself – for the present.'

The Grenadiers' positions in the woods at Zwarteleen were systematically shelled on a daily basis in an attempt to break the line and force a gap through which the waiting German infantry could advance. So far, German infantry attacks had repeatedly failed to make an impression against the resolute rifle and machine-gun fire that the British front line troops poured into the advancing waves of infantry. Lieutenant Colonel Wilfred Smith, commanding 2/Grenadier Guards, noted in a letter to his wife that 'we have killed hundreds in the last few days and these woods are full of them, poor things.' But far from giving up, German infantry were now seen to be entrenching a new line only some 300 yards away, clearly another infantry assault was being planned.

The attack came after the early morning mist had cleared on Friday, 6 November. The French infantry under the overall command of General De Moussy were holding the defensive line that ran roughly from the Ypres-Comines Canal to the Klein Zillebeke road. North of the French were the Irish Guards and beyond them the Grenadiers in position along the line of the Brown Road. With the clearing of the mist came the expected artillery bombardment which was followed after two hours by German infantry attacks all along the line. The initial wave was repulsed everywhere leaving heaps of enemy dead and wounded in the now bright sunshine of the morning. The second, far more determined attack, which appeared to be focused on the French positions, succeeded in breaking the resolve of the French and opening up a considerable gap. The French retirement in the face of this attack was the beginning of a collapse that impacted directly on the now exposed right flank of the Irish Guards and it was not long before the Irish line gave way completely, leaving the Grenadiers' trench line open to a similar flanking attack. The whole house of cards was now in great danger of collapsing and it was only the fortitude of the Grenadiers who stood their ground and managed to swing their threatened flank back to the relative security of the Brown Road that prevented a total disaster.

As soon as news filtered through that the Irish Guards' line had broken, Colonel Smith sent Harry Parnell and Number 3 Platoon with Carleton Tufnell and his machine-gun section to open fire on the infantry who were advancing through the gap. While this did not hold them up, it did slow the advance down as the Grenadiers fired down one of the wide rides in the wood directly into their right flank, exacting a heavy toll on the German infantrymen. But the situation was far from being contained. Once in position it would have been immediately clear to Tufnell that, despite the fire power of his machine guns and the additional support of Harry Parnell's rifle platoon, more support was going to be needed if the breakthrough was to be halted. But help was at hand; an urgent call had been sent to Kavanagh's 'Fire Brigade' to come to their assistance. There is some difference of opinion as to who exactly ordered 7 Cavalry Brigade to assist Lord Cavan's forces on the afternoon of 6 November 1914. An article in *The Times* in 1924 suggested that Haig himself gave the order while other contemporary sources insist Lord Cavan, as the local commander on the ground, sent word to Kavanagh's Brigade which was in Sanctuary Wood. Whoever was responsible for the order it set in motion a dismounted cavalry action that many feel was more brilliant than, and just as crucial as, the charge of the Worcesters a week earlier at Gheluvelt. In fact if the German breakthrough had succeeded at Zwarteleen there were precious few, if any, reserves to have prevented Ypres from falling.

Kavanagh's troops were directed to approach over Observatory Ridge to avoid revealing themselves too much before they deployed across the line of the French retreat. Just short of the village of Zwarteleen the brigade dismounted under fire and with the Blues held in support, both Life Guards regiments advanced at the double astride the Zillebeke-Zwarteleen Road towards the Klein Zillebeke Ridge to meet the enemy. With them went Harry Parnell and Carleton Tufnell together with some Irish Guards and those French troops that could be found. 1/Life Guards with Regy Wyndham and Howard St George attacked the trenches that had been abandoned earlier in the morning by the Irish Guards; their spirited bayonet charge was enough to expel the occupying German troops and regain the lost position. Realizing just how weak the line was at this point, Harry Parnell confirmed his cool and rational behaviour under fire by collecting together several Irish Guardsmen to both strengthen his own platoon and link up with the Royal Sussex on his left. The Irish Guardsmen were completely devoid of weapons and ammunition, having abandoned everything when they had left their trenches in near panic but Harry went out personally and collected rifles and ammunition from casualties to re-arm the Irishmen. Placing them amongst his own men, he was able to hold the gap all through the hours of darkness until relieved the next morning.

While this was taking place 2/Life Guards and William Petersen advanced along a line that ran from the edge of the railway line across the open ground to the village of Zwarteleen. 2/Life Guards, war diary is almost certainly the most accurate account of the subsequent fight:

'The regiment ... was ordered to establish itself on the Klein Zillebeke Ridge keeping in touch with the 1st Life Guards on the right, who were to conform with the right of the Guards Brigade. Major Hon Dawnay ordered B Squadron across the open [to] occupy the high ground in front. D Squadron was sent across the Zillebeke-Zwarteleen road to secure the right flank by moving parallel to the railway. C Troop and machine guns were kept in reserve ready to support B Squadron. The latter squadron succeeded in reaching the edge of the wood on the ridge after some fighting owing to the enemy being in possession of several houses. Almost at once the right flank of B Squadron became open to enfilade fire which caused Major Dawnay to order the squadron to fall back slowly by troops. ... The squadron was then ordered to fix bayonets and charge the wood while C Troop was taken by the CO to fill the gap which had occurred between the two squadrons.*

This troop vigorously attacked the village of Zwarteleen using the bayonet with great effect, taking a certain number of prisoners. B Squadron meanwhile drove back the enemy several hundred yards and occupied a ditch 200 yards from their position.'

The village was filled with British, French and German troops fighting at close-quarters; the aggressive energy of the cavalrymen had stirred their allies and French and British fought alongside each other to push the enemy back along the road. They were successful; the gap was closed and Zwarteleen recovered. But the fight was far from over. Just when it appeared the situation had been restored to some resemblance of normality, the French on the right of 2/Life Guards gave way again, opening up yet another gap which the enemy was quick to capitalize on. 2/Life Guards' war diary again:

'Owing to the French infantry again falling back, B Squadron and the Blues were ordered by the Brigadier to move across the Zwarteleen-Verbrandenmolen road and support C Troop which was occupying a small ridge south-east of the hamlet. The fighting in this vicinity became very involved owing to the somewhat precipitant retreat of the French and on consequence several casualties were incurred. Part of the ground gained including a part of Zwarteleen was lost.'

With the daylight beginning to fade, the exhausted cavalrymen had yet again met the German advance head on and for a moment or two the outcome had hung in the balance. Incredibly they managed to stand firm and despite having to abandon some of the hard won ground gained earlier in the afternoon by Dawnay's men, the line was once again securely in British hands. At 9.30 pm that evening the cavalry began to be relieved by 3 Brigade, which had marched from Bellewaarde Farm, and 22 Brigade who had been brought up from reserve at Dikebusch in motor buses.

The extent of the cavalry's casualties would not have been immediately apparent to the men of 7 Cavalry Brigade as they returned to their billets at Mud Farm. Only when the roll calls were completed the next day would the full human cost of the afternoon's action become evident. And what a cost! There is no doubt that this bold and inspiring charge by the cavalry had saved the day and prevented 4 (Guards) Brigade from being annihilated, but the casualties had been heavy. From a brigade which on 5 November had been unable to muster more than 600 men in total, casualties amounted to six officers killed and a further eleven wounded with sixty-seven other ranks killed, wounded or posted as missing, and this coming less than a week after the fight at Zandvoorde. Amongst 1/Life Guards' casualties was Regy Wyndham, three of his men had been wounded and he had been killed leading his beloved troop

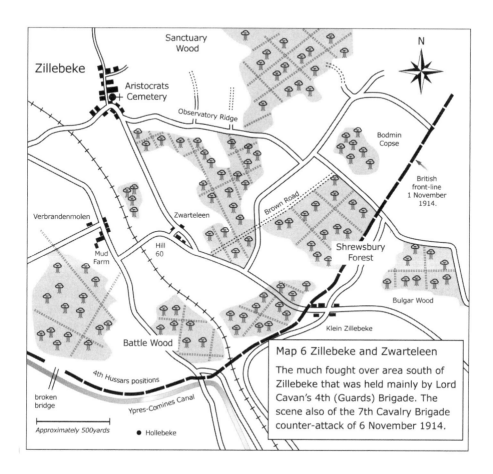

Map 6 Zillebeke and Zwarteleen

The much fought over area south of Zillebeke that was held mainly by Lord Cavan's 4th (Guards) Brigade. The scene also of the 7th Cavalry Brigade counter-attack of 6 November 1914.

into action. Lloyd and his fellow NCOs considered Regy's death the saddest loss of the day:

> '*So well liked was Sinbad amongst the troops that when darkness fell that same night, two drivers from the machine-gun section, Rubber Reeves and Tinker Underwood, got two horses and a half-limber, galloped up to the scene of the counter-attack, and brought back his body for burial in a near-by churchyard. They received no official recognition for this action but Sinbad's brother, Lord Leconfield, sent them both a token of his gratitude and a letter of thanks.*'

2/Life Guards had borne the brunt of the day and it was during the advance through Zwarteleen that Hugh Dawnay and Arthur O'Neill were killed. Exactly where William Petersen fell will probably never be known but as most of the regiment's casualties occurred during the final British counter-attack of the day by B Squadron and C Troop, it is highly likely he was shot by German infantry who were firing from the shelter of outlying houses on the eastern edge of the village. Accounts of the action tell us that he was killed leading his troop as they advanced under heavy fire and that shortly before his death he and his men were 'keeping back a very strong attack of the enemy.'

Precisely when and where Gordon Wilson was killed is also difficult to pinpoint as there are conflicting accounts of his death. The Official History of the Household Cavalry, written by Sir George Arthur, describes Gordon Wilson with a rifle and bayonet in hand leading his men into the woods with a 'cheery laugh bubbling up.' Moments later a bullet 'pierced his brain, and without word or a moan he sank to the ground.' This account is very different to that of the Blues' war diary:

> *'We drove the enemy back through the wood, the edge of which was held after by the 3rd Cavalry Division. Captain Lord Gerard was wounded but otherwise we had few casualties in the advance. When it got dusk we were ordered to withdraw to the trenches about 80 yards in the rear. In doing this we came under fire from some of the enemy who were in advance of their line and Colonel Wilson and Lt. A de Gunzburg were killed and Captain E P Brassey and Captain Lord Northampton were wounded.'*

An account written by General Kavanagh in a letter to Lady Sarah on 8 November 1914 suggests he was killed during the advance the Blues made in support of C Troop towards the end of the afternoon, rather than later in the evening when the Blues were withdrawing after being relieved:

> *'The Brigade had successfully carried out the main part of its task and regained a lot of ground, when I ordered it to halt, and urged the French commander to reorganize his troops and reoccupy the trenches they had left. This he said he would do, and sent about 400 of them forward. They had, however, only advanced about 100 yards when they seem to have been seized by a panic, and came hurrying back saying the Germans were making a counter-attack. I called one squadron of the Blues and one of the 2nd Life Guards to meet this attack, but they were practically swept away by the retreating French and it was at this moment that most of the casualties occurred and that your husband was shot. He was shot through the head, and his death must have been instantaneous.'*

Of the three accounts I am more inclined to accept the version in the Blues' war diary. Kavanagh was correct in describing where on the battlefield Gordon Wilson was killed but his timing was out. Arthur's account – published in 1926 – was, I suspect, the subject of an overenthusiastic pen and at the very least must be considered to be inaccurate. But whatever the version of Gordon Wilson death, General Kavanagh's final words to Lady Sarah are a fitting tribute to a brave and professional soldier:

'He is the greatest loss to the Brigade in general, and his regiment in particular, and his absolute coolness and indifference to danger has been the admiration of us all. I have met a good many brave men, but have never seen one quite apparently so indifferent to danger as he was.'

There is a similar lack of firm information regarding the death of Alexis de Gunzburg. Contemporary accounts describe him being shot down while running across an open field under fire. The war diary describes his death taking place at the same time as Gordon Wilson's, which would be in keeping with the view that de Gunzburg, as official interpreter, would be close at hand should his commanding officer require his services. Other sources have de Gunzburg acting as a runner and relaying Gordon Wilson's orders which would be consistent with him being killed crossing an open field. However, I tend to lean in favour of the war diary; Alexis de Gunzburg was probably killed close to his commanding officer while the Blues were being relieved from their positions.

Norman Neill's death, which occurred less than a week after he had returned to duty, was another great loss to the brigade. 'His death, I think', wrote Kavanagh, 'must have been instantaneous and without pain, as I saw him two minutes after he was hit.' Neill had been sent by Kavanagh to order the Blues into action in support of 2/Life Guards after the French had given way on the second occasion. He was hit while returning to brigade headquarters. The last thing Norman Neill would have seen before he fell was the brigade advancing towards the enemy.

So what of the Grenadiers who were fighting for their survival along the Brown Road? Once through the gap created by the French retreat, the advancing German infantry quickly enfiladed Number 1 Company which accounted for most of the seventy-five NCOs and men who were killed and wounded. After the timely arrival of 7 Cavalry Brigade both Harry Parnell and Carleton Tufnell had advanced in support and at some point during the counter-attack Carleton Tufnell was shot through the throat and died of his wounds soon afterwards. Writing on 8 November, Captain Eben Pike, the battalion's Adjutant, mourned his passing:

'Poor young Tufnell was killed the day before yesterday. He is the second machine gun officer we have had killed and was engaged to a girl in England. Poor chap, he was always so excited about the post coming and getting his letters.'

The Grenadier Guards' war diary described the events of 6 November as a 'trying and critical day'; a view shared by John Lee Steere, in what was his second day of front line action, agreeing 'we had it hard yesterday.'

Dawn on 7 November heralded another misty and dull start to the day. Late the previous evening 1/Gloucesters had arrived as part of the reinforcements that had been drafted in to bolster the Zwarteleen frontage. Like 3 Brigade, 22 Infantry Brigade was desperately under strength. Of the 4,000 officers and men that had marched into battle in October 1914 only three officers and a few hundred men remained. As for the Gloucesters, despite being reinforced a few days previously by a further 200 men, 1/Life Guards' war diary noted they were still unable to muster enough rifles to effectively occupy all of the front line allocated to them. It was only at 2.30 am on 7 November that 1/Lifeguards were finally able to leave the positions they had fought so hard to regain the previous day. The actual frontage allocated to the Gloucesters was at the eastern end of Zwarteleen which included a portion of the woods further to the north. But even when reinforced by a scratch force of Irish Guards, Royal Munster Fusiliers and Royal Sussex, their line had to be divided up into sectors and held by batches of men with the surviving officers placed at strategic points. Robert Rising was now second-in-command of the battalion and must have felt apprehensive at the thought of his very tired troops having to mount a counter-attack the next morning against infantry who were relatively fresh and in strongly held positions.

At 6.00 am on 7 November orders were received by the Gloucesters from Lord Cavan to assist in the 22 Brigade attack on Zwarteleen. These orders were later countermanded with fresh orders for 3 Brigade to advance and occupy the apparently empty enemy trenches that been abandoned after the 22 Brigade attack. Lieutenant Grazebrook's account describes Robert Rising's last battle:[2]

'The battalion pushed forward in two lines, Captain Rising leading the first and Major Ingram the second about 50 yards behind. On issuing out of the village of Zwarteleen the battalion was met by an intense rifle and machine-gun fire and it was found the enemy were holding some of the outermost houses of the village ... Officers and men were much too exhausted to do more than clear a few of the houses. Most of the men had to lie down in the open all day and only a few could get back to the trenches they had dug the night before. Major Ingram and Lieutenant Halford tried to check the tendency to retire to the cover of the houses but there were not enough officers left to lead the men forward. Lieutenant Kershaw with his platoon of A Company on the right had been cut off and nothing more was ever heard of him. Major Ingram was wounded in the knee whilst crossing the road under full view for the fifth time when attempting to point out the line to be held. He was able however to reach Captain Rising and discuss with him the situation before being taken back to the dressing station. Captain Rising himself was carried back to the dressing station a few minutes later, mortally wounded.'

While this attack was being carried out German artillery kept up their daily bombardment of the British and French positions; the Grenadiers, who were now dug in along a fresh line parallel to the Brown Road, reporting that they had been shelled for most of the day. Casualties in the battalion for 7 November were nineteen killed, forty-six wounded and three missing. One of the dead was 20-year-old Private Walter Siewertsen who, on the day of his death, had completed one year and 214 days in the service of the Crown. He was buried soon after at Zillebeke churchyard with Robert Rising who had died of his wounds at the battalion dressing station. They joined the casualties of the previous day which included Carleton Tufnell, Gordon Wilson, Regy Wyndham, William Petersen, Alexis de Gunzburg and probably Arthur O'Neill.

The story of the battle from 8 November up until 10 November continued with the German commanders continuing their attacks on every sector of the line with the intention of preventing the Allied forces from consolidating their defences. Having being checked at Zwarteleen there were German successes further south at Le Gheer and in the north where units of the German Fourth Army re-took Kortekeer. The Coldstream Guards at Polygon Wood continued their wet and shell-torn existence and although the Germans had sapped very close to the Coldstream trenches, any demonstration of force was quickly repulsed. It was a different story at Zwarteleen. Tuesday, 10 November was a bad day for the Grenadiers. The line had been reinforced a few days earlier by the London Scottish who, fresh from their fight on the Messines Ridge, were now sharing the daily artillery barrages alongside the Grenadiers. On that Tuesday the shelling began at daybreak and lasted most of the day. The Grenadiers' trenches on their right flank were thrown back and there were several direct hits on their positions. In the case of a direct hit, those that were not blown to atoms were often buried under tons of soil and debris. One of these was Captain George Powell who was completely buried by a large shell and was only just dug out in time. Casualties in these circumstances were unavoidable and one of the first was Bernard Gordon Lennox who was killed by a high explosive shell near Bodmin Copse:

'For three months he had been in the thick of every engagement, always cheerful and making the best of every hardship. He was one of the most popular officers in the Brigade of Guards, and his death was very keenly felt by everyone.'[3]

At around midday the intensity of the barrage increased significantly and Michael Stocks was killed with a number of his platoon by a shell. Harry Parnell, who had fought so brilliantly four days earlier, was shot through the heart by a sniper and young Hervy Tudway, who had joined the battalion with John Lee Steere only a few days before, was badly wounded in the head, later dying of his wounds. In all, the battalion had twenty-one killed, thirty-seven wounded and sixteen missing, the trenches had been reduced to a series of shell holes and the whole line was covered in the shattered remains of trees that had been brought down by the bombardment. Even if the Germans had mounted an infantry attack they would have had great difficulty penetrating the confusion of destroyed woodland that now masked the British line. At 10.00 pm the first of the relieving troops finally came to the Grenadiers' assistance having themselves had great difficulty in finding their way through the obstacles in the dark. The relief was finally completed at dawn and the Grenadiers, magnanimous with their patience, marched back to their reserve location at Bellewaarde Farm. Contrary to expectation there was to be little rest

The Allied forces had little in the way of intelligence to warn them of the preparations that were being made by the Germans to conclude the battle for Ypres. A new army group headed by General von Linsingen had been assembled with the sole purpose of ending the stalemate at Ypres by delivering a final decisive blow along a nine-mile front that ran from the Coldstream Guards' positions at Reutel down to Messines. Von Linsingen's forces included the XV Army Corps, Linsingen's own 4th Pomeranian Division and Winckler's Guard Division which had been brought up from Arras. The new German offensive coincided with a change in the weather; a strong westerly wind brought an icy rain sweeping across the battlefield turning the already soaked ground into a sea of mud. Trenches quickly filled with water and defensive parapets had to be raised above ground level, increasing the risk of death and injury from shell fire.

At dawn on 11 November the German offensive opened under leaden skies with a bombardment from both the Fourth and Sixth Army's guns. Those who survived it swear it was the heaviest yet, and far worse than that delivered at Zandvoorde and at Gheluvelt. Between 8.00 and 9.00 am it increased in intensity and as the barrage began to lift from the front line positions any suspicions that were being harboured of an imminent infantry assault were swiftly confirmed when line after line of German infantry appeared out of the morning fog. At Klein Zillebeke the German 30th Division pushed the French back again and captured Hill 60 and for a moment the flank of the London Scottish looked as if it was about to be overrun. Colonel Malcolm had only a few reserves left but managed to strengthen the line with the men of Headquarters Company; the moment passed and the line held. During the fierce close-quarter fighting in the woods, William Gibson, the 29-year-old commercial clerk from Ilford, was killed. The London Scottish war diary does not specifically record the casualties for 11 November but during the five-day period up to 13 November they lost two officers and seventy men.

The twelve battalions of Winkler's Prussian Guard that attacked across the Menin Road looked unstoppable as they took all the 1 Brigade front line trenches between Veldhoek and Hooge. In several places they succeeded in breaking through in large numbers but inexplicably failed to capitalize on their success; perhaps caught in that dangerous state of relaxation that sometimes follows when initial objectives have been reached. Such was the case in Nonne Bosschen Wood, a small copse between Polygon Wood and the Menin Road. Some 900 of the German 1st Foot Guard broke through General FitzClarence's front and were advancing through the undefended wood threatening the 2nd Division's flank. A potentially disastrous situation was only averted by a gallantly improvised defence and a vitally important counter-attack in the afternoon which unnerved the German forces and pushed them out of Nonne Bosschen just as the rain, which had been threatening all day, began to pour down. At 5.00 pm the energetic General FitzClarence was in the process of gathering together enough men for a counter-attack to regain the lost positions in Polygon Wood. Major General Landon, who was still in temporary command of the 1st Division, sent him 2/Grenadier Guards and the Irish Guards to support the Gloucesters and the Munsters. Some time after 3.00 am on 12 November the assembled force was approaching Polygon Wood with FitzClarence leading them personally along the track towards the wood. Hearing rifle shots close by FitzClarence moved ahead of the main column to investigate, moments later he was hit by rifle fire and mortally wounded. The attack abandoned, the Grenadiers marched back to the Menin Road and spent the remainder of the night in Herenthage Wood.

From the relative security of Herenthage, John Lee Steere found the time to write to his father. Number 2 Company was now being commanded by his cousin and he was the only other officer remaining:

'We have been having some very stiff fighting lately which has taken a good toll of officers and men, but I'm glad to say I'm still fit and well ... and though the men have been splendid, they are feeling the strain now rather ... Had an awful shelling 2 days ago, Bernard Gordon Lennox, who commands my company, was killed. I am sorry, as though I had only seen him for a week, I thought him absolutely splendid and the men all liked him awfully. Simeo [Captain Symes-Thompson] now commands the company. We have a Captain and a subaltern in each company that's all. Recent casualties among officers are, killed: Bernard Gordon Lennox, Tufnell, Stocks, Congleton. Wounded: Pike, Powell, Tudway (who came up with me) Rose ... By the way, I've killed a German or two, not with revolver, rifle of course.'[4]

On 13 November the Grenadiers were still in reserve and were moved to Sanctuary Wood. Arriving at midnight they dug in just before German artillery began to fire on the wood at dawn. In John Lee Steere's letter to his mother dated 14 November he comments amongst other things on the accuracy of the German artillery and the dangers of being buried in collapsing dug outs:

'We are still having a well earned rest, but only just behind the firing line and ready to move in at any moment to any part of the line which wants support ... The Germanoids, as we call them, have a nasty way of finding out where the reserves are and shelling them, so we've been hard at work this morning making dugouts to keep out splinters. I hear it was put in Divisional Orders and even in 1st Army Corps Orders that this battalion was to be given a rest at all costs, but we are so frightfully outnumbered that little rest is possible for any troops. They all say this last 10 days or so (since I've been out here) have been the worst of all, as bad as the retreat from Mons for hard fighting and little rest. All the Brigade and divisions are frightfully mixed up ... they [the Germans] must be getting short by now, their ammunition supply is marvellous, artillery wonderfully accurate. They had our trenches absolutely to the yard the other day. Their infantry very plucky but fire badly, except snipers. [Their] machine guns vastly outnumber ours ... Gilbert Hamilton's [Major Gilbert Hamilton, OC No. 1 Company] dug out has just fallen in and he is gone back to hospital, having been half buried, so you see we have other dangers to face than bullets and shells. This leaves us with enough officers for two per company (full strength 5ish each). Men [are] proportionally low and yet we are comparatively strong, as battalions go out here.'

7 Cavalry Brigade had also been summoned to take part in General FitzClarence's counter-attack on the night of 11 November. Earlier that day the brigade had been reinforced by the three squadrons of the Household Brigade Composite Regiment returning to their parent regiments from 4 Cavalry Brigade. Although the break up of the Composite Regiment was viewed with some sadness by its surviving members, the addition of reinforcements was a much needed boost to the depleted ranks of Kavanagh's Brigade. As it turned out they were not required at Polygon Wood and were ordered to Zwarteleen to relieve the men of 6 Cavalry Brigade. Dawn on 15 November began with the usual shelling of the British positions, 1/Life Guards' war diary noting that no damage was done. At about 3.00 pm Howard St George arrived at headquarters from the advanced trenches to report that in response to the British and French bombardment of the German forward trenches, the enemy appeared to have evacuated from the edge of Zwarteleen Wood. He never made it back to his own trench. On crossing the Zwarteleen-Klein Zillebeke road he was shot dead by a sniper who was lodged in one of the houses overlooking the British line.

Tuesday 17 November 1914 was the last attempt of the German High Command to break the resolve of the Allied defence and end the battle. The Grenadiers were once again back in familiar territory along the Brown Road and despite the shelling that lasted most of the morning, John Lee Steere managed to write what was to be his last letter home:

'*Yesterday was a red letter day for me, 4 letters and a parcel in all … it rains here most days and the trenches are not very comfortable. My feet have not been dry for a week, washed my face once in the last fortnight and have not shaved since I left St Nazaire. Quite a nice beard I can assure you. I looted this pencil off a German dead man, it writes better than my own!*

Today we've been in some very exposed trenches, can't show a finger above ground till it gets dark … I fear this will be a long business, the Germans have so many fresh troops they keep flinging in while we only just have enough to keep them off. All [the] battalions I've seen or heard of are at very low strengths. No more now as its lunchtime and I must help Simeo along the trench.'

It was at lunchtime that the German infantry assault began with the brunt of the attack falling on Number 1 and 2 Companies. Colonel Wilfred Smith's letter to John's parents described the events that led to their son's death:

'*Poor boy! He was killed during a strong infantry attack by the Germans which his company repulsed with considerable slaughter. You will be glad to hear that owing to the steadiness of No. 2 Coy and of No. 1 on the right, the Germans failed to break our line, though at least one German got through and had to be shot behind the trenches. The ground in front of the Grenadier trenches was covered with fallen Germans. No. 1 Coy could count 80 in the first 50 yards. They could not see further owing to the wood. No. 2 must have killed at least as many: and we think the two companies (about 180 rifles) must have killed about 300 Germans.*'

A little more detail was provided by Maurice Arbuthnot, a Grenadier officer and friend of the family who was ADC to General Gough in 1914:

'*I was talking to Beaumont Nesbit the other day and he told me Symes-Thompson was killed by a sniper and word was passed down the trench for John to take command of the company. He came straight up the trench to where Symes-Thompson was lying to make certain he was dead. He then himself tried to do in the sniper who had killed Symes-Thompson, but was shot through the head himself attempting it.*'[5]

In his letter to the Lee Steere family Wilfred Smith concluded by saying that John had done:

'*Outstandingly well during the short time he had been with us, and was rapidly making a valuable officer. He was always happy and cheerful under the most trying conditions … He was buried last night in the small village churchyard of Zillebeke where I am sorry to say six Grenadier officers lie side by side. I hope it may help you to bear your loss to know that your boy was hit doing his duty and doing it well in the presence of a dangerous and heavy German infantry attack.'*

His promotion to lieutenant was published in the *London Gazette* on 9 December 1914.

Tuesday 17 November was also the day that the Coldstream Guards finally left Polygon Wood with orders to move to Zillebeke. Arriving under shellfire all thoughts of a rest were quickly dispelled when the main German attack began and Coldstream companies from both the 2nd and 3rd Battalions were sent up in support. But as to the circumstances of Lance Corporal James Whitfield's death there is no mention in the war diary of any of the battalion being killed in action on that day. We can only assume that he was part of Number 4 Company that was sent to reinforce the Grenadier and Irish Guards in the firing line and was killed sometime during the afternoon or evening. Strangely, Richard Dawson's death is another that went unrecorded in 3/Coldstream Guards' war diary. The rumours that the French were about to relieve 4 (Guards) Brigade became reality on 19 November when the brigade received orders to hand over their trenches the next day. Leave passes were issued to the first batch of officers and NCOs and it looked very much as if the long suffering Coldstream battalions were finally going to have a rest. But the heavy hand of fate had not finished. German shell fire continued throughout the day on 20 November and the regimental history records four men killed and ten wounded, one of dead was Richard Dawson who was struck by a 'high explosive shell that burst some fifty yards away from him.' It was incredibly bad luck; he had been at the front for thirty-four days and was only hours away from being relieved. At 8.00 pm on 20 November 3/Coldstream Guards were relieved by the 122nd French Infantry Regiment and as they marched out through Zillebeke and past the churchyard there would have been many in the battalion who bowed their heads as they passed the wooden cross that marked Richard Dawson's grave.

4/Hussars had missed the Prussian Guard attack of 11 November, having been further south in the Messines area since their relief from the Hollebeke trenches. The regiment returned to the Ypres sector on 19 November to relieve 9/Lancers in the now shell-torn Hooge Chateâu on the Menin Road. It was bitterly cold and owing to the close proximity of the German trenches no fires were allowed; wet clothing soon became as stiff as board and to make matters worse, the Germans opposite were a particularly aggressive bunch. Mortar fire and regular sniping kept the Hussars pinned down in what must have been some of the most miserable conditions they had yet faced. When dawn appeared on 20 November the shelling began and a small trench running from the stable buildings to the chateâu was badly damaged along with the stable buildings. It was in this trench that Alfred Schuster and his troop were deployed and in the ensuing mêlée to escape the shellfire, Alfred fell victim to a German sniper and it was not until it became dark that Captain H Scott, his squadron commander, was able to retrieve his body. Alfred Schuster's death marked the last of the men commemorated in Zillebeke churchyard to be killed in action in 1914 and, like those who had fallen before him, his passing touched the lives of many,

> '*But, perhaps to those who were lucky enough to know, it was his domestic qualities, which to observant eyes, shone with the most steady brilliance, his unselfishness and companionability whether as son, grandson, brother or friend, the mixture in him of thorough education with natural taste, quick wit with the kindliest sympathy, physical courage with the gentleness of a woman, and a modesty of mind such as it rarely met with. He was one of the few who made nearly as many friends as acquaintances.*'[6]

On 22 November GHQ issued a special order of the day from Sir John French to be read out to all ranks of the BEF:

> '*I have made many calls upon you, and the answers you have made to them have covered you, your regiments, and the army to which you belong, with honour and glory. Your fighting qualities, courage and endurance, have been subjected to the most trying and severe tests, and you have proved yourselves worthy descendants of the British soldiers of the past, who have built up the magnificent traditions of the regiments to which you belong. You have not only maintained those traditions, but you have materially added to their lustre. It is impossible for me to find words in which to express my appreciation of the splendid services you have performed.*'

Although written for the living, his words were a fitting epitaph for the dead who now rested in the Zillebeke churchyard.

Chapter 11

After the Battle

How wealthy families chose to commemorate their loved ones killed in the Great War is worthy of a book in itself. The profusion of stained glass windows and memorial tablets which appeared in churches across the land is, even to this day, not fully documented. Memorials came in all shapes and sizes at home and, once the war had been concluded, soon spilled over to the abandoned and shattered battlefields of France and Flanders. The notion of permanent memorials to the fallen became so deeply embedded in the post-war psyche that Winston Churchill seriously advocated that the piles of rubble that had once been the splendour of Ypres should not be rebuilt but remain as a memorial to the hundreds of thousands of British, Empire and Dominions soldiers who had died in defending the Salient. Fortunately good sense prevailed and Ypres was almost rebuilt when the German Army entered the city in May 1940; a feat that had eluded them during the four years of the Great War.

The research into the whereabouts of memorials in the United Kingdom commemorating the men of the Zillebeke churchyard developed into a fascinating and intricate piece of detective work. Apart from the more obvious national memorials, I expected there would be inscriptions on local war memorials and occasional tablets in local churches; but rather naively perhaps, I did not fully appreciate the extent of the national outpouring of grief that accompanied the casualty lists and how that manifested itself into remembrance in the post-war years.

The news of Robert Rising's death in action reached Norfolk via the usual telegram expressing the sorrow and sympathy felt by the King and Queen in 'the loss you and the army have sustained by the death of your husband in the service of his country.' Constance had expected him home for Christmas, but being a realist, Robert would have recognized by late October 1914 that the likelihood of the war being over for Christmas was remote. His last hours before he died on 7 November were spent in the battalion dressing station which had initially taken over a cottage in Zwarteleen. The battalion had sustained another ninety casualties during the day and at roll call on the evening of 7 November only 213 men and four officers were present. The story of the Gloucesters at Ypres did not end there, they were fighting again on 11 November alongside 2/Grenadier Guards when the Prussian Guard attacked either side of the Menin Road and it was only six days later, on 17 November, that they were finally taken out of the front line.

Captain Harold Richmond's tour of duty in 1914 as a staff captain with GHQ ended abruptly in late November when Lieutenant Colonel Lovett asked that he rejoin the depleted ranks of the 1st Battalion. Most of the battalion's veteran officers had been either killed or wounded and Richmond's experience was badly needed to assist in rebuilding the battalion. Ten days after Robert Rising's death he took over command of D Company and was killed less than a month later at La Bassée. Colonel Lovett did not remain in command of 3 Brigade for long; in December 1914 he was back in command of the 1st Battalion but in February 1915 he was sent home ill. Appointed to the Home Command as GOC Yorkshire Coast Defences, Brigadier General Lovett died on 27 May 1919. Brigadier General Landon after taking over temporary command of the 1st Division was appointed to command the 9th (Scottish) Division in 1915 and despite Haig writing in his diary in August 1915 that, 'he daily goes down in [General Gough's] estimation as a commander, on account of his indecision and lack of thoroughness,' he later commanded both the 33rd and 35th Divisions.

Robert's promotion to Major was announced in the *London Gazette* on 18 January 1915 and a month later his name was mentioned in despatches for his leadership and gallantry at Gheluvelt. Constance Rising became a wealthy woman when her father died but never remarried; eventually settling in the Somerset village of Winscombe with the children. Passenger records tell us that she travelled widely between the wars with her daughter Elsie to destinations in Europe and others such as Egypt, South Africa and Madeira. Little more is known of the children. Robert Edis Rising married in 1931 and again in 1947; he died in 1970 aged 65. Constance lived at Bridge House in Winscombe until April 1961 when she died aged 84. She now rests in the churchyard of St James the Great. Elsie remains a mystery, although there is some evidence to suggest she died before her mother and both mother and daughter are in the same grave at Winscombe. In Norfolk, Robert's brother, Arthur, continued in the family business and does not appear to have fought in the Great War. He died in December 1955 aged 83 and is buried in the churchyard at Ormsby St Margaret with his wife Ellen and his parents. Robert Rising's name is commemorated on the Ormsby War Memorial and on the Charterhouse Roll of Honour.

The *London Gazette* of 17 February 1915 also carried the names of Gordon Wilson, Richard Dawson, Harry Parnell and Charles FitzClarence, all of whom had been mentioned in Sir John French's sixth despatch of the war for 'gallantry and meritorious conduct in the field.' After Gordon Wilson's death Lord Tweedmouth took over command of the Blues and one of his first duties was to write to Lady Sarah. Sarah was still in France running her hospital at Bolougne which complicated matters a little in that the regiment was unsure how to get in touch with her:

> *'I sent you a telegram yesterday but did not know your address in France so thought it would be forwarded to you [from London]. I cannot express my sympathy sufficiently with you over poor Gordon's loss, and it was a great disaster to us as a regiment: he was so active and keen, brave as a lion and full of sympathy for the men and officers. I feel his loss tremendously, as we had been so much together during the last month, and he has been very kind to me ... I wish I could offer you more comfort: but you can think that he died like a brave man and that his loss is impressed most deeply on us all.'*

There is an interesting letter dated 30 November 1914 written by Surgeon Major Basil Pares to Lady Sarah that provides a hint of the precarious state of the British line on the night of 6 November:

> *'I can't tell you how we miss our Colonel; but I'm glad we were able to take him to Zillebeke the same night. I doubt if we could have done so afterwards.'*

The fact that Pares felt recovering Gordon Wilson's body would have been difficult, if not impossible, underlines the closeness of the German lines. A detail which makes the midnight dash by two Life Guard troopers to recover Regy Wyndham's body all the more courageous an act.

Wilson's effects were gathered together by his brother Bertie and sent back to England with an officer who was returning home on leave. When they were finally unpacked by Lady Sarah a small newspaper clipping was discovered in his writing case containing two lines of the James Handley epitaph: 'Life is a city of crooked streets.' After the war when she was contacted by the CWGC and asked for a suitable epitaph for Gordon's headstone at Zillebeke she used James Handley's words:

> *'Life is a city of crooked streets*
> *Death the market place where all men meet.'*

Gordon Wilson had in effect written his own epitaph. His brother Bertie was killed during the battle of Arras on 11 April 1917 when the regiment was fighting at Monchy-le-Preux. He is buried at the Faubourg D'Amiens Cemetery near the Citadel at Arras.[1] In 1925 the surviving Wilson family members paid for a stained glass window to be erected in the Commonwealth

Church at Great Audley Street in Mayfair. The window was dedicated to Jean Wilson and her three soldier sons who had given their lives.

Sadly for Lady Sarah her husband was not the only member of her family to give his life during the battle for Ypres. Brigadier General Charles FitzClarence, the VC winner she knew during the siege of Mafeking in 1899 and had earlier introduced to her cousin Violet, was one of the few British senior officers to be killed in the Great War. In the four years of fighting almost eighty officers holding the rank of brigadier general and above were killed in action or died of wounds. Charles FitzClarence was 49-years-old when he died and is the highest ranking officer inscribed on the Menin Gate Memorial at Ypres. He is also remembered with a tablet in the Guards Chapel in London. As for Lady Sarah Wilson, she remained a widow and died in October 1929.

The Guards Chapel on Birdcage Walk is also where the Tufnell family chose to remember their dead. A brass plaque commemorates three members of the family: Carleton Wyndham Tufnell, his nephew, Hugh John Tufnell, who was killed in North Africa in 1944 serving with the Grenadier Guards, and his eldest brother, Neville Charsley Tufnell, who died in 1951. Neville was commissioned into the 1st Volunteer Battalion (later 4th Battalion), Queen's (Royal West Surrey) Regiment in 1908, transferring to the Grenadier Guards Special Reserve shortly after war was declared. He joined the 3rd Battalion at Simencourt in December 1917 and commanded Number 3 Company for the remainder of the conflict. In 1939 he was appointed lieutenant colonel and transferred to the King's Royal Rifle Corps. He perpetuated the family sporting ability and played for Cambridge University and the Marylebone Cricket Club. He also played one Test Match for England at Cape Town against South Africa in 1909.

Richard Dawson had no other immediate family except for his mother Jane and only surviving sister, Norah. His uncle, Vesey Dawson, the 2nd Earl of Dartrey, had married in 1882 and had two daughters. He was succeeded in the Earldom by the Hon Anthony Lucius Dawson, youngest and only surviving son of Richard's grandfather, the first Earl of Dartrey. The 3rd Earl died without issue in 1933, after which all the family honours became extinct. Had Richard survived the Great War he may well have become the 4th Earl of Dartrey. His name is commemorated along with thirteen others on the Holne War Memorial, as is young Arthur Pearce, the Hall Boy from Holne House who was killed on 27 May 1918 in the fighting around Marfaux. After the war Richard's mother had a stained glass window put in the south-eastern corner of the church of St Mary the Virgin at Holne, together with a marble tablet in memory of her son. By 1984 the window was in a poor state of repair and the Coldstream Guards regimental fund contributed £100 for its maintenance.

Harry Parnell was mentioned in despatches for his part in holding the line at Zwarteleen on 6 and 7 November 1914. He was highly regarded by his commanding officer and since joining the battalion in September 1914 had shown on a number of occasions his potential for battlefield leadership. Had he lived, promotion to captain and the command of a company would not have been long in coming. Writing to Lady Congleton in 1915, William Spooner remembers his former student at New College as, 'an honourable and kindly man, very loyal to his friends and with a fine courage.' It was to the family's Mayfair address in London that the telegram carrying the news of Harry's death was sent and it was from there that the official announcement was made that the heir presumptive to the title, John Brooke Molesworth Parnell, had succeeded him as the 6th Baron Congleton. Educated at the Royal Naval College at Dartmouth, John was a serving naval officer during the Great War and had followed in the footsteps of his grandfather who fought in the Battle of Navarino in 1827 as a midshipman aboard HMS *Glasgow*.

But the indelible mark of the Great War had not finished with the Parnell family. Harry's youngest brother, William Alastair Damer Parnell, joined his brother's old battalion on 21 August 1915, just in time to take part in the battle of Loos.[2] Like his brother he was quickly recognized as a brave and resourceful officer and in December 1915 was awarded the Military Cross for his leadership and gallantry during a fighting patrol into enemy trenches. Tragically he was killed nine months later on 25 September 1916 during the Somme offensive; he was 22-years-old. The Somme also claimed the life of one of Harry's cousins, Major Geoffrey Brooke Parnell, who died fighting with the 1st Battalion of the Queen's (Royal West Surrey) Regiment on 15 July 1916.[3] Poor Lady Congleton never really recovered from losing two of her sons and a nephew and she died fifteen years later in 1931. Both Harry and his brother William are commemorated on one of the panels in the Royal Gallery of the House of Lords.

The death of Bernard Gordon Lennox was widely reported in the home and international press. He was mentioned in despatches in the *London Gazette* of 7 April 1915 and the *New York Times* of 13 November 1914 carried an article entitled 'Duke's Son Killed in Battle in France,' but erroneously reported his elder brother, Charles Henry, the Earl of March, was serving at the front as a major in the Sussex Yeomanry. In November 1914 the Sussex Yeomanry were still in Sussex and would not see action until they arrived on the Gallipoli Peninsula in 1915. Charles Henry sadly became ill on the eve of departure and was never to command his regiment in action.

Esme Gordon Lennox recovered from his wounds received at Zandvoorde and after the battle of Loos in 1915 took over command of the 1st Battalion Scots Guards. Shortly before the Somme offensive began in July 1916, he was seconded to Fourth Army Headquarters and soon after was given command of 95 Infantry Brigade. He was wounded on a second occasion in April 1918 but survived the war having been mentioned in despatches twice and decorated with the DSO. He died in 1949. Bernard's nephew Charles Henry Gordon Lennox, Lord Settrington, joined 2/Irish Guards in July 1916 as a Second Lieutenant. In March 1918 he was taken prisoner when fighting with the 3rd Battalion at Vieux-Berquin and only returned to England in December 1918. However, his war was not over. Attached to the Fusiliers as a signals officer he was dispatched to Russia with the North Russian Relief Force in May 1919. This disastrous foray into Russia was prompted by the fear of Bolshevism spreading across Europe in the wake of the 1917 Russian Revolution. Allied forces openly intervened in the Russian Civil War by giving support to the pro-Tsarist, anti-Bolshevik White forces. Charles died of wounds in August 1919 and was buried at the Archangel Allied Cemetery. He was only 20-years-old.

Both Charles and Bernard are commemorated with a plaque on the Waterbeach Lodge gate to Goodwood Park. In addition to being present in the Royal Gallery of the House of Lords, Bernard's name is also on the Boxgrove Priory War Memorial in the northwest corner of the priory church of St Mary and Blaise. Charles has a separate memorial on the west wall. The final memorial to Bernard is located in the small Gordon Chapel, tucked away behind the High Street at Fochabers in northeast Scotland. Here there is a stained glass window dedicated to Bernard depicting St George killing the dragon which was probably made by William Morris & Company. Bernard's wife, Lady Evelyn, did not remarry and continued to live at the family home at the nearby Halnaker House until her death in 1944 when she tragically fell victim to a German air raid.

There was one other Gordon Lennox who fought with the Grenadier Guards in the Great War. Victor Charles Gordon Lennox was a cousin to Bernard and was appointed to the 5th Reserve Battalion in early 1915. Posted to the 1st Battalion he was wounded in one of the last skirmishes of the Somme offensive at Gueudecourt. He subsequently returned to duty and survived the war.

Petworth House, where Regy Wyndham was born, is a twenty minute car journey from Goodwood and basks in the Arthur Mee accolade of being described as the 'greatest house in Sussex.' Set in a vast Capability Brown landscaped deer park, the house was considerably developed by the 3rd Earl of Egremont during the early part of the nineteenth century. Regy's grandfather, the 1st Lord Leconfield, made very few changes to Petworth and it was left to Regy's father Henry to complete the alterations at the south end of the house. In 1947 the 3rd Lord Leconfield gave the house and park with an endowment to the National Trust although the current Lord Leconfield, John Max Henry Scawen Wyndham, 2nd Baron Egremont and 7th Baron Leconfield, continues to live in the south wing with his family.

Edward Scawen Wyndham, who had been wounded at Messines serving with the Composite Household Cavalry Regiment, recovered from his wounds and was mentioned in despatches in November 1914. A month later the *London*

Gazette reported his award of the DSO. Edward returned to France in May 1915 and survived the war. Regy's death gained coverage in the national and local press; the local Grantham paper printed his obituary a week after his death, highlighting his love of horses and racing, while *The Times* of 14 November 1914 drew attention to his 'delightful humour' and wrote of his selfless behaviour towards others, a facet of his character that so endeared his men to him in Belgium:

> *'Among his intimates he was called, after his favourite horse, The White Knight ... but to those who knew him best the name had a deeper meaning ... his thoughtfulness for others, his forgetfulness of himself – all indeed, that may be summed up in the old word chivalry, while along the difficult paths of colonial life, the turf and society, he maintained those high standards of conduct and honour that are looked for from the stainless knight.'*

Before the war Regy was resident for much of the winter in the Lincolnshire town of Grantham where he had a house on the North Parade. Being resident at Grantham gave him the opportunity to pursue his great love in life by riding with the Cottesmore and Belvoir Hunts. In 1929 his mother, Lady Constance, donated £1,000 towards a memorial to perpetuate the memory of her son. In response Grantham Town Council elected to create the Wyndham Memorial Park by changing the name of the town's Slate Mill Park. The scheme, begun in 1922, cost about £5,000, whereby about 400 unemployed, many of them old soldiers, were paid by the Board of Guardians the standard unemployment rate of 1 shilling (5p) an hour. In July 1924 Lady Leconfield officially opened the park in memory of her son. Apart from Regy's name being commemorated on the St Wulfran War Memorial at Grantham and in the Royal Gallery of the House of Lords, his name is also inscribed on the Petworth War Memorial which stands outside the parish church of St Mary.

*   *   *

Generally speaking, war memorials before the two conflicts with the Boers in South Africa, were designed to celebrate victory in battle. With the advent of the citizen volunteer, particularly in the second South African War of 1899–1902, this trend was to some degree reversed with the first ever mass raising of war memorials in this country. In 1918, after the Great War, an event which saw the creation of the largest army ever fielded by a British government, war memorials appeared on village greens, market squares and churchyards in every town, village and hamlet in the UK. Numerous memorials along the lines of the Wyndham Memorial Park were built and funded by those with more wealth, who perhaps envisaged a more lavish and communal memorial to their loved ones.

Such was the case with the Lee Steere family at Ockley when they designed and paid for the village hall in 1923 as a permanent memorial to John and the others of Ockley who were killed in the conflict. The hall still serves its community to this day and inside there is a large painting of John in the uniform of a Grenadier Guards officer, below which is a plaque which reads:

'To the dear and honoured memory of John Lee Steere, Grenadier Guards, and his cousins. Died 1914: Philip Van Neck, Grenadier Guards, Charles Van Neck, Northumberland Fusiliers and Cholmeley Symes-Thompson, Grenadier Guards. 1915, A. Phipps Turnbull, 10th Light Horse, West Australia; 1918, Edward A. Roberts, 44th Battalion, West Australia and, 1919, Chauncey Stigand, 1st Royal West Kent; who all fell in action.'

Cousin Alexander Phipps Turnbull was a Second Lieutenant serving with the 10th Australian Light Horse Regiment when they were sent to Gallipoli in April 1915.[4] The legendary 3rd Light Horse Brigade's dismounted charge at The Nek on 7 August 1915 resulted in 372 casualties of which 234 were killed including Alexander Turnbull. Fellow Australian Private Edward Augustus Roberts was killed with the 44th Australian Infantry Battalion during the German offensive on 28 March 1918.[5] Major Chauncey Hugh Stigand died in the Sudan attached to the Egyptian Army in December 1919.[6] There is a further memorial to John in St Margaret's Church at Ockley consisting of a marble mosaic in the chancel and a tablet on the south wall.

In 1915 John's mother commissioned the well-known portrait painter Sir Phillip Burne-Jones to paint a likeness of her son from a photograph. In order to provide some authenticity she also arranged through her sister, Grace Van Neck, to have his dress uniform delivered to Burne-Jones at his London address, presumably for the artist's model to wear. Burne-Jones was the son of the famous Pre-Raphaelite painter Sir Edward Burne-Jones who died in 1898 and was an established society painter of wealthy socialites. It appears from correspondence between Anna Lee Steere and Burne-Jones that he offered to paint the portrait but the final work was rejected by Anna. In an intriguing letter dated 5 May 1915, Burne-Jones wrote to Anna apologizing for his failure in producing an acceptable likeness of John:

'There does not seem anything for me to say, except to express my very real regret that I have failed so unhappily in the work I had such bright hopes about. Perhaps the sad and unusual circumstances may be some excuse for me ... and in frankly telling me that I have not succeeded in recalling the face you loved, you have filled your part of the bargain.'

There is a final instalment to the Lee Steere story. Twenty-six years later, when the next generation donned uniform to complete what had been started in 1914, Flanders was destined to be the last resting place of another family member. Flying a Hurricane with 601 (City of London) Squadron, Flying Officer Charles Augustus Lee Steere was posted missing on 27 May 1940 while taking part in one of the many air operations that covered the BEF's retreat to Dunkirk. He is the only British airman buried at the Oostkerke Communal Cemetery, a short forty minute car journey from his young cousin at Zillebeke churchyard.

John Lee Steere's cousin, Cholmeley Symes-Thompson, is remembered with a tablet on the south wall of the nave at the church of St Michael at Finmere in Oxfordshire. His name is also on the village war memorial. The Symes-Thompson family is still remembered in the village to this day despite having finally moved in 1967 and although the estate was sold off, the house is still standing, albeit unoccupied and in a poor state of repair. Cholmeley's parents, Edmund who died in 1906 and Elizabeth who died in 1920, are buried in the village churchyard, as is his wife Grace, who died in 1940. Grace's headstone also records the death of Sybil Laura Lassen in 2005, the small child that Cholmeley last held in his arms just before he embarked for France in August 1914.

Many families were inconsolably torn apart by the deaths of their sons. As heir to the Petersen shipping empire, William's death in November 1914 was a severe blow to his parents. His death at Ypres may well have been an underlying factor in his mother's tragic death in 1918 by drowning in her bath at the family residence at Portland Place. Known for his prodigious work ethic, Sir William Petersen dealt with this double tragedy by immersing himself further in his work; which probably contributed to his sudden heart attack in June 1925 while in Canada. The previous year his island home on Eigg had been totally destroyed by fire and this, and the fact he had been ill for a while before his death, could only have exacerbated matters. His body was brought back to England on board the SS *Melitia* accompanied by the Canadian Prime Minister's secretary. His memorial service was held at the Church of St Clement Dane in London. Second Lieutenant William Petersen's name is to be found on the Glenalmond School War Memorial which was unveiled in 1922 at the east end of the school chapel. Designed by Sir John Ninian Comper the memorial contains the names of the 157 old boys of the school who lost their lives in the Great War.

Another family which was shattered by the death of their soldier son was the Stocks family. Michael Stocks and his cousin Francis Levita are commemorated on the rather dramatic broken column in the churchyard of St Helens at Boultham, Lincoln that was erected by Michael's maternal grandfather Sir George Ellison. Francis was the only son of the Levita family; the broken column indicating he was the last of the male line. The inscription on three sides of the monument is dedicated to three members of the family: George Paget Ellison who, as a Captain in the 9th Lancers, died of enteric fever in 1902 at Kroonstad in South Africa, Francis Ellison Levita and Michael George Stocks.

I can only imagine the despair at the Gibson household in Ilford when the news of William's death arrived by post. The long casualty lists that featured daily in the pages of the press would have already listed several of William's friends, prompting fears for their own son, particularly as the London Scottish had already lost heavily at Messines in October. The family was a large one and apart from William's father, John, who was employed as a Managing Clerk at a local Ilford tea merchant, four of the grown-up Gibson children still lived at home along with William's mother, Janet. She must have had her heart in her mouth when she waved goodbye to William's younger brothers, John and Sydney Gibson. John joined the 22nd Battalion London Regiment and Sydney the King's Royal Rifle Corps and in 1918 it was only John who returned home to 38, Mayfair Avenue. Sydney was killed serving with the 18th Battalion on 15 September 1916 on the Somme battlefield and as his body was not recovered his name was added to those on the Thiepval Memorial to the Missing.[7] Anxious that Sydney should have a headstone his parents had his name engraved on William's headstone at Zillebeke. At the London Scottish Regimental Headquarters at Horseferry Road in Westminster, William's name is included on the huge memorial that surrounds the fireplace in the main hall.

Walter Siewertsen's death also affected his parents deeply and the family home displayed a photograph of him up until his mother died in March 1954. Walter's father died heartbroken in 1946 and family legend has it that he was buried with Walter's campaign medals. They are both buried in pauper's graves at the City of London Cemetery at Manor Park. The name of James Whitfield, the Coldstream NCO who was killed ten days after Walter Siewertsen, is inscribed on the Medomsley War Memorial that was unveiled in March 1921 by Stanley Robert Vereker, who later became the 7th Viscount Gort. Strangely, the memorial cross was first erected in a field on the outskirts of the village but was eventually relocated in the centre of the village near the church. The Whitfield house in the row of terraces where the family lived still stands but the Medomsley Pit was closed in 1972.

In 1914 the St George family was living at the Ashorne Hill estate near Leamington Spa in Warwickshire when they received the news that Howard had been killed near Ypres. Inconsolable at her son's death Evelyn St George used her immense wealth to bequeath a number of memorials to commemorate his memory. The first of these was inside the church of St George the Martyr at Newbold Pacey where Evelyn paid for a wall plaque to be erected. Howard is also remembered on the village war memorial, but these were small tokens of remembrance in comparison to those that followed. One of the more noteworthy was the Ivan Mestrovic wood carving 'Descent from the Cross', which was exhibited in the Victoria and Albert Museum in 1915. The significance of the relief in the context of the war was not lost on Evelyn and she purchased the work directly from the artist. The Mestrovic relief recently sold at Sotheby's for over £200,000. Evelyn was an enthusiastic and knowledgeable collector of art and before her death in 1936 she had amongst her collection several works by Cezanne, Van Gogh and El Greco. Apart from the stained glass window at Zillebeke church, she also financed the St George ward of the American Women's War Relief Hospital at Oldway House, near Paignton in Devon.

* * *

The culture of celebrating and honouring the war dead was very much part of the public school ethos. In the Great War between thirty-five and forty per cent of all officers from the leading public schools were decorated for gallantry and some twenty per cent were killed or died of wounds. Twenty-six public schools had two or more recipients of the Victoria Cross with Eton and Harrow winning thirty-one between them. Over 3,500 Old Carthusians served in the Great War and by the end of 1914 the school chapel was no longer large enough to comfortably accommodate the growing numbers of boys and masters who had been killed in action. In 1917 a War Memorial Fund was inaugurated and post-war a new chapel, Memorial Chapel, designed by Sir Giles Gilbert Scott, was built in honour of the fallen. Their names are commemorated on stone panels set in the eastern half walls of the antechapel and included amongst them are Robert Rising and Alfred Schuster.

Both Alfred's brothers survived the war. Edgar began his military service in Salonika as a lieutenant and after contracting a severe bout of malaria was brought back to England in a very poor state. Eventually he was seconded in 1917 to work with the Medical Research Committee after some considerable string-pulling by the MPs Sir Samuel Scott and the Hon Waldorf Astor. After the war he remained part-time with the council until 1938. Edgar died in 1969. George Schuster arrived in France on 22 August 1915 to join the Oxfordshire Hussars. A series of staff appointments followed with the artillery, eventually culminating with an appointment at First Army Headquarters with the rank of major in 1918. He was awarded the Military Cross in the King's Birthday Honours List in June 1918. In 1919 he was promoted to lieutenant colonel and sent to North Russia with the Expeditionary Force as Chief Operational Staff Officer. A long and illustrious political career followed; he was knighted in 1925 and died aged 101 in 1982 at the family home at Nether Worton in Oxfordshire.

Apart from the plaque inside Zillebeke church and the Charterhouse Roll of Honour, other memorials that were erected by the family to perpetuate Alfred's memory were difficult to find. However, it was almost completely by accident that a stained glass window commissioned in his memory was found in the small church of St Brendan in the Devonshire village of Bredon. The inscription in the left light of the window reads, 'Well done good and faithful servant. In memory of Alfred Schuster – Lieut 4th (Queen's Own) Hussars'. In the right hand light is inscribed, 'Enter thou unto the day of our Lord. Born 30th July 1883 Killed in action near Ypres 20th November 1914.' We shall probably never know why the rather remote village of Bredon was chosen, maybe there was a family connection there, or it was a place he was particularly fond of, especially as he regularly hunted with the Devon and Somerset Staghounds. It was a family connection that led to the second memorial. In the Nether Worton parish church of St James is a rectangular marble family tablet dedicated to Sir George Schuster's son Richard who was killed in 1941 serving with the Middlesex Yeomanry and also to the uncle he never met, Alfred Schuster.

The memorial to the fallen at Eton College takes the form of a striking bronze frieze in the Colonnade below Upper School which honours the 1,157 Old Etonians who died in the War. This is in addition to the War Memorial Chapel and the memorial plaques that are to be found on the walls of the Cloisters. The Cloisters provide a rather sombre, almost neo-classical backdrop to the seemingly endless names of war dead. On the left of the entrance are the names of Bernard Gordon Lennox, Michael Stocks, Carleton Tufnell, Chomeley Symes-Thompson and Harry Parnell on the Grenadier Guards memorial plaque.

At Harrow School the old boys are commemorated in the War Memorial Building which was completed in 1926 and contains the school Roll of Honour together with the VC banners commemorating the holders of the Victoria Cross. John Lee Steere's cousin, Charles Hylton Van Neck, and Captain Norman Neill are remembered on the Harrow Roll of Honour. Norman Neill's name is also amongst the thirty-nine men inscribed on the Merrow village War Memorial in Surrey. The Harrow School memorials to its dead include those of its former students who were killed in the Crimean War; in the school chapel there is a window over the door of the crypt to the memory of one of Richard Dawson's soldier ancestors, Lieutenant Colonel Hon T Vesey Dawson, who was killed at Inkerman in 1854.

I could find no memorial placed by the family, apart from the bells at Zillebeke Church, which remembers the name of Alexis de Gunzburg. However, the Holy Trinity Church at Windsor contains memorials to the Household Cavalry and Brigade of Guards. The chancel screen was specially made to remember those of the Household Cavalry who fell in the war and was unveiled by Lieutenant Colonel Tweedmouth on 6 October 1921. Alexis de Gunzburg, together with all those of the Household Cavalry and Brigade of Guards who fell in the Great War, is recorded in three books of remembrance.

* * *

The Great War of 1914–1918 was a tragedy which was experienced by individuals, communities and whole nations In Great Britain it was remembered and commemorated at each of these three levels. For many individuals who had suffered the loss of loved ones in the conflict, a pilgrimage to the battlefield cemeteries and memorials was the only way of finding closure and consigning the dead to memory. Apart from the Baroness de Gunzburg who made the journey to see her son's grave when the bells were hung in the new church, exactly how many of the other relatives of the Zillebeke churchyard men made the journey is impossible to tell. But some would have undoubtedly made the journey and possibly travelled with organizations such as the British Legion, Salvation Army and the YMCA. Between November 1919 and June 1920 the Salvation Army conducted over 5,000 relatives to France and Belgium while the YMCA assisted some 60,000 people to make the pilgrimage up to the end of 1923. However, for the very poor, such as the Siewertsen family, even these subsidized travel arrangements would have been beyond their means.

For the more affluent families the cost of travel would not have been an issue and I would be most surprised if the Zillebeke churchyard was not visited after the war by Evelyn St George and Henry and Anna Lee Steere. Continental travel was a pastime that individuals such as Lady Elizabeth Congleton would have been quite familiar with, so a relatively short journey to Belgium with other family members would have been easily accomplished. We know that Constance Rising travelled widely between the wars, and again, it is unlikely that she did not visit her husband's grave.

A number of regimental associations organized their own visits to coincide with the unveiling of battlefield memorials. Typical of this was the Household Cavalry party that travelled to Ypres for the Household Cavalry Memorial ceremony at Zandvoorde on Sunday, 4 May 1924. Arrangements were made with Thomas Cook to convey the group and organize the travel arrangements. Regimental funds were made available to assist those who were unable to afford the £3 to travel third class (£4.15s for First Class). Lady Sarah Wilson and Regy Wyndham's sisters and mother, Lady Constance Wyndham, may well have been in this party. The memorial to all the Household Cavalrymen who fell between 4 August and 31 December 1914 was unveiled by Field Marshal Earl Haig and was erected on the spot where the body of Lieutenant Lord Worsley was found after the war. The memorial is said to have been paid for by Charles Worsley's father, the Earl of Yarborough. Standing in front of the memorial today the battlefield visitor can look out over the ground that was defended by 7 Cavalry Brigade on the morning of 30 October 1914. Behind are the names of Gordon Wilson, Norman Neill, Regy Wyndham, Alexis de Gunzburg, Howard St George and William Petersen which are amongst the host of names inscribed on the stone column. Be there early on a cold October morning and you can almost hear the sounds of battle.

From the Zandvoorde Ridge it is a short journey across to the Menin Road which still runs along its original 1914 course. Just east of Hooge, where the road bends slightly, is a spot which was known by the troops as Clapham Junction. The memorial to the men of the Gloucestershire Regiment is here, very close to the point where Robert Rising crossed the Menin Road with the 1st Battalion on his way to Zwarteleen on 6 November 1914. A similar memorial on the N365 road between Wytschaete and Messines was unveiled in May 1924 by Albert, King of the Belgians and remembers William Gibson and the London Scottish. The memorial is in the form of a large St Andrew's cross which is on, or very near, the site of the mill which marked the point where the battalion made their charge on 31 October 1914. Present at the ceremony were relatives of those men who fell in 1914 and very possibly the Gibson family was there also.

By far the largest of the memorials in the Ypres Salient is the Menin Gate which was designed by the British architect Sir Reginald Blomfield and officially inaugurated on Sunday, 24 July 1927. Blomfield's design combines the architectural images of a classical victory arch and a mausoleum and contains enormous panels into which are carved the names of the 54,896 officers and men of the British and Commonwealth forces who died in the Ypres Salient area and who have no known graves. Alfred Schuster has his name here as does the Hon Arthur O'Neill and Cabby Dawes, Regy Wyndham's troop sergeant.

In 1939 a new group of visitors arrived at the memorials and cemeteries around Ypres. This time it was the soldiers of a second BEF who saw first hand the sacrifice made by their fathers in the 'war to end all wars.' One young Royal Engineers officer, who was later to become better known as the writer and poet, Anthony Rhodes, recorded his visit to the war graves at Ypres with a poem he entitled 'Repetition'.[8]

'Dirty grey of the day at a Flanders dawn
Breaks down on the graves where old Englishmen born
For the earth of old England store up their infinite days
Never knowing their sons in similar ways
Will shatter themselves, their marrow and rust
In search of a similar dust'

Perhaps it was just as well that the men who lie in Zillebeke churchyard would be 'never knowing' that despite their sacrifice, the generation they hoped would enjoy a lasting peace was about to take up the gauntlet once again.

Other Burials at Zillebeke

Lieutenant Colonel Arthur de Courcy Scott: 1st Battalion, The Cheshire Regiment

Grave: H.3.

Arthur de Courcy Scott is one of only two officers with a headstone at Zillebeke who was not a casualty of 1914. The 1st Battalion Cheshire Regiment (1/Cheshire) spent October 1914 on the II Corps front until 7 November when it arrived in the Ypres sector just in time for the Prussian Guard attack on 11 November. The battalion was still desperately short of experienced officers and Scott was transferred from the 2nd Battalion to be its new commanding officer in late November 1914. This appointment, from all accounts a popular one, was to last less than six months.

On 4 May 1915, 1/Cheshire was resting in dugouts under the ramparts that surrounded Ypres. At 8.45 am the Germans released a gas attack on the British line enabling the German forward troops to take over a substantial portion of the now abandoned British positions on the lower slopes of Hill 60. The Second Battle of Ypres had begun and 1/Cheshire was rushed up to help fill the gap in the line. Arthur De Courcy Scott was killed two days later on 6 May. The regimental history recorded his passing thus:

> 'The regiment suffered a very severe loss when Colonel A de C Scott was killed. 'Bro' Scott was much loved by all ranks. His abilities were of a scholarly type, all too rare in our service.'

Born in 1866, Arthur de Courcy Scott was the son of Major General Alexander de Courcy Scott of the Royal Engineers. He was educated at Wellington College from 1879 until 1883 after which he entered Sandhurst as a gentleman cadet. In 1885 he was commissioned into the Cheshire Regiment, joining the 2nd Battalion in India. His marriage to Phyllis Katharine Wilson came comparatively late in life and took place in Madras during October 1905. Scott was 39 and his young bride was 20. Two years later Rosalind Enid was born and in 1907 Phyllis gave birth to their son, Herbert.

12647 Lance Corporal Neil Thomson: 11th Battalion, The Royal Scots

Grave: J.1.
Neil Thomson was killed on 9 December 1915 whilst his battalion was at Dickebusch providing 'large fatigue parties under brigade orders'. This could have been anything from digging trenches or erecting and repairing barbed wire defences to unloading and transporting stores. Well aware that this type of activity was carried out during the hours of darkness, gunners on both sides would target likely communication routes and assembly areas behind the lines opposite with high explosive shells in the knowledge they were bound to hit something eventually. Neil Thomson was a victim of this random shell fire. The 11th, 12th and 13th Battalions were raised in August 1914 in Edinburgh, with the 11th and 12th being allocated to the 9th (Scottish) Division. They moved to France in May 1915 and first saw action at the Battle of Loos, where the 11th Battalion was almost wiped out. The Thomson family farmed Crosscroes Farm at Fauldhouse, West Lothian.

13239 Private William Stewart: 11th Battalion, The Royal Scots

Grave: Special Memorial 2.
William Stewart was born at Harwich in 1896 where his father worked as a boatman for the Customs and Excise Service. His parents, William and Susannah Stewart, returned to Scotland with their five children at the turn of the century where William was employed as a second class boatman at the port of Greenock. His work with the customs service included 'rummage' duties as part of the prevention of smuggling by ships and their crews arriving from foreign ports by searching vessels for contraband. During this period the family lived at 2, Wemyss Bay Street. It is probable that on the outbreak of war in August 1914 the 19-year-old William was also working with his father as a boatman before enlisting in the 11th Battalion, Royal Scots. By December 1915 William was in Sanctuary Wood where the battalion was ordered to supply working parties to repair trenches. He was killed on 16 December 1915 when his working party was shelled.

27611 Corporal Charles Coyde: 15th Battalion (Central Ontario), Canadian Expeditionary Force (CEF)

Grave: C.4.
Charles Coyde was born on the island of Guernsey in November 1892 and was the only son of Charles and Isabella. In 1901 the family were living at 41, Upper

St Jacques Road, St Peter Port but by 1914 the address had changed to Queen's Road. His father worked as a market gardener and his mother was employed as a housekeeper. Charles worked initially as a commercial traveller but in June 1914 he left Southampton on the SS *Ascania* for Quebec. On arrival in Canada Charles found work as a lumberjack in the Quebec area before enlisting on 9 September 1914 at Valcartier.

The battalion embarked at Quebec on 3 October 1914 aboard the SS *Megantic*, disembarking in England on 14 October 1914. Four months later on 14 February 1915, they landed in France becoming part of the 3rd Canadian Infantry Brigade, 1st Canadian Division. The 15th battalion was initially in the La Bassée area before moving north to the Salient. In June 1916 the battalion was involved in the battle for Mount Sorrell, the low ridge between Hooge and the crest line of Hills 62 and 61. As a vantage point it rose approximately ninety feet higher than the shallow ground at Zillebeke, affording any occupying force excellent observation over the Salient and all approach routes. Possession of the ridge was a great prize and at 6.00 am on 2 June 1916 German artillery began a massive bombardment of the Canadian positions. Just after 1.00 pm German engineers blew up four mines and attacked the ridge. By the end of the day the ridge had been taken and the Canadians driven back over half a mile. A Canadian counter-attack the next day, which included the 15th Battalion, was unsuccessful and it was not until ten days later that German forces were pushed off the ridge back to their original line. Although eventually successful, it had been a costly engagement for the Canadians. Between 2 and 14 June, Canadian forces lost over 8,000 men.

On 3 June the 15th Battalion and other units of the Canadian 3 Brigade were in position at 3.27 am and awaiting the signal to attack, however by the time the attack began at 8.55 am there had already been numerous casualties from German artillery targetting the Canadian assembly positions. The 15th Battalion war diary also reported several shells from their own artillery dropping short onto Canadian lines. The battalion war diary takes up the story:

'*Upon the signal being given the officers and men behaved most courageously immediately getting out, forming line and rushed forward in the face of a perfect hell of artillery and machine-gun fire. It did not seem possible that anything could live through it. The right of the line was held up by a thick hedge and before a way was found through it, the first line was all shot down … it soon became apparent the objective could not be reached. Accordingly the men fell back to the starting point.*'

It had been a costly day for the men of the 15th Battalion, the official casualty figures recorded eleven officers and 297 other ranks as killed, wounded or missing. It is not possible to pinpoint exactly when Charles Coyde was killed; he could have been one of the casualties sustained before the attack began or he may have been killed during the attack itself. However, his body was recovered and buried at Zillebeke.

445160 Private William John Croft: 24th Battalion (Victoria Rifles), CEF

Grave: B.3.

John Croft was an 18-year-old tailor's apprentice when he enlisted in July 1915 at Chatham, New Brunswick. The battalion left Canadian shores on the SS *Cameronia* and arrived at Devonport on 20 May 1915. Four months later, after a further period of training in England, the Victoria Rifles landed in France on 16 September. On the evening of 7 June 1915 the battalion was transported to a point close to Vlamertinghe and were en-route to the trenches in the vicinity of Maple Copse:

> 'On the way to the front line from Ypres, the Battalion was harassed severely by enemy fire. At approximately 11.45 pm, 'B' Coy., under Lieut. C S B White, was passing in single file along the road in front of the church in Zillebeke when a heavy shell burst in the midst of No. 5 Platoon, no warning preceding it, as the sound of its approach had been drowned by the noise of a field battery clattering hurriedly towards the front. When the shell burst, the company commander was hurled into the roadside ditch, but soon recovered his feet and dazedly sought his men. For a moment it seemed that No. 5 Platoon had disappeared, but eventually, from a carnage of torn and riven bodies on the road, Lieut. G V Walsh and Company Sergeant-Major L A Sewell reported themselves unwounded. Lieut. Walsh was suffering from severe concussion, but was able to report the disaster and summon assistance from the rear ... Twelve men lay dead on the road, including two of 'B' Company's Signallers, and eleven severely wounded lay amongst them. Arms and legs were strewn around and in the darkness the nightmare task was to separate the wounded and dying from the dead.'

One of those who could be still identified from the carnage was William Croft.

65891 John Carron Sime: 24th Battalion (Victoria Rifles), CEF

Grave: D.4.

John Sime was born in 1897 at Crail, a small village on the east coast of Scotland. James and Catherine Sime, together with John and his three sisters, lived at 5, Temple Crescent. James Sime was a successful butcher in Crail and the family employed a servant. Nevertheless John decided against joining his father in the family business and emigrated to Canada with his cousin Hugh Sime. Travelling on the SS *Scotian* they arrived at Halifax, Nova Scotia in February 1913. John enlisted in Montreal in October 1914 a month after his

22nd birthday, his occupation is noted on his attestation papers as 'bank clerk'. Along with William Croft, John joined the 24th Battalion and on 7 June 1916 he was with 5 Platoon when they were hit by the high explosive shell by the church at Zillebeke. He was buried with William Croft in what remained of the shattered churchyard across the road.

438053 Sergeant Walter William Davison: 52nd Battalion (New Ontario), CEF

Grave: B.5.

Walter Davison was a stenographer who, before he enlisted in December 1914, worked at the Grain Exchange at Fort William. Canadian born and unmarried, he lived at 331, Bathurst Street with his parents, John and Rachel Davison who ran a small grocery business. The 52nd Battalion was raised in northern Ontario during the spring of 1915 with its mobilisation headquarters at Port Arthur. The battalion landed in France on 20 February 1916 and three days later joined 9 Brigade of the 3rd Canadian Division. Just over three months later, the battalion was part of the Canadian Mount Sorrel action and on 7 June 1916 was ordered to relieve the 43rd Battalion in the trenches at Maple Copse:

> *'Battalion rested during day. 3.00 pm orders received to move to the relief of 43rd Bn. Then occupying trenches extending from Maple Copse to Gourock Rd ... This relief successfully carried out and completed by 1.30 am. Draft of 20 OR reinforcements reported with transport. A shell bursting where rations had been dumped inflicted several casualties amongst the men of this battalion and must have made a direct hit on 438053 Sgt. Davison, Orderly Room Clerk, reporting for duty, as no trace of him could afterwards be found. His death was a severe blow to Orderly Room Staff.'*

Despite the rather grim account of Walter's death in the war diary, some remains must have been found and later buried in the Zillebeke churchyard.

568 Sapper Charles Preston Ilsley: 6th Field Company, CEF

Grave: H.2.

Charles Ilsley graduated from McGill University in 1915 with a Bachelor of Science degree in Civil Engineering. In February of that year he travelled from Ottawa to Montreal to enlist in the 6th Field Company. Over half the volunteers were from Queen's University, Montreal, the remainder travelling from all over Canada to enlist. The Company left Canada on the SS *Northland* on 24 April 1915, arriving five days later at Avonmouth. By 15 September they were in France deployed in the Kemmel sector as 2nd Canadian Division

Engineers. The Company moved into the Zillebeke area in March 1916. Charles Ilsley's death on 23 March was the work of a German sniper:

> *'Another one of our splendid lads, Sapper 'Red' Ilsley, of Section 2, was killed by a bullet at 8.00 pm while loading material at Bull Dump in Maple Copse on the 23rd. Sapper Ilsley was buried in Zillebeke churchyard alongside a cross that marks the grave of Lieutenant [sic] Gordon Lennox, killed in 1914.'*

Born in September 1892 in South Dakota, Charles Ilsley was 24-years-old when he was killed. He left a widow, Adelia Blance Ilsley.

Lieutenant Frederick Johnston Watson: 43rd Battalion (Cameron Highlanders), CEF

Grave: F.3.

Born in Arbroath in 1888, Frederick Watson studied Law at the University of St Andrews from 1908–9 and was admitted to the Glasgow Institute of Chartered Accountants in 1912. In November 1912 he sailed on the SS *Cassandra* for Montreal and on the outbreak of war in 1914 was working in Winnipeg with Messrs Riddell, Stead, Graham and Hutchison. He initially enlisted in the Winnipeg Rifles but was soon commissioned into the 43rd Battalion which was formed on 16 December 1914. In June 1914 the battalion sailed for Devonport on the SS *Grampian*, ultimately joining 9 Brigade of the 3rd Canadian Division. By February 1916 the battalion was in France and four months later it was engaged in its first action at Mount Sorrel. Lieutenant Frederick Watson was killed in action on 10 June. The battalion war diary for that date records his death:

> *'43rd relieves 52nd Bn. [Battalion] HQ at Dormy House. 2 platoons 52nd relieved 2 platoons 53rd Maple Copse. Both sides artillery active all evening, extraordinary number of enemy's shells blind. B Coy [Company] bombers beat off enemy bombing party at dusk at Block Hill Street. Our artillery opened heavy bombardment. Bn. Scouts went over the parapet to reconnoitre and reported both going out and coming in. 101 OR [other ranks] reinforcements arrived from base. Wind North. Casualties. 4 killed, 29 wounded (killed includes Lieut. F J Watson).'*

Frederick was not the first in the Watson family to feature in the casualty lists. His younger brother, Stanley Lee Watson, had been killed in the Battle of Loos on 25 September 1915 whilst serving as a Captain in the 4th Battalion, Black Watch.

Frederick Watson is commemorated on the University of St Andrews Roll of Honour and on the Institute of Chartered Accountants of Scotland Roll of Honour.

Appendix 2

Summary of 1914 Deaths

Name	Rank	Regiment	School	Commission	Date of death	Grave Reference
Neill, Norman	Captain	13th Hussars (Brigade Major 7 Cavalry Brigade)	Harrow 1894–1897	Militia 1902	6.11.1914	A.4.
de Gunzburg, Alexis George	Second Lieutenant	11th Hussars (attached RHG)	Eton 1901–1904	Direct 1914	6.11.1914	B.1.
Wilson, Gordon Chesney	Lieutenant Colonel	Royal Horse Guards	Eton 1879–1884	Militia 1887	6.11.1914	B.2.
Petersen, William Sinclair	Second Lieutenant	2nd Life Guards	Glenalmond 1906–1908	UOTC 1914	6.11.1914	C.3.
Tufnell, Carleton Wyndham	Lieutenant	2nd Grenadier Guards	Eton 1905–1911	Sandhurst 1912	6.11.1914	D.1.
Wyndham, William Reginald	Lieutenant	1st Life Guards	Eton 1889–1893	Sandhurst 1894	6.11.1914	SM 1.
Siewertsen, Walter Frederick	Private	2nd Grenadier Guards			7.11.1914	E.4.
Rising, Robert Edward	Major	1st Gloucestershire Regiment	Charterhouse 1885–1889	Sandhurst 1891	7.11.1914	E.5.
Stocks, Michael George	Lieutenant	2nd Grenadier Guards	Eton 1906–1910	Sandhurst 1911	10.11.1914	E.1.

Name	Rank	Regiment	School	Service entry	Date	Reference
Parnell, Henry Bligh Fortescue (5th Baron Congleton)	Lieutenant	2nd Grenadier Guards	Eton 1904–1909	UOTC 1912	10.11.1914	E.2.
Gordon Lennox, Lord Bernard Charles	Major	2nd Grenadier Guards	Eton 1891–1896	Sandhurst 1898	10.11.1914	E.3.
Gibson, William	Private	London Scottish			11.11.1914	A.3.
St George, Howard Avenel Bligh	Second Lieutenant	1st Life Guards	Eton 1908–1913	Probationer 1914	15.11.1914	A.2.
Lee Steere, John Henry Gordon	Lieutenant	2nd Grenadier Guards	Eton 1908–1912	Sandhurst 1913	17.11.1914	F.1.
Symes-Thompson, Cholmeley	Captain	2nd Grenadier Guards	Harrow 1896–1898	Militia 1899	17.11.1914	F.2.
Whitfield, James William	Lance Corporal	2nd Coldstream Guards			17.11.1914	A.1.
Dawson, Richard Long	Captain	3rd Coldstream Guards	Eton 1893–1895	Sandhurst 1897	20.11.1914	E.6.
Schuster, Alfred Felix	Lieutenant	4th (Queen's Own) Hussars	Charterhouse 1896–1901	Special Reserve 1905	20.11.1914	Tablet

References

Introduction

1. Cited in Brown M, *1914, The Men Who Went To War*.
2. There is no hyphen used in the family name of Lee Steere.
3. There are several shortened versions of his name in print. I have used the version that was used extensively by the Wyndham family in their letters to each other.
4. There is no hyphen used in the family name of Gordon Lennox.

Chapter 1

1. Correspondence with CWGC, 22 May 2008.
2. Certain cemeteries with fewer than fifty burials do contain a Cross of Sacrifice.

Chapter 2

1. Cited in Strawson, J, *Gentlemen in Khaki*.
2. Sir George Charles Gordon Lennox, the son of Lord Bernard Gordon Lennox, held the post of Sandhurst Commandant 1961–63.
3. Chamber's *Book of Days*.
4. He signed all his letters 'Harry' and his mother used this shortened form when she wrote to him.
5. French, D, *Military Identities The Regimental System, the British Army, and the British People c.1870–2000*.
6. Smith was killed while commanding the 2nd Battalion on 19 May 1915. He is buried at Le Touret Military Cemetery. Grave Reference: II.D.14.
7. Beckett, I W, *Ypres the First Battle 1914*.

Chapter 3

1. One of the school's boarding houses. Each was titled with an adaptation of the name of their first housemaster, such as 'Weekites'.
2. 'Gownboys' was the boarding house for scholars, who were entitled to wear gowns.
3. Schuster, Sir G, *Private Works and Public Causes*.
4. He became Lord Louis Mountbatten.
5. 2nd Dragoon Guards.

6. In 1916 William Orpen became an official War Artist alongside Paul Nash, Muirhead Bone and Wyndham Lewis. He was knighted in 1918.
7. Lieutenant Colonel Alfred Dykes is commemorated on the Memorial to the Missing on the Marne at La Ferté-sous-Jouarre.

Chapter 4

1. Lloyd, R A, *A Trooper in the Tins*. Hurst and Blackett. 1938.
2. Sergeant R J Minahan was killed in action on 25 July 1916. He had been recommended for a commission but was killed before leaving the front line to take it up. He is buried at Contalmaison Chateâu Cemetery. Grave Reference: II.D.3.
3. Terraine, J, *Mons, Retreat to Victory*.
4. Lloyd, R A, *A Trooper in the Tins*. Hurst and Blackett. 1938.
5. Arthur Pearce is buried at the Marfaux British Cemetery. Grave Reference: V.I.3.
6. Captain, later Major, Douglas Reynolds died of wounds on 23 February 1916. He is buried at Etaples Military Cemetery. Grave Reference: I.A.20. His son, Lieutenant Peter Reynolds of the 2nd Battalion, The Irish Guards, was killed on 23 May 1940 during 20 Brigade's defence of Boulogne. Peter Reynolds is buried in Outreau Communal Cemetery. Grave Reference: B.4.
7. Captain Guy Maxwell Shipway is commemorated at Etreux Communal Cemetery. Memorial Reference 50/51.
8. Lieutenant Robert Vereker is buried at Landrecies Communal Cemetery. Grave Reference: B2.
9. Ponsonby, F, *The Grenadier Guards in the Great War. Vol 1*.
10. Lieutenant Francis Ellison Levita is buried at the Meteren Military Cemetery. Grave Reference: II.N.348. Captain John Kirwan Gatacre is also buried at Meteren. Grave reference II.N.32.
11. Died of wounds on 18 November 1914. Buried at Bolougne Eastern Cemetery. Grave Reference: II.B.13.

Chapter 5

1. Major General 'Tommy' Capper was killed at Loos in September 1915.
2. On 6 September 1914, 3 Cavalry Brigade (then under 1st Cavalry Division) and 5 Cavalry Brigade (an independent command) were placed under the orders of Brigadier General Hubert Gough. A week later they were formed into the 2nd Cavalry Division – Gough is promoted – and other units required to make up the divisional structure were added as they arrived.
3. Llewellyn Alberic Price-Davies was awarded the Victoria Cross in 1901 at Blood River Poort whilst a lieutenant in the Kings Royal Rifle Corps (60th Rifles).
4. Fergusson was brought back in December 1914 to command II Corps but was removed again in 1916.
5. Militia or non-regular troops.
6. German artillery attacks on Ypres were an almost daily occurrence from this date but it wasn't until 22 November that the Cloth Hall was set on fire and ultimately destroyed. The town also suffered from occasional bombing by German aircraft. By 1918 little, if anything, remained of the town's buildings.

7. Sir John French estimated that on 19 October there was only one German Corps between Menin and the English Channel.

8. Samuel Holt Lomax died of wounds on 10 April 1915. He was cremated and his ashes were buried in a plot at the Aldershot Military Cemetery, where he was later joined by his wife under a private headstone.

9. Only eighty-four Gordon Highlanders took part in this charge which included drivers, cooks and store-men.

Chapter 6

1. After Alexandria the regiment was granted the privilege of wearing their regimental number on the back of their headdress as well as on the front, a perpetual reminder of the occasion when they had fought back to back on 21 March 1801 against the French.

2. Harold Christopher Richmond was mentioned in despatches on 31 May 1915.

3. The graves of the Irish Fusiliers and the Gloucesters that have been in place since 1900 were recently vandalized. An entire stone cenotaph marking the fallen from the Gloucester Regiment has disappeared. In 2004 a four-year contract to maintain the graves of the 25,200 soldiers who died fighting for Britain in the second Boer War given to the Commonwealth War Graves Commission. It is the first time the Commission will take responsibility for the fallen from a conflict that pre-dates the Great War.

4. Lieutenant Baxter was subsequently awarded the MC for his gallantry on 23 October.

5. Sergeant T J Knight was killed in action on 29 October 1914. He is buried at Harlebeke New British Cemetery. Grave Reference: XVIII.D.4.

6. Philip Van Neck is buried at Zantvoorde British Cemetery. Grave Reference: V.H.14.

7. Charles Hylton Van Neck is buried at Cabaret-Rouge British Cemetery. Grave Reference: XVI.B.17.

8. Cited in *The Coldstream Guards 1914–1918*.

Chapter 7

1. Frederick William Joseph Miller is commemorated on the Menin Gate, Panels 9 and 11.

2. The Royal Dragoons.

3. Later promoted to command the 8th Battalion South Lancashire Regiment, Harold Brassey was killed on 15 July 1916. He is buried at Bouzincourt Communal Cemetery Extension. Grave Reference: II.F.1.

4. Ponsonby, F, *The Grenadier Guards in the Great War. Vol. 1*.

Chapter 8

1. Viscount Henry William Crichton is buried at the Zantvoorde Military Cemetery. Grave Reference: V.B.11.

2. So called because of the colour of their uniform.

3. Corporal Wallace Walter Rhodes is commemorated on the Menin Gate. Panel 3.

4. Lieutenant Sir Richard William Levinge is buried at the White House Cemetery, Ypres, Grave Reference: I.D.28.

Chapter 9

1. Private E Lawson is commemorated at White House Cemetery. Special Memorial 5.
2. Corporal of Horse Herbert William Dawes is commemorated on the Menin Gate. Panel 3.
3. Major Lord Charles George Francis Fitzmaurice was on the staff of 6 Cavalry Brigade. He later used the surname Mercer-Nairne and is buried under that name at Ypres Town Cemetery. Grave Reference: E.I.10.
4. Sergeant John Arthurs is commemorated on the Menin Gate. Panel 5
5. Both Alex Vandeleur and Hugh Grosvenor are commemorated on the Menin Gate. Panel 3.
6. Charles Sackville Pelham is buried at Ypres Town Cemetery. Grave Reference: II.D.4.
7. Royal Scots Greys.

Chapter 10

1. One of the Langhorne sisters, her sister Nancy became Nancy Astor.
2. WO 95/1278.
3. Ponsonby, F, *The Grenadier Guards in the Great War of 1914–18. Vol. 1.*
4. John Lee Steere obviously did not know that Hervy Tudway had died from his wounds.
5. Captain Beaumont Nesbit took command of the company after John Lee Steere had been killed.
6. *The Carthusian*, October 1915.

Chapter 12

1. Grave Reference: V.A.1.
2. The Hon William Parnell is buried at the Guards Cemetery, Lesboeufs. Grave Reference: I.C.I.
3. Major Geoffrey Parnell is buried at Flatiron Copse Cemetery, Mametz. Grave Reference: VII.H.2.
4. Buried at the Ari Burnu Cemetery, Gallipoli. Grave Reference: E.16.
5. Buried at Villers-Bretonneux Military Cemetery. Grave Reference: III.E.3.
6. Buried at the Khartoum War Cemetery. Grave Reference: 10.C.5.
7. Sydney Allan James Gibson is commemorated on the Thiepval Memorial. Pier and Face 13A and 13B.
8. Rhodes, A, 'Repetition', in M Stephen (Ed.) *Never Such Innocence: A New Anthology of Great War Verse.*

Bibliography

Unpublished sources

The National Archives
Unit War Diaries in WO95
Service Records in WO 339
Naturalization papers in HO 144

Private Papers
The letters of John Lee Steere
The letters of Gordon Wilson and officers of the Royal Horse Guards
The letters of Lady Constance Wyndham and Hon William Reginald Wyndham
The letters of Lady Elizabeth Congleton
The letters of Harry Parnell, 5th Baron Congleton
The diary of Major Lord Bernard Gordon Lennox
The diary of Lieutenant Hon William Reginald Wyndham
The diary of Lieutenant Colonel Howard Ferguson Murland

Published Sources
Anglesey, Marquess of, *A History of the British Cavalry 1816–1919* (4 vols), Leo Cooper 1973–1982.
Arthur, Sir G, *The Story of the Household Cavalry Vol 3*, Heinemann 1926.
Atkinson, G, *The Seventh Division*, John Murray 1927.
Banks, A, *A Military Atlas of the First World War*, Leo Cooper 2004.
Beckett, I, *Ypres – The First Battle 1914*, Pearson 2004.
Brice, B, *The Battle Book of Ypres*, Spa Books 1987.
Brown, M, *1914, The Men Who Went to War*, Sidgwick & Jackson 2004.
Blunden, E, *Undertones of War*, Penguin 1938.
Cave, N, *Hill 60*, Pen & Sword 2000.
Clayton, A, *The British Officer*, Pearson 2006.
Coombes, R, *Before Endeavours Fade*, After the Battle 2006.
Crookenden, A, *The Cheshire Regiment in the Great War*, Privately published 1956.
Craster, J, *Fifteen Rounds a Minute*, Macmillan 1976.

Cust, L, *A History of Eton College*, Duckworth 1909.

Daniel, D, *Cap of Honour*, White Lion 1951.

Dunn, J, *The War the Infantry Knew*, Abacus 1994.

Evans, H, & Laing, N, *The 4th (Queen's Own) Hussars in the Great War*, Gale and Polden 1920.

Evans, M, *The Boer War*, Osprey 1999.

Farrar-Hockley, A, *Death of an Army*, Arthur Barker 1967.

Fetherstonehaugh, R, *24th Battalion CEF; Victoria Rifles of Canada 1914–1919*, Gazette Printing 1930.

French, D, *Military Identities. The Regimental System, the British Army, and the British People c.1870–2000*, Oxford University Press 2005.

Gardner, N, *Trial by Fire*, Praeger 2003.

Gliddon, G, *VCs Handbook*, Sutton 2005.

Gliddon, G, *The Aristocracy in the Great War*, Gliddon 2002.

Hamilton, Lord E, *The First Seven Divisions*, Hurst & Blackett 1916.

Liddell Hart, B, *History of the First World War*, Book Club 1973.

Lloyd, R, *A Trooper in the Tins*, Hurst & Blackett 1938.

Morton, D, *When Your Number's Up: The Canadian Soldier in the First World War*, Random House 1993.

Otley, C, Militarism and Militarization in the Public Schools 1900–1972, *British Journal of Sociology*, Vol. 29, No3, 1978.

Otley, C, The Educational Background of British Army Officers, *Sociology* Vol. 7, No. 2, 1973.

Ponsonby, F, *The Grenadier Guards in the Great War of 1914–1918*, Macmillan 1920.

Ross of Bladensburg, Sir J, *The Coldstream Guards 1914–1918*, Oxford University Press 1928.

Razzell, P, Social Origins of Officers in the Indian and British Home Army 1758–1962, *British Journal of Sociology*, Vol.14, No3, 1963.

Roynon, G, *Massacre of Innocents*, Sutton 2004.

Schuster, G, *Private Works & Public Causes*, Privately Published 1979.

Sheffield, G & Bourne, J, *Douglas Haig War Diaries and Letters 1914–1918*, Orion 2005.

Simpson, A, *The Evolution of Victory*, Donovan 1995.

Stephen, M, (Ed.), *Never Such Innocence*, Buchan & Enright 1988.

Strawson, J, *Gentlemen in Khaki*, Secker & Warburg 1989.

Strawson, J, *Beggars in Red*, Hutchinson 1991.

Symonds, J, *Buller's Campaign*, Book Club 1963.

Terraine, J, *Mons, Retreat to Victory*. Wordsworth 2002.

Thomas, H, *The Story of Sandhurst*, Hutchinson 1961.

Weatherbe, K, *From Rideau to the Rhine and Back*, Hunter-Rose 1928.

Wyrall, E, *The Gloucestershire Regiment in the War 1914–1918*, Methuen 1931.

Index

Index of Individuals

Individuals in **bold** are those commemorated at Zillebeke.